Vertical Development

A personal story about how the ability to reflect and take risks will transform the way you lead, live, and create results

Kim Háfjall

The events and conversations in this book have been set down to the best of the author's ability, although names and details have been changed to protect the privacy of individuals.

Copyright © Kim Hafjall, 2021

Cover Design by Linda Balle

First Edition: October 2021

ISBN 978-1-7398091-0-2 (paperback)
ISBN 978-1-7398091-2-6 (hardcover)
ISBN 978-1-7398091-1-9 (eBook)

www.hafjallconsulting.com

'Life itself is the most wonderful fairy tale'

Hans Christian Andersen

Dear Henry,

dec 2021

Thanks for all your support and help throughout my book project period.

It has meant a lot to me, that you have supported, helped and provided honest feedback.

The results is better due to your support.

I therefore dedicate this book to you with a big thank you.

Much Love,
your eternal friend.

Contents

Introduction

Are you tired of reading management books full of textbook examples and the seven keys you need to be a good leader? Or how to drive change and transformation by following ten simple steps? Are you bored of books that churn out the same advice on how to improve yourself?

I hope this book will give you something different. Over my working life, I have known the power of story-telling. And this is what this book is – me telling my story. You'll get my honest learnings and observations on leadership, culture, driving transformation, and, not least, personal development. As a senior professional with more than 20 years of work experience, I can tell you that I haven't just learnt my most valuable lessons in the office, but through all the different areas of my life, which I also share here.

I say 'honest' because in no way am I perfect. I have managed some situations well but I could have done much better in others. I share times when I have patted myself on the back for a job well done and times when others have too. I talk about times when I have been disappointed in myself and in others, and they in me – when I have made mistakes or taken my eye off the ball. It is human to fail, but only by acknowledging and reflecting on those times have I been able to learn and grow – indeed, to grow 'vertically'.

This story covers a decade of my life from the ages of 35 to 45. Over these years, my career took me across the globe from Denmark to Argentina, the UK, back to Argentina, Venezuela, Romania, and finally, back to Denmark. I worked as a General Manager (GM or CEO), Finance Director (FD or CFO), Group Treasurer, Change Manager, and Finance Manager. I had the opportunity to learn about and from cultures vastly different to the one I grew up in. I share these cultural learnings here as well as cultural sensitivity is a critical element often forgotten and not widely taught as a fundamental life skill.

As I have written this book, it has become increasingly clear to me that what has *most* impacted my personal and professional growth is my ability to continually reflect, learn from my mistakes, remain curious and take calculated risks. These are core elements of what I have come to know as 'vertical development'. It has been so critical in my own development that I have made it the title of this book. I hope that my story teaches you something, inspires you, or at least spurs you on to reflect or on your own life.

This book is not a story about the companies I have worked for or about any specific individual I have worked with. I don't refer to company or people's names, and identifying characteristics have been changed. Still, it would be difficult to tell my story without referring to situations and the people I have encountered, to whom I am so grateful.

Outline of Book

My life isn't more interesting than others' lives or more worthy of having a book written on it, but I have had the opportunity to see and experience things many have not. Through the book, I share my personal experiences, observations, and learnings as I encountered them through a critical period of my life and career as a senior executive working across the globe. I particularly share situations that taught me something valuable and caused me to grow vertically (more on what this exactly means later). Many learnings are interweaved through the narrative, but I have structured the book into five parts, which would ideally be read as a whole.

Part 1 looks at the topic of **change**, which I experienced both personally and professionally. Many people see change as a threat, but change is one of the few inevitable things in life. By understanding the emotions and reactions that are triggered by change in you and others, you can better manage it. I also touch on risks – taking risks and managing change are interdependent.

Part 2 covers **culture**, especially the differences that exist between what is considered right and wrong behaviour in different countries. I share some of the key elements of cultural understanding and how being mindful of these upfront will help you avoid some of the mistakes I made.

Part 3 focuses on **transformation**. This covers the transformation – professionally and personally – that you need to go through in order to adapt to and operate effectively in the new and unfamiliar environment you find yourself in. But also, this section of the book looks at the transformational change that an organisation, at times, needs to go through in order to survive in a given business environment and the complexity embedded in orchestrating organisational changes.

Part 4 contains some of my thoughts on **leadership**, and specifically the importance of leadership agility. Many people hit a ceiling in their leadership ability. Understanding vertical development and its various developmental stages can help you to identify, without judgement, how you are doing and prioritise growth areas. As your appreciation for differences in leadership capabilities and limitations grows, you'll be able to lead more effectively and intentionally.

Finally, in Part 5, I reflect on what I have come to know about my **purpose in life**, which is based off getting to know my true values. I cover the importance of reflection in order to do this. As you read my book, you'll see that my personal circumstances required that I ask these questions of myself, but you don't need to wait until those questions are forced on you to consider why you are doing what you do. For me, it was, once again, time to take a risk and seek the unknown.

I hope you enjoy the story. It starts in my home city of Copenhagen…

Copenhagen, Denmark

Preface

It was a cold day in January 2018. I was only in Copenhagen for another three days before I would be returning to Bucharest, Romania. It would be even colder there but I missed my work and colleagues, and I was looking forward to the buzz I always felt stepping into the office building after having been away for a while.

As usual, I had spent the Christmas holidays visiting friends and family, and stocking up on Danish products I couldn't get in Bucharest. I'd just come back from the supermarket armed with three full bags of Danish cheese, fish cakes, liver pâté, rye bread, and liquorice. It was already dark outside and I was looking forward to pouring myself a freshly brewed cup of coffee to warm myself up.

I stood on my doorstep, dumped my bags on the mat and hunted for my keys. I felt my phone vibrate in my pocket but didn't manage to pick it. It clicked over to voicemail.

Strange. Three missed calls from my dad. I must not have noticed whilst I was cycling home.

Now, my mum was calling me. But it was my dad's crying voice that rang through: '*Kim, Kim, I think Mum is dying*'. I could hear the siren from the ambulance in the background.

'What do you mean? What's happening?' I asked.

'I'm not sure. When I got back to the living room, I found her paralysed in her armchair', he responded.

In an instant, it felt like someone had sucked out all life from my body. I knew it was true, but I was still confused. 'Which hospital are you going to?' I asked.

'Glostrup', Dad said. But the paramedics corrected him, 'No – I mean Bispebjerg. We're going to Bispebjerg Hospital', he stumbled. I had never heard him talk this way before. I told him I would drive and meet him there as soon as possible.

I hung up and got into my car. As I was about to turn the ignition key, I realised I had left my shopping, much of which needed to go into the fridge, on the floor in the hallway. I went back to sort it, placing all of the items in their rightful place. Isn't it strange what you can do on auto-pilot?

I headed back to the car and started driving. It was strange. I felt numb; my emotions were shut off. I only repeated aloud to myself: 'She'll be OK, she'll be OK'.

Bispebjerg Hospital was one of the few hospitals in Copenhagen that had not undergone any expansion or refurbishment. It opened in 1913 and on that hazy night, it looked like a hospital straight out of a Hollywood horror movie. Or perhaps that was just my emotional state that night.

Mum had been admitted into the intensive care unit. The room was bare and the ceilings were unusually high – no homely comforts to tempt you into spending any more time than necessary there. The only sound I heard was the regular small *beep* coming from the machine that monitored her heart. I was thankful for this little sign of life.

I found Dad pacing up and down in the hallway. Mum was stable now, but it was too early to know how she would do in the medium term. It could go either way, the doctors told us. We would have to monitor her progress week by week and then, if we got there, month by month.

My mum had always had a strong will like no other person I knew, and an immeasurable calm. Looking at her now, the outlook was poor. She couldn't move. She couldn't speak. When she wasn't asleep, she just laid there with her eyes open looking out into empty space. She still wore her own clothes – a crumpled sand-coloured shirt. Earth tones had always suited her warm complexion and warm character, but now her skin was pale and drained of all expression. It was horrible to see.

My brother stood on the other side of the bed and my dad stationed himself at the end of it. We all had empty expressions on our faces. None of us dared to say what we were thinking.

Two nurses came in. They looked tired, but managed to smile. They needed to do some tests, so we were asked to leave the room. We went into the hallway and got ourselves a cup of coffee from the vending machine.

I have never liked hospitals. Who has? Bad news and grief hang in the air. The doctors and nurses try their best to bring assurance and good news, with a smile, but there remains a lot that is unsaid. Relatives hang around looking like spare parts. Another family down the hallway seemed to be in the same state of shock as us. The nurses came out into the hallway, smiling again, and said we could go back in. They had changed her into a white hospital gown. It looked more comfortable and more fitting to her new status as patient. They had even smoothed out her hair.

I looked deep into her eyes, trying to reach her. I caressed her cheek, hoping to bring her comfort. The only thing I could see looking back was fear and sadness. What was she thinking? Was she using all her strength to try to move her body? To communicate to us?

It was past midnight now. We could do nothing more and she had fallen asleep again. We left the ward. On the parking lot, we embraced each other. My brother would drive my dad home and I would drive myself home. Driving through the empty streets in the cold car, I began to cry. The emotions that followed were overwhelming. I felt devastated and empty. Profoundly sad and lonely. How life can change in a second.

In the past, whenever I was under enormous pressure, I would reach out to my mum. She was always ready to listen and support, speaking sense and coaching me back to seeing hope, solutions, or both. She had so much strength and energy for this. She supported many others like this as well. It was something I always admired of her and, up until that moment, hadn't realised how much I relied on her for it.

When I was a child, I was bullied in school. When I would come home upset, my parents would comfort me. Dad's advice was to 'Just punch them straight in the face!' He was sure that would stop the bullying. Mum, on the other hand, would sweep me up and give me a big, loving hug like only a mum can give and just the comfort I needed. Then, she would ask me, 'Why are you sad?' I would try to explain to her with the typical filter most of us apply when describing tough experiences. Often, instead of probing for details or questioning my actions, she would ask open questions like 'Why do you think they said that?', 'Why do you think they did what they did?' or 'Could you have done anything differently?' Since I was a child, I had been asked these questions over and over again. Eventually, it had become natural for me to think this way and often, I could coach myself with the same open questions.

Besides this helpful part of my upbringing, Mum had never held back any of her love, support, and acceptance of whatever I wanted for my life. She was young when she had me, so I'd always imagined she'd be by my side *well* into my old age. She was only in her mid-sixties and I wasn't ready to let her go yet. Not at all.

I began to think back to more than ten years earlier, when life was so different for all of us. The years when her coaching helped me make that difficult decision to leave Denmark and embark on a journey that would take me on work and personal adventures across the world. That decade would teach me a lot about who I was as a person and what really mattered to me in life. It would teach me about different cultures, about dealing with continual change, and about how to continue developing both personally and professionally. It would mature and strengthen me. Ultimately, those ten years hugely influenced how I would now cope with this unforeseen and sudden change, although only the future would tell how it would really go.

Part 1

Change

Copenhagen, Denmark

Chapter 1: If the Furniture Goes, I Go with it

It was a good day. June 2007. The sun was out and I was on my way to my parents' house. I had bought a bottle of champagne and celebration was on the agenda.

I had just landed my first senior position in a top-20 Danish company. I was proud and excited. I had just turned 35 a month earlier and what better gift could I get than landing a senior job full of new challenges. I was moving up in the world!

I drove up the driveway to my parents' house and walked round to the garden, where they both were. They were a little surprised to see me on a weekday afternoon, but when they saw my beaming smile and champagne, my dad shouted: 'You got it?'. 'Yes!' I proudly confirmed. 'Meet your Group Treasurer son.' They were so happy for me and, I think, proud as well.

Their son, coming from an ordinary working-class family had landed an attractive senior job in a top company. We toasted with the champagne and Dad asked if I would stay for dinner. Absolutely, I would! He left to pick up some good steaks from the local supermarket.

My mum, still smiling, was washing some strawberries to go with the rest of the champagne on the terrace. She looked fabulous as usual. Nicely tanned and pairing a classic black skirt with an elegant grey shirt. She had always dressed well, making an effort to look contemporary. She was always being mistaken for someone younger, but she was in her mid fifties. She kept healthy and vibrant. A subtle use of make-up gave her a natural calmness and mildness to her face and smile. Today was no exception.

We sat down and she asked me again, 'Tell me more about the position and what precisely your responsibilities will be'. I began to explain again. She smiled and asked questions. She wanted me to enjoy my day and she knew what better way than to let me have the spotlight, sharing more about my new job and why I was so excited.

After my dad returned, we chatted more outside until it was time to prepare dinner. I joined him in the kitchen. He was wearing faded jeans and one of his t-shirts. Every Christmas, he wanted nothing else from us but a new t-shirt. This one was dusty blue with a big white Superdry print on the front. He always liked wearing casual clothes and since he had lost weight, he could easily pass for a guy in his late forties with that look. He had short dark blond hair, coral blue eyes, a warm complexion, and a broad smile. I could see why Mum had fallen for him forty years ago.

While Mum set the table, my dad asked me to pick the wine I wanted from their humble collection. I chose an Italian Chianti to go with the steaks. My success had to be celebrated with a feast. And it was!

Having worked out the notice period with my existing company, I started at the new one. It was a well-established company with solid earnings and its last 'crisis' was many decades ago. Despite being a listed company, most of its shares were held by a few rich Danish families who were effectively running the company. Many large Danish companies are owned in this way – either by family funds or independent investment funds.

After many years of stability and limited development, the company had just implemented an integrated business management software system (also known as an 'Enterprise Resource Planning' or 'ERP' system). This would also support the change transformation journey that they were about to embark. The aim was to drive efficiencies and synergies based on economies of scale.

With a background in Corporate Treasury from one of Denmark's largest treasury departments, I was familiar with the transformation journey. Over the ten years I had served in the company, the treasury team had been transformed into a professional, driven, and efficient function. No doubt this was one of the main reasons I was hired by the new company.

During the job interview process, I had spoken with the Group FD about the challenges of the position. Elisabeth was an elegant tall blond woman in her late fifties. Well dressed in her dark conservative suit, as to be expected for a woman in her position. She had an appealing but loud voice. You sensed she could make herself heard with that voice. And perhaps this was needed being FD in a mostly male-dominated world.

Having been brought up by a strong woman myself, I always appreciated other strong women. Elisabeth explained the proud history of the company and how it was organised. There were operations in 15 countries across Europe and the Americas. She explained how the Group GM had recently joined the company and how they were embarking on a transformational change journey. It was clear from her description that this was a company that had historically operated with the mantra: 'This is how things have always been done so why change a thing?'

She wanted me to build a centralised treasury function, leveraging the experience I had from my previous company. I was excited and felt this was a challenge I would enjoy. Before I had accepted the role, we looked at the current team structure. I shared how I believed it had to look for me to successfully deliver results. With ten years of experience under my belt, I knew what set-up was or wasn't going to work.

To my surprise, she approved my suggestions on the spot. I could expand the function by two additional people. This would bring the team to ten direct reports, of which seven would be working within treasury and risk management. It wasn't a large function but enough to make a significant contribution. The company was incredibly lean. Many people were juggling two different roles ('double-hatting'), which meant seven were officially in the team but in reality, there would be more than seven involved in treasury activities across the company.

Lean organisations can be superb when you have a stable workforce, which the company did. However, it can also make a company vulnerable when changes inevitably occur. Knowledge and procedures are known by and reliant on a few skilled people. These people hold a lot of history and are less inclined to write that knowledge down in handbooks or follow formal systems of working.

Shortly after starting at the company, I kicked off the hiring process with an external head-hunter to look for the two new team members. It took longer than anticipated but we eventually found two solid people with the right background and characteristics to join us on the change journey. They would start three months later. For now, I had my existing team and together we pushed ahead with multiple new transition projects.

As with all change, there was resistance from across the organisation. This was expected. Many in the company had been used to managing their areas themselves, without outside interference. Suddenly, we were talking about centralising certain areas (e.g. banking and currency exposure management) from the local subsidiaries into the central holding company. Understandably, people felt we were taking work and territory away from them.

Despite pushback, we managed to implement some easy wins early on in the process – this would be important to gather momentum. However, soon the resistance also began to pick up momentum and was being noticed at the company's headquarters (HQ), where we were based.

As in all organisations, there are formal and informal networks. The informal ones were powerful in this organisation. It soon resulted in questions and pointed comments from some senior managers, such as 'your predecessor tried the same, but…'. Irrespective of this, we kept moving on.

The New Office

As part of landing in the new company, I wanted to make my office personal and enjoyable. I am someone who needs to have things well organised and tidy around me to concentrate. I appreciate having an office with a modern contemporary look and feel, rather than an old or classic one.

The company had recently celebrated its 100-year anniversary. For decades, the interior style was of low lighting and dark mahogany wood, both in the public and private areas of the office. It matched the company's profile of stability and conservatism. Still, I preferred a brighter Nordic look in the form of oak, light colours, and contemporary art.

I spoke with the Head of Procurement and he handed me a catalogue to select new furniture from. I ordered the usual pieces (e.g. table, drawers) but chose white oak rather than mahogany. I didn't think much of it. The price was the same.

They would take six weeks to arrive and I continued working on various projects with the team, getting to know the organisation and building up my own network within the company.

The day eventually came when the furniture arrived. I was excited. The 30-year-old-plus dark scratched wooden furniture had seen better days. The new white oak furniture looked great with the freshly painted white walls and lighter carpet. There was an adjustable-height table which, was a mandatory offering in Denmark.

I brought some artwork in from home – a large black and red abstract piece I had painted myself. I picked up some vases and other small items from IKEA at the weekend to add some style. It looked amazing and I felt energised in the room. My team commented a lot on it, mostly out of positive recognition and even suggested we should have more meetings in there. The new office certainly indicated that change was coming.

It only took a few days before I noticed that more and more people were passing by my office. Even people who wouldn't normally be on the Finance floor. Some would just peer in but others made explicit comments on the furniture: 'This doesn't look like what we normally consider to be standard'. I just smiled and didn't spend much thought on it. It wasn't the first time I had experienced people using sarcasm to poke at change. In later organisations, even wearing a new jumper was enough to elicit a whole team conversation.

A few weeks later, Elisabeth came back from a period of extended sick leave. I heard her voice clearly through the hallway before I saw her body. She greeted me as she entered my office and closed the door quietly. She seemed a bit tense.

'I see you have ordered furniture that is not in line with company policy'. She continued, 'This has caused noise in the management team and we need to find a solution'.

I looked at her with surprise and responded with, 'I don't understand'. I felt tension building up in my body.

After a short pause, she continued, 'I think the best solution is to have it replaced with what we've always used'. My jaw hit the floor. I was fuming and I could not believe what I was hearing. My body language had gone from relaxed to tense in a moment and, despite all of my previous learnings about being in control of one's emotions as a leader, I could not.

I looked for signs that she was joking, but couldn't find any. I replied, 'You have been away for several months. I am entirely new to this organisation. Yet, I have managed myself, settled in well and taken tough business decisions without needing to consult with you on them. You return and the *first* thing you say is: the furniture in my office is not what people have historically ordered'. Gesturing at the room, I asked, 'Has this made you *so* uncomfortable that you come into my office and throw this at me?'

Elisabeth looked puzzled at my reaction.

I was on a roll now. 'Let me be clear... If you would like the furniture to be replaced with the dark wood that you have used for decades, feel free to do so. At the same time, you can go and find another Group Treasurer because... *if the furniture goes, I go with it*'.

Elisabeth began to raise her voice and responded with, 'No reason to get so upset, Kim'.

I interrupted her. 'Yes, there is. What I would have expected would be your full support upon your return and to catch up on areas of genuine business importance. As well as to see how I'm generally getting on as a newcomer to this organisation. Instead, the first thing you come to talk to me about is the furniture?'

I cannot tell you what she thought at that moment, but before she could respond I added, 'All change is difficult. You asked me to join this group to lead change within my area. The first visible change you see, you ask me to reverse it. What impact will this have on all the other initiatives that my team and I will carrying out? What will people say when I say we need to do things differently? For that exact reason, …the furniture stays and I hope that you will support me.'

To her credit, she started smiling and said, 'You're right. My apologies. I had not seen it from that angle. No more talk about the office furniture and now, tell me more about what else has been happening whilst I was away.'

As I gathered my emotions, we turned our attention to business and we ended up having a great catch up. I gave her an update on key areas and got her advice on a few topics where I had outstanding questions. As she got up from the chair and opened the door, she said loudly, 'I really like your new interior. It feels very *refreshing*!' and left the office smiling.

From that day onwards, there was no more talk about my office. People continued to walk past and take a look, but the comments became more and more positive. Elisabeth and I also worked well together, now that we understood each other better. This would not be the last office I would change in my career or, believe it or not, the last time changing my office furniture would lead to talk and controversy.

Food for Thought

☞ Have you ever had a manager treat you unfairly?

☞ What feelings were triggered?

☞ How did you react?

☞ How would you describe a good manager (e.g. characteristics, behaviours, values)?

Chapter 2: Opening a Juice Bar in Buenos Aries

Three months had passed and the two new hires had started. I was more than excited. They were seasoned professionals and both brought a breath of fresh air to the organisation. I had originally thought to hire people in their late twenties or thirties who would bring new energy into this settled organisation but these two candidates had so much personality and drive that they clearly outperformed the younger candidates in the interview process. They would be more robust and dependable in driving forward the radical change that was required through the organisation. Whilst they were more expensive, it was worth it. You get what you pay for and we definitely did here.

After a month or so, we had a team-building offsite day with a professional coach. Meeting at a hotel, we worked through different exercises that strengthened our ability to work as a team, drive change and enjoy ourselves whilst doing so. We bonded over a superb dinner that evening and at the end of the night, we jumped into taxis to get home, satisfied and ready to start the next day as a new team.

Early the next morning, I received a call from Elisabeth. She was brief: 'Please be in the office no later than 8 a.m. and make sure the team is there no later than 8.30 a.m.'

I didn't know what to expect but arrived early to be told that another company had bought us. By 8.30 a.m., the other employees were gathered in the canteen and told the news. A foreign company had offered to buy a large part of the group and 90% of the employees at HQ would be transferred to the new company.

I was in shock. Everyone was in shock. After the announcement, I gathered my team in my office. They immediately asked, 'Did you know about this?'. 'No', I said honestly. The two new joiners were not happy – this isn't what they had signed up for. I felt terrible and I didn't know what to say.

Later that morning, I went and challenged Elisabeth. She said, 'This deal went fast and although I participated in the negotiations, I could not have stopped the hiring process of the two employees. It would have indicated something was underway.'

I had to acknowledge that this was true, but asked for her assurance that they would be looked after, especially as they had not passed the three-month cut-off period for statutory corporate redundancy support that exists in Denmark. Elisabeth promised.

I didn't leave the office in a good mood that day. I was frustrated. The many dreams and aspirations I had for the new job had evaporated and I felt bad for the team, not least for the new hires.

That evening I had a few drinks at home and talked with good friends and family. I was frustrated but there was little else I could do. I myself had only been in the role and company for nine months. As one of the senior team, I would be driving the transformation, shaping and leading my area into new directions. I had so many plans and ideas. Now, I would be just another employee in a much larger pond, subsumed into the London-headquartered multi-national corporation.

It was late February. The deal was conditional on EU approval so it was not expected to go through until three or four months later. I hadn't had a vacation for almost a year. I had postponed all of my vacation until the full team was in place. With the holiday days that I had built up, I had been planning a five-week vacation in Argentina for months. I had never been in South America before and in my previous company, a good colleague who had married an Argentine had convinced me that I would love it there.

Given the company situation and with the change agenda on hold, I could do nothing but park my frustrations and try to enjoy the break.

After eighteen hours travel, I arrived in Buenos Aires, capital city of Argentina. It was not at all what I expected. I shouldn't have been surprised. After all, I had heard from my former colleague and his wife about how vibrant and cosmopolitan it was there. Still, my brain had not really computed this. I expected something far less developed. In fact, Buenos Aires is a major city with more than 15 million inhabitants. Many of the areas reminded me of Spain in the 1990s, although a little tired and with worn-out infrastructure. Seeing some of the impressive buildings, boulevards, and parks, I understood why the city was popularly known as the Paris of Latin America. It was amazing and I was hooked!

I was renting a flat in a new 14-storey building with a large pool and sundeck on the roof. It was in Recoleta, a part of the city mostly populated by richer, older Argentinians. It was very affordable compared to European prices.

I had also signed up for a four-week Spanish course. For four hours each day, I would try to improve my beginners Spanish. Luckily, the school was only three blocks away from the flat. It was in an old building with classrooms facing onto the inner courtyard. During the breaks, we would all gather there for *mate* (a traditional South American tea in a bulbous cup drank through a metal straw), or coffee and tea for the rest of us. This was always accompanied with *galletitas* (small cookies) to fuel the brain cells.

Our teachers were young, warm and charming. I loved it. My main teacher, Claudia, was a 30-year-old Argentine girl. She was slim, tanned and had long black hair. Her English was fluent but she rarely chose to use it. From the first moment, it was all Spanish. Although I felt very uncomfortable that first week, I had high hopes of improving my spoken Spanish and Claudia's warm smile and good humour made it easier.

The other pupils were a mixed crowd – young adults from Europe taking a sabbatical year after high school and more mature working adults, predominantly from the US, who just loved the Argentinian life. They came back year after year to improve their Spanish during the daytime and dance Tango during the night. I couldn't blame them.

On the first day, I met John. He was around the same age as me and had come from New Zealand. He'd worked in the capital and financial markets for many years and had gotten out just before the financial turmoil started in 2008. He had plenty of money and had chosen to quit work and move to Argentina. With no firm plans about what to do but enough funds for some years, he said he would chance it. I was inspired and his story got me thinking: should I do the same?

Apart from school, I spent many hours exploring the city. The combination of architecture, the daily noise and chaos, wild night life, history, and the charm of the Argentines did it for me. I went out every weekend and met lots of different people. I liked the emotions of the country.

The Global Financial Crisis had hit Argentina hard. They had hardly gotten out of their previous crisis that had resulted in a major devaluation of the Argentine Peso currency in 2002. On many nights, people would go onto their balconies and noisily hit their pots and pans for an hour. It was the Argentine way of demonstrating daily and making the politicians hear that they were not content with the way the country was being run. This was a country and a people full of expression – a major contrast to the mostly reserved Danes from back home.

The five weeks flew by. I know they say you look back with rose-tinted spectacles, but I enjoyed every single day there. I took the opportunity to ask Claudia about general life in Buenos Aires and about the rules and opportunities for working and living there. I sensed I wasn't the first to ask her. I also asked John. I didn't know what exactly I was exploring but I knew that Buenos Aires was the first place I had visited in the world where I felt an immediate connection, both with the people and the place.

The Management Buy-out

Through our daily life, all of us are hit by a multitude of core emotions like joy, fear, sadness, disgust, and anger. Different emotions are triggered by different situations, and those emotions will be different for different people.

Sometimes we can be hit by the whole spectrum of emotions within just a few hours. Something similar happens when it comes to change. The interesting thing, however, is that with change, the emotional triggers come from how our ego reacts to different threats. In other words, our ego perceives change to be a threat.

According to research, our ego is built on our life experiences and serves to protect us[1]. Each person's ego is different and has been built gradually as we learn from life's experiences. No two people will experience a given situation in exactly the same way. The ego's six core issues are:

- Safety
- Inclusion
- Power
- Control
- Competence
- Justice

Which issues are triggered differ from person to person. Where a given change may activate the need for safety and inclusion in one person, the same event may activate the issues of control and competence in another. This is one of the reasons as to why leading change is so difficult and explains why resistance often arises in situations where people are exposed to change. Their ego is simply responding to protect themselves against a threat they perceive and moreover, their particular response has been learned through previous experiences of threat through change. In light of that, resistance is perhaps the only logical response.

During my stay in Argentina, I thought a lot about why I reacted so strongly to the acquisition offer on my company. It had triggered an immediate demotivation and negative spiralling of my mood. I reflected on it and tried to figure out what had happened.

I thought I was used to change and generally dealt with it pretty well. At my previous company, there were constant changes. At first, it was shifting from a state monopoly into a service-oriented company as the sector had recently been opened up for market competition. This change transformed the organisational mindset from one that was fixed to one that was frequently dealing with constant changes and learning on the job.

After a couple of years, there was another drastic change. The company was bought by an investment capital fund. The control of the company changed overnight. Young and ambitious investment guys arrived with strong views about every single thing. Their sole focus was to generate a return on their investment. Employees' and customers' well-being was towards the bottom of the priority list and only included if there were financial benefits to be reaped. It certainly triggered negative reactions in people with ego issues around justice and inclusion.

Gradually, most of the strategy was set outside the main operating company and all decision-making had to be cleared with the new board. It was not a pleasant period. For people liking power and control (which, to be fair, is most people) it was a nightmare.

Thankfully, the situation was a bit different in the corporate treasury department, where I worked. Debt management, cash flow and currency movements were suddenly elevated and got a lot of air time with the new board. The buyout had resulted in high levels of debt and the existing corporate treasury team was best placed to manage these. Still, it triggered a lot of negative emotions in people sensitive to feeling competent and being in control. It did in me.

One of the saddest things was to see the entire organisation lose its momentum. Previously, the company was the market leader in Denmark and growing in several international markets. The new owners, however, adopted a sell-off and streamline strategy. Soon the company would shrink its international presence to a third of its original size and pour all of its focus onto the home market. Many who worked in foreign subsidiaries were sold off to new companies and for many others, the safety and justice issues they encountered were just too great.

Many had joined a large and growing company, only to now find themselves in positions that had less responsibility, autonomy and limited growth opportunities in the future. By the time I left, the company was stable. Most of the international subsidiaries had been sold and the focus was entirely on the Danish home market. The mood, especially in the HQ, had been decimated.

Perhaps it was a flashback to that time that triggered my strong reactions. I had taken a job where I was senior, had great responsibility and management trust in my abilities, and had an exciting mandate to lead a major transformation across the company's 15 international market operations. In a moment, my remit was taken away and I saw the company it would become.

It was not surprising that I felt dejected. As the company acquiring us was substantially larger and already had their own Group Treasurer and 30-strong team of treasury analysts and managers at the HQ alone, I would have to take whatever offer, if any, was made to me. It was out of my control and it triggered feelings of justice, or rather injustice. I could do nothing but wait and see how things would unfold. That did not suit me.

On the plane back to Denmark, I found myself thinking over my situation. The lightness I had felt for almost five weeks was rapidly being replaced by tension. Was this the opportunity to try something new? To take a chance? In theory, I had lost my job – the job I had agreed to anyway.

I had always been career-motivated. I had my first job at 12 years old and worked through my holidays. I went from school to high school, university and onto full-time work without a break. I even started my first full-time job a month before I handed in my master's thesis. I had never given myself a sabbatical year or time to just do nothing. Was this a sign from above? An opportunity to take time out and explore other things?

I landed in Copenhagen and was picked up by my parents. I shared my holiday experiences with them. They clearly sensed that I was more excited about Buenos Aires than anywhere else I had been in the world. I spoke about the people I had met, including John, who I said had really inspired me with his story of giving everything up to move across the world. Needless to say, my parents were not cheering.

I shared my thoughts about the job situation and my mum, in her usual coaching style, asked me questions rather than directing me to a solution or answer. It was great to talk out loud and share with her. She asked many helpful questions and showed her support, yet I sensed that the idea of me leaving Denmark was not her first choice.

The Impact of Forced Change

The next morning, I arrived back in the office and what a change five weeks had brought. Whilst I had been away (and before smartphones on holiday were the norm), 30% of the finance department had resigned, including one of my team. The atmosphere was awful –people were extremely negative and all the energy had gone. Most water cooler chats were about how terrible the future looked and how they were all updating their CVs.

This was not an organisation accustomed to change and I could see that all the core ego issues were at play. Some didn't like losing power or not being in control. Others were afraid they would not be competent enough to meet the new challenges. Some felt there was a lack of justice and hoped they would be included in the 10% of people staying with the existing company. Others simply feared they would lose their jobs.

News of this had reached the acquiring company. As they were keen to take over a well-functioning business, they sent over a few heads from their London HQ to attempt to build bridges between the two organisations.

It could not have gone more wrong. Everyone was gathered into the canteen for a Q&A session. The senior visitors went on stage and made a presentation about how global the company was, how well they paid their staff were, how good bonuses had been and how international careers were open to the employees. One talked about how he had travelled the world and experienced many different cultures, and how that had enriched him as a person. The problem is they didn't know their audience.

The typical profile of an employee at the company was in their forties or fifties, had worked the same company for 20 years or more, lived nearby to the office and was married with grown-up children and even grandchildren. They had a good quality of life and craved stability from their 8 a.m. – 4 p.m. jobs, ready to collect a good pension in due course. Clearly, the presentation was not met with a standing ovation. To the contrary, people were even more upset. Apart from not knowing their audience (their first and most obvious mistake), the visitors did not address any of the audience's core ego issues. In fact, most left feeling a greater sense of threat!

There were four senior managers in the finance top team reporting to Elisabeth, including myself. As Elisabeth was on leave, we all reported to the GM, Michael. After a few weeks back in the office after my Argentinian holiday, he called me in for a meeting.

After the usual small talk, he told me that one of the other top team managers had resigned. It was not official yet but he would like me to take over their function whilst they searched for a permanent replacement. I was puzzled. I had been in the company less than a year. Surely there was someone else more familiar with the work and team. Whilst I took it as a compliment, I suggested it would be better if he asked one of the other two managers. In addition, I was not planning to stay around either.

I could see the shock on Michael's face. He asked politely if I could elaborate. I told him about my plans to move to Buenos Aires. About how I'd been inspired by a guy called John who had just done the same.

Over the few weeks I had been at home, I had become more and more convinced about the move. I had even contacted a real estate broker and had had my house valued. It would be going on the market any day. With the proceeds, I would be able to live well for several years. It would enable me to live out my new dream of moving to Buenos Aires and opening a juice bar!

Michael smiled and said, 'Juice bar? Sounds different but exciting. Why now?'

I explained that with my experience of buy-outs and need to control my own future, this seemed the best course of action. Michael complimented me and said that while he was sad I wanted to leave, he respected my decision. We agreed he would ask one of the other managers to temporarily manage the orphaned function. More time for me to plan my move to Argentina!

Food for Thought

☞ Are you aware of which core ego issues (safety, inclusion, power, control, competence, and justice) are triggered in you by changes?

☞ Have you ever experienced having change forced you that throws your career or life plan out of the window?

☞ What did you do or what would you do in this case?

☞ Do you have a dream (fall-back or otherwise) that you want to pursue?

☞ Who might be able to help you?

Chapter 3: A New Beginning

After some weeks and continued depressed mood in the company, the acquiring company flew in more senior managers to visit us. They wanted to meet with different employees from all the various functions – those who would be among the 90% moving over to the acquiring company (the Group).

I would be among the 90% of staff transferring to the new company while the other two senior finance managers would remain in the old company. With the fourth senior manager leaving altogether, I was the only senior finance manager expected to join the new organisation. They wanted a one-to-one meeting with me.

This would be my opportunity to talk about my plans to move to Argentina. I would stress that I had nothing against the new company but I just didn't see a role for me there. Yes, that was my decision.

After some small talk, I was asked about my plans. They had already been informed by Michael about my plan to move to Argentine and wanted to hear more about it. What was I going to do there? Did I already have a job lined up?

Great – no beating about the bush. I shared my plans excitedly and when I had finished, I heard someone say, 'That sounds great. Would you consider moving to Argentina to work for our local subsidiary there?'

I wasn't expecting that. I tried to bring to mind the picture I had of me juicing oranges in shorts, impromptu dinner plans with new friends on days that I closed the shop early, followed by live music and dancing at the tiny bar John had taken me.

'What would I do for you there?' I asked.

'Well for now, I don't know, but something in finance. As you're willing to move there without a job, going there on an expatriate (expat) contract wouldn't be worse, would it?'

He smiled. He had a point. I replied that it sounded interesting but I needed to understand the timing and conditions. Hmm. We agreed that I would think more about it and he would come back in a week's time with a more tangible proposal.

I couldn't help but start to imagine it. It wouldn't be juicing but did I really think that was me anyway? I drive an Alfa Romeo and read about politics and economics in my spare time. It seemed almost too good to be true.

If I moved to Argentina as an expat, I would be back in control. I would be back in beautiful Buenos Aires and as a professional, with an expense account and perks to boot. I may not know exactly what type of job I'd be doing in the short term or the long term, but I'd be there! I felt the energy that had vanished that day in February rushing back. I was taking control of my life and it was going in my way.

The company rang me the following week. The deal would be the following: once the acquisition was approved by the EU over the summer, I would stay for six months in the newly established Danish subsidiary to lead the integration of all the finance functions. After that, I would move to Buenos Aires on a three-year contract for a non-specified finance role to be decided on my arrival. I thought about it. A few seconds later, I accepted the offer. I had addressed my ego's core issue – being in control.

Fast forward a few months, the acquisition was approved and separation with the old company took place. The 10% who would continue in the old company would leave the premises and the new management team (all expats from various countries) would move in. It was an exciting period.

Aligning organisations

The core ego issues framework can be helpful to understand what can trigger reactions to change. Combined with this, I find the Kübler-Ross change curve[2] helpful to better understand the actual reactions that the core issues trigger. It is a great tool for informing change management strategy because it breaks down how people process change in general. The five stages, also known as the five stages of grief, are as follows:

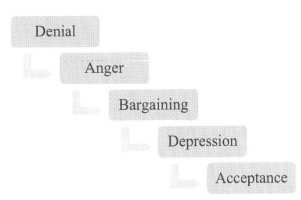

Figure 1. Kübler-Ross Change Curve

The initial denial and disbelief of the acquisition offer had now passed and many had moved onto anger and bargaining. I had managed to bargain a better outcome, which meant the depression phase passed quickly and I readily accepted my new situation.

Many others were not there yet and, because the stages are not necessarily neatly sequential, many who had gone through the depression phase were now back at anger or bargaining. Whilst individuals' responses to handling change will influence the length and extent to which these stages are felt, the K-R change curve also provides a framework to understand the combined reactions of groups to change. Clearly, the organisation can help or hinder this process.

I now double-hatted as treasury and integration lead for finance. The challenge for me was to be a sounding board between the finance groups in the former Danish organisation and the Group. I had to help build bridges between the two distinct cultures but also be mindful of where different people were on the grief curve.

For instance, Danes prefer to be upfront and discuss things openly, even if it's uncomfortable. Most people feel free to air their views and frustrations. As a manager, you would have to listen to and manage these different views. Sometimes you would adapt your plans to get better buy-in from the staff. This is the way of doing things in Denmark and seeking broad agreement is deeply rooted into many Danish organisations.

This is different from the British work culture, where the obvious is not always explicitly articulated. In this case, the situation was made even more difficult because certain UK laws prevented senior management from talking about certain business changes (e.g. that had potential impacts on employment). This meant that much of the communication went through me. I would take the messages from the London HQ and translate them into blunter messages that the Danes would understand and be accustomed to.

I began addressing the core ego issues in a proactive way. In order to do so, I tried to tailor my communication to address people's specific ego issues. As many people are generally not aware of their own issues (as I wasn't previously), it wouldn't be easy for them to articulate exactly what the change was triggering in them. Instead, it showed up as a lot of frustration and anger.

For example, for those where safety was especially important, I reassured them that no one would lose their job and to the contrary, that new jobs would be created as the Group ran a fatter organisational structure. This would mean new opportunities for some. For those for whom feelings of justice were triggered, I was open around how the process for determining how new job positions post-merger would be filled and on what criteria the selection would be made. Over the months, the approach brought more and more people into the bargaining and depression stages, and indeed the anger dissipated.

The integration continued and new problems popped up. This is to be expected in change management. The cultural differences between the old company and the Group were stark. The Group had a hierarchical structure. There was a grading structure from grade 22 to grade 30. Someone at grade 23 would report to someone at grade 24, who would report to someone at grade 26, and so on. This led to a lot of noise and dissatisfaction, with some employees who had worked for decades suddenly told they were a grade 23 and would be reporting to someone 10 years their junior. These grades had great power – salaries, bonuses and other benefits (e.g. cars) were granted based on these grades.

By contrast, most Danish companies operate with flat management structures and often seniority is granted based on years of service rather than simply rank. You may have a lower salary than others, but because you have many years of service, you rank higher in the organisation and people pay attention to what you have to say. For the same reason, it would not be unusual in Denmark to be a manager but lead a group of peers based on your credentials and seniority. With the new grading structure, many felt they were being downgraded and this led to some of the most vocal objections across the Danish subsidiary.

The new management team couldn't understand why. They had operated for years in their hierarchical structure and saw the set-up as the only correct and logical way of organising people – a classic clash between two distinct corporate cultures, with country-specific differences to boot. Ego issues of justice, power and control were triggered. Some reacted by taking a bargaining stance. Where it made sense, the Group were forced to waive some of the grades. Some people were appointed 'personal grades' that were higher than the Group's role-specific grades. This also addressed the compensation packages and some of those affected soon joined the acceptance group of employees. Progress.

Over the months, I let people air their frustrations, as was the culture in Danish organisations. There were definite signs of depression, especially among those employees who had been in the company for many years. Energy levels and moods were low. After a while, the other colleagues and I were tired of it. I took a few people aside for a frank conversation, making it clear that their disapproval had been noted, but that their conditions and package had been retained so it was time to move on. Eventually, all did seem to accept the change. Over the six-month long integration, only one person left finance, so overall, we managed to stabilise the team and new ways of working and interacting between the Danish subsidiary and the new Group were established.

We'll Meet Again

As we approached December 2008, my assignment in the Danish subsidiary was coming to an end. I was ready to start my new life on the other side of the world. My adventure to Argentina! I couldn't wait.

It was a strange Christmas that year. I was excited about the move but was also aware of how my family and closest friends were feeling about my move. My mum comes from the Faroe Islands – 18 small windswept islands situated in the middle of the North Atlantic Ocean. She moved to Denmark when she was only 15 years old with her cousin (and best friend). Today, the islands are only a two-hour flight from Copenhagen but at that time, the only way to get there was by ship and the journey took 36-40 hours.

As I am very close with my friends and parents (who I also consider my friends), the move impacted us all. They were stressed and so was I. In 2008/09, prices for long distance calls were incredibly high. Travel subscriptions with mobile phones were non-existent and roaming charges would be bankrupting. I am someone who can speak with friends on the phone for hours. Voice over IP calls like Skype had only just begun but were unreliable – you spent half the time asking if the other person could hear you clearly. This was pre-FaceTime and WhatsApp, let alone Zoom, so moving to Argentina meant a high degree of isolation from my loved ones.

Up until then, I had not used Facebook. It was fairly new and I wasn't interested. Why would I sit and scroll to see what my friends were doing instead of being with them? Now that I was moving to another continent, it seemed to be the only easy way to stay in touch with Denmark. I could keep them updated on the journey and adventure. Equally, I could follow their lives while I was away. Still, at that time, Facebook was in its infant stages and most people only posted news once a month.

Over my final month in Copenhagen, I was out every weekend with my best friends. My mum, having moved to another country at a young age, understood what I was embarking on and the many thoughts and emotions that I had at the time. She provided a lot of support during the packing and moving phase. It was tough on her and Dad, but largely, she managed to regulate her own emotions. I spent the last few nights at their place as my own home had been packed up and all the furniture shipped to Argentina early. Those last nights were difficult for all of us. It was the first time I was moving away from Denmark. I felt like I was leaving behind everyone and everything I knew. It was incredibly exciting and terrifying at the same time.

I wasn't bringing a partner or family. I was moving by myself. Whilst this meant I wouldn't have to worry about whether my spouse or children would be happy in the new country, it also meant no daily support and company for me either. I was starting completely afresh, with no continuity apart from my furniture!

I had many thoughts prior to my departure. I thought I had foreseen most of the challenges and emotions. Of course I hadn't. How could I? It was all uncertain and new territory.

The clock showed 3.30 a.m. It was dark and cold. A fresh winter's day in January. I got up and took a shower. When I was done and dressed, I came out and found both my parents up. We sat in the kitchen and had a quick cup of coffee. We didn't speak much but I sensed they wanted to send me off in the best possible way. I just wanted to enjoy their company a little bit longer. This was really happening now!

To some extent, my family is not a typical Danish family. We hug and kiss each other, at least on my mum's side of the family. Perhaps this is because she comes from the Faroe Islands, where families are very close. It is much more similar to how families are with each other in the Latin world. I love it.

When it was time to head to the airport, my mum gave me one of her typical warm hugs but this one was much longer than usual. It was like she stock-loaded me with a bigger dose of her love and comfort, as it would take a long time before I would get another hug.

My dad drove me to the airport. The highway had already been cleared of the snow from the night before. We spoke about practical things like how long the flight was and how nice it was to leave winter and be arriving in the 35-degree-celsuis Argentine summer. It was simply too difficult to talk about how neither of us knew when we would see each other again. It could be in a year, or longer. At the airport, my dad gave me a long and tight hug too.

I said goodbye and went through check-in, passing security and boarding the plane. Finally, I sank into the seat and tried to relax as the airplane got ready for take-off. My emotions were all over the place. No turning back. I had given up my life in Denmark for a new one on the other side of the world. It had all been triggered by the discomfort my ego had felt about losing control over my work decisions. This deep desire and need to stay in control had led to a chain of events that eventually placed me on this flight bound for Buenos Aires, 7,493 miles away.

To-date, I had always chosen the stable and known life. I was leaving a warm and incredibly caring family, many amazing friends, my house, job and community – yes, my entire life as I knew it was about to change. It would be a new beginning, but I had chosen it myself. That it was *my* choice and not someone else's made the change more exciting. I had to get the best out of it and I resolved that I would.

I dug out my Spanish grammar books from my bag, eager to practice as much as I could before I would really *need* it on the ground. I couldn't concentrate. My thoughts were everywhere as the plane took off – as I closed my eyes, I drifted off to sweet sleep.

Food for Thought

☞ Can you recall a work situation where you experienced the five stages (Denial - Anger - Bargaining - Depression - Acceptance) when exposed to change?

☞ What did you learn about yourself?

☞ Have you ever moved city or country on your own?

☞ What would be the greatest challenges for you?

☞ Have you ever had to build a network from scratch?

☞ Do you think you could do it?

Chapter 4: My Home is My Castle

The noise and chaos was incredible. The line for immigration was long and it felt like no-one had moved for an hour. I'd managed to sleep on the plane so I was fresh and exited. The company had arranged for a car to pick me up and it was already waiting for me outside. When I finally got through immigration and walked out from the heavily air-conditioned airport, I felt the warm sun on my face. Finally, I was here!

Denmark is an incredibly quiet country. Most Danes consider loud people boorish and irritating. As a nation, we cherish silence and calm. If you were to take the metro during rush hour, you would hardly know it was packed. People don't talk to strangers and if you are with someone you know, you will speak in hushed voices and definitely not attract unnecessary attention or irritate the others on the train.

Buenos Aires could not be more different! People were shouting into their mobiles like they were walkie talkies, not phones. People used the car horn at least every five minutes and if someone complained or shouted, others would jump in and join in on the complaint. I loved it! I had been there less than a day and I felt energised and happy.

For the first few months, I would be staying in a rented flat. My furniture from Denmark would take another six or seven weeks to arrive, so there was no rush to find a new home. The company had arranged for everything, from ensuring I got my visa, an airport pick-up and a rented flat. It was all taken care of.

I would eventually get a company car but to start with, I would have a driver so that I could get used to the city and its different traffic culture. The Argentine subsidiary used a *remis*, a typical private non-marked taxi company in Argentina. They didn't have the best cars but they had a dedicated group of drivers who were incredibly flexible when it came to waiting, driving, running errands, and so on. Because it was always the same group of drivers, they were more like colleagues.

A slim gentleman in his fifties by the name of Carlos drove me every day. He spoke a lot and he only spoke Spanish. His voice was deep and rusty from the 40 cigarettes he smoked on a daily basis. At the start, I didn't understand much of what he shared. Often, I just responded '*si si*', but soon enough he began to repeat what he was saying and insisted that I understood him. Carlos was key in helping me improve my Spanish during our daily car rides which, during rush hour, took an hour or longer each way. And slowly, as my language improved, I began to understand him!

My first day in the office went well. I landed the same day that the new FD, Patricia, came on a pre-visit. Patricia would not assume the role until a few months later but was there to agree the handover process. This also meant that the existing FD, Maduro, had no time to see me. As part of the agreement made in Denmark, I would be there on a three-year expat contract, paid by HQ in London. Apart from rent and car, the Argentine subsidiary would have me for free.

The first day was primarily spent with the Human Resources (HR) team and some of my new finance colleagues. They showed me around and generally took me under their wings. It was strange to arrive in a company without a specified job. I wondered what my colleagues thought, especially as I was the second most senior finance employee (the FD being the most senior) in the company, according to the Group's grades structure.

On my second day, Maduro called me into his office. An old-fashioned, alpha male type manager in his late forties. The type, I could tell, who shouted in the office, threw his weight around and was generally unreasonable. Something in his demeanour and approach triggered something negative in my ego. I hadn't come across this type of manager in Denmark. They are almost extinct there, but here was one fine specie still alive!

He started by saying, 'I don't know why you are here or what you are supposed to do, but HQ have told me that I have to find something that you can do. So, tell me about yourself and I will figure it out'. His accent revealed that he wasn't Argentinian. I began to share my treasury background and that I was an economist, not an accountant, by training.

He thought briefly and said, 'You will join the planning and reporting department. It will teach you something about accounting and how to work with finance in a company.'

He opened his door and shouted through the entire finance department for Matias (Matias led the Planning and Reporting department). As Matias entered the office, Maduro said, 'You will have Kim on your team. He knows *nothing* about budgeting and planning but you will teach him.'

I didn't leave the office feeling appreciated and in less than ten minutes, my fate was sealed. The entire situation was thoroughly anxiety-provoking.

Matias kindly took me into his team. He was also new to the Group, having started less than six months earlier. He himself was in the process of landing in the Group, building relationships, getting to know how things worked, and so on. He was in his early thirties, dark-haired, tall and slim. He spoke calmly with a deep voice. The contrast to Maduro was striking. I would soon connect well with him and he was a brilliant manager. He would teach me a lot about budgeting and planning in the finance field. His team consisted of six young professionals and they were all incredibly helpful, patient and warm. I could not have asked for a better welcome.

The hunt for *hygge*

I was on my way to view my sixth flat in Buenos Aires. The first five had been horrendous – dark, old, and not at all to my taste. I had filled in the form with what type of flat I would like and even sent pictures of my house in Denmark. At a minimum, I wanted the kitchen and bathrooms to be modern and bright. The real estate broker kept showing me flats that could not have been more incompatible. It began to be a joke that just wasn't funny.

For some, a house is just a house – a place where you sleep. For me, it matters much more than this. As I reflect back, I realise that I had a greater need for control at that time given the complete lack of control I felt in my work or daily life. Even basic communication was exhausting with my basic Spanish. Several core ego issues had been activated, and so my home had to be just right – the place where I would feel safe, recharge my batteries and recuperate after another challenging day. The place where I would find *hygge*.

Most Danes cherish *hygge*. If you're unfamiliar with it, *hygge* is an abstract concept. It can be obtained in good company with friends and family and in *hygge* places, which can be your home or other spaces where it feels cosy, informal and welcoming. An atmosphere where you relax, recharge, and just be yourself.

If you know the showrooms of the Swedish furniture chain IKEA, you will have an idea of what I mean by *hygge*. Nicely decorated and functional home, with many lamps in the rooms and selective soft furnishing to create a cosy atmosphere. Open fireplaces and candlelight on a dark cold winter's day rather than a single 60W light bulb dangling from the ceiling. According to Danes, this instantly kills *hygge*.

Living on the other side of the world alone, I knew I couldn't find *hygge* with friends and family so my flat had to hold all the *hygge* I needed. I could not see myself finding it in any of the flats I was being shown though. We continued to look.

After a few weeks, the real estate broker rang me. She had found three new flats. One was more than the housing budget the company had allocated, but I could top it up myself. The other two were still under construction, but would be finalised around the time my furniture would arrive. We went and visited them straightaway. One of them was outstanding - a brand new 40-storey high-rise with a beautiful garden and pool, all made to a high quality. I signed up on the spot and just hoped it would be ready before my furniture arrived some months later. In the meantime, I would stay in a small furnished flat.

Several months later, my furniture finally passed the customs checks and was delivered. The flat was ready and I moved in. It felt so good to see my things. I felt much more myself surrounded by my own furniture – a little bit of home. A new life in a new country and my home would be my castle! Somewhere I could rest and get my energy back, and it addressed my core need for feeling safe.

Food for Thought

☞ Have you tried to learn something new (e.g. a language or skill) as an adult?

☞ Did you notice a difference in your learning ability as an adult?

☞ What does your home mean to you and what surroundings are required for you to feel safe and at ease?

Chapter 5: A Sense of Belonging

At work, I had begun to settle into the Reporting and Planning function. I really loved working with the team. It was intense and I learned a lot in a short period of time. We also had great fun, not least during the late hours during busy seasons. They quickly became friends as well as colleagues.

Having settled more into my stride, I began to see that the office culture was very different from Denmark. My Argentine colleagues would engage with their colleagues at a personal level as well and this made it easy for me to feel welcomed. Danes are the opposite – they are at work to work. Whilst they are polite and friendly, they usually don't want to hang out with colleagues after work or engage in lengthy personal chats in the office. It isn't that Danes do not like their colleagues. Some will become friends but the majority will have well-established friendships from childhood. They don't expect or want to make other friends at work.

Many have busy lives, with a partner that also works full-time. They strive to be as efficient at work as possible so that they can leave the office on time to pick up their children from nursery. They may have hobbies after work or do sports (sports associations are very popular). Furthermore, it is uncommon, even for well-paid professionals, to have domestic help for chores like cleaning or cooking. In Argentina, on the other hand, if you can afford it, domestic help is very common.

This all means that a good work-life balance is a priority for Danes and ensures that there is a clean cut-off between people's work and personal lives, which is how most Danes like it. Unfortunately, it also means that it is difficult for foreigners to integrate into the Danish culture and make friends. Luckily for me, I was a Dane in Argentina. I got up every morning looking forward to going into the office and working with my team – they were friends and I felt enveloped into the culture and community.

On top of the day job, I received Spanish lessons in the office twice a week. The company was supportive of their employees developing language skills and many of the locals received English lessons. I tried to use my Spanish whenever I could and we would help each other out. Often, I found myself in uncomfortable situations in supermarkets, or calling utility firms and carrying out everyday chores with much more effort than usual.

The Spanish spoken in Buenos Aires is very different from that spoken in the rest of Argentina or in other Spanish-speaking countries. Known as *Rioplatense Spanish*, the language had inevitably been heavily influenced by the large Italian immigration to Buenos Aires. It is spoken incredibly quickly and I found it extremely uncomfortable asking locals for help. Often, it was easier to skip items I couldn't find in the supermarket rather than risk the impatience of a local. This was before you could look everything up on a smartphone. My colleagues helped me with making calls and various other administrative tasks, which meant I managed OK in the first few months. Gradually, my Spanish improved and I could manage on my own. Still, I was never able to grasp the language to a professional level.

After some months, Maduro left the company and was replaced by Patricia. In many ways, she reminded me of Claudia, the Spanish teacher I had during my five-week holiday. Due to that fact alone, I already liked her. She had an entirely different approach to Maduro. She was more well-rounded as a leader. During one of the first conversations we had, we spoke about my ten-plus years of treasury experience and my economist background. She expanded my areas of responsibility to include supporting the treasury department. This definitely made my day job more exciting and I began to remember what it felt like to bring value rather than feeling like a trainee using up other people's time asking probably annoying questions! Treasury was my specialist area. Something I was really good at.

At the time, treasury activities in Argentina were highly regulated. Lots of people were employed to manage the numerous paper forms and legal requirements in connection with buying and selling currency. More sophisticated financial products were not permitted. Most people working in the area were therefore not experienced in the more complex parts of treasury. In particular, my knowledge of capital injections and funding came in handy. It helped me feel useful and appreciated – two things which, I increasingly realised, I needed to feel comfortable.

The New Kid on the Block

The Argentine subsidiary had a long-standing culture of proud employees. It had been the market leader in the past. However, over recent years, increased competition and several failed strategies had pushed the company into loss-making territory. The mood was not great amongst the management team as they felt the constant pressure from UK HQ to turn the business around.

For reasons unknown to me, this ended up impacting how directors treated me, notably with much scepticism. Given my grade, I was invited to the top team meetings, but they were conducted in Spanish even though everyone knew that I would barely understand what was being said. I raised it several times with Patricia, but was told that she could not force them to speak English. It went further than that though. It was clear they didn't trust me. Time after time, as I arrived in the room or approached a group, voices would be lowered and subjects changed. It was not pleasant.

Whilst I had become friends with some of my co-workers, our difference in seniority meant that I couldn't discuss this with them. I began to really miss having close friends and family around me to discuss things like this with trusted loved ones. I was sure my mum's helpful coaching sessions with open-ended questions would have helped my brain to think rationally and reach a workable solution – to see, for example, that this wasn't really about me and that I shouldn't take it personally.

I called friends and family every so often, but during these calls, I was eager to sound happy and reassure them that everything was going well. Somehow, both parties needed to hear this, even though we both knew life was probably more up and down in reality. Pretending everything was OK somehow made it OK, at least during the calls. Plus, we didn't speak long enough to warrant wasting the precious time on bad news and there wasn't much either of us could do from the other side of the world. For now, I would have to find new ways to address the issues I was struggling with. I came to accept that this was just part of the experience of moving away and indeed, it forced me to dig deeper more than ever.

Eventually, with much sensitivity, I did speak with my team. Matias mentioned that he had at times felt the same. Not with the Spanish language, but the secrecy of conversations, general mistrust and switching of topics. Others in the team were empathetic. It provided me with some comfort to know I wasn't entirely on my own.

As the Orchestra Played On...

As time passed, I got to know the company better and it began to resemble a poor remake of the Hollywood hit movie, Titanic. The ship was obviously sinking but the existing management refused to acknowledge it, at least publicly. The delivery of bad news was heavily downplayed or carefully scripted. Many functions focused on reporting positive trends, however marginal the success.

The wider Group started to notice the early-warning signs. They demanded a radical restructuring of the Argentine subsidiary. We were given the option to come up with a sensible turnaround plan ourselves or have one given to us from London. Unsurprisingly, we chose the former.

It was decided that the restructuring project would be overseen by the Finance department, with Matias leading it. I would take over the Planning and Reporting team. I had only been at the company for four months, but I knew how strong the team was and I was delighted and excited for the responsibility. Gradually, things were making more sense – why I had risked the move to Argentina and how it fitted into my longer term career plans. I could see progression and again, began to be useful and deliver value to the Group.

Over the following months, the company came up with a new strategy. It was an overhaul. In order to have a major impact on the organisation, we would have to address key areas like culture, mindset, and behaviour. Whilst many managers, including myself, had seen this coming, it came as a surprise to the vast majority of the employees. Unsurprising given the leadership team had been opaque about the troubles that the company was in. At monthly performance meetings, they highlighted small positive stories of success and ignored the deteriorating bigger picture.

The mindset of the leadership team was one of protection and close-mindedness to perspectives that differed from their own. They were reluctant to respond to new information and change direction. There was little reflection on why strategies were failing and even their expectations of a turnaround seemed to be lacking. Sadly, it had not created a fertile ground for innovation, risk-taking or a coaching or mentoring culture.

Admittedly, the company had operated in a difficult political and economic environment, with tough competition from rivals. As most of the leadership team had been in their roles for many years, they operated with fixed mindsets and their behaviour matched this. I was only able to see this after a few months in the company and observing how differently Patricia, who was new to the company, acted and led.

The mindset and behaviour of the management team had fostered a culture where mistakes were not seen as constructive learning opportunities. Often failed strategies would lead to blame and a search for external excuses, while minor positive results would often be excessively celebrated and praised. Employees with matching values and behaviours typically got on well with senior managers and were held a small select group of insiders. They were favoured and thus became (negative) role-models for how others should act.

All great leaders make mistakes. Making mistakes is a great way of learning, but only if you actually learn from them. Those who admit their errors (sometimes publicly) and learn from them are the ones who create an environment where others in the organisation can also take chances and learn from their mistakes. All too often, I find leaders do not do this because they are too proud or believe they are, or should at least appear to be, infallible. This is a dated version of leadership.

My manager in Copenhagen, Elisabeth, had been one of the exceptions. When she realised her mistake for criticising the new furniture, she promptly apologised and even stood up for me in the face of continued disapproval from her peers. Subsequently, we were able to move beyond the initial disagreement and a fruitful partnership followed. It was something I respected her for and took onboard myself when leading others. Frustratingly, that sort of mindset was rare among the top management team here.

On the surface, it looked like the company was doing OK. The GM drove one of the most expensive Audis you could buy in Argentina at the time. The Head of Marketing could often be found in his sports car. The annual off-site meeting for the management team was held in the fanciest of locations, with no expenses spared. It was a textbook example of how *not* to manage a failing business.

The new strategy would require some changes to the group of Directors. With Patricia having only recently started in her role, it was the other Directors' positions that were at stake. This did nothing to improve the mood in the company, with Directors being territorial and playing their own playground games.

With time, I began to understand their behaviour better and why they had kept me at a distance. In their view, I had been placed in their company by London HQ – the very HQ that was demanding improvements be made. It became increasingly clear that some of them saw my placement as related to the company's poor performance.

Perhaps they thought I was feeding information back to London. While this wasn't the case, seen from their point of view and without asking me outright, what other conclusion would they have logically come to? Why would HQ place a senior manager in the company with an undefined role for three years, especially one with extensive background in funding and capital restructuring? It spelled change and external influence. It couldn't only be because of a deal made with the Danish subsidiary – it had to be something bigger. It wasn't, but perception is reality and it made my life much more difficult there.

Food for Thought

☞ How comfortable are you with making mistakes?

☞ How do you react to your own mistakes?

☞ How do others around you react?

☞ How do you learn from your mistakes?

☞ Have you ever been excluded from a group?

☞ What did you do about it?

☞ Have you kept certain others at a distance?

☞ Are there some people who you just trust less?

☞ Why do you think this is?

Chapter 6: So, You Said *"No"* to the Group Treasurer?

It was June 2009 and I had been in Argentina about half a year. I had established a good rhythm to my life.

I really loved my flat and the part of the city it was in. The security situation had deteriorated since the major crisis of 2002, but I felt safe. My routine included going to the gym and exercising in the local parks. I had my favourite grocery shops. And I had even made a few friends outside work who I would see during the weekends. Life was good.

I began to practice my Spanish with the security and cleaning staff in the building. They were great fun and I felt at home. Plus, I found the most amazing lady who helped me with my home. As I've said already, in Denmark, only the very wealthy people have help around the house – at least a lot of help. People take care of their own cooking, ironing, and cleaning, and children are brought up to learn that this is the right way. In state school, both girls and boys are taught to cook.

The average quality of life in Denmark is incredibly high. This is partly as a result of relatively high earnings for service staff and other jobs typically low-paid in other parts of the world. Of course, some people in Denmark would argue that the salaries are not that high but, compared to most other parts of the world, they are. Whilst this means taxation rates are also high, healthcare, education, and social care for the elderly is usually free. Nursery, day-care, dental and other services are also heavily subsidised.

A different system operates in Argentina. The wage gap between white-collar jobs and manual or service labour is much greater. Many will therefore have hired help for the home – often daily or live-in help. As I worked long hours, I embraced this set-up.

One of the security guards in the building recommended Lucia to me. She was in her early fifties, but she had aged very well (i.e. not aged at all). Tall, tanned, well-dressed and not at all how

I'd imagined a typical Argentine housekeeper would look! She would not accept the job unless I hired her for three full days a week. Going from no help to three days is somewhat of a treat, especially for someone like me who by nature is tidy. Three days a week meant I had all of my windows cleaned once a week, the bathrooms three times a week, and so on. I didn't need it but those were her conditions for taking the job! Basically, Lucia could not survive by only coming to my place once a week. It made sense to me. A shift in mindset but I didn't complain. I felt incredible spoiled.

We instantly hit it off and I saw her more as a friend who helped me take care of my home while I worked. I tried to help by paying above-average wages. I think it worked well for both of us and I was super grateful to her. At the start, I barely understood what she was saying – she spoke so fast! When I didn't understand her, she would speak even faster and use even more words (that I didn't know) to explain herself! I would be totally lost. Often, I just said '*si si*' but she knew I didn't get it. Somehow, we muddled through!

Do you want a career in the Group or not?

I was settling in well into my new Argentine life. It was all I thought it would be to live in that part of the world, and more. But, as I was getting accustomed to it, I was about to receive a call from London that would throw it all up in the air.

It was late June when I got a call from Miles, the Group Treasurer based at HQ in London. I had only met Miles once, during the handover of treasury activities from the Danish company to his team at HQ. I didn't know him well at all.

He came across as an Eton boy and indeed, as I later found out, he had gone to one of the best and most expensive boarding schools in the UK. He was well-groomed and good-looking, with an expensive tailored suit, floppy hair, and beautiful English accent. He had risen swiftly through the ranks of the company and was seen as one of the stars.

When I met him, he was just on his way back to HQ after an assignment in Asia and paid little interest in me, having come from little Denmark. I was surprised to receive a call from him. He got straight to the point, 'Kim, I'd like you to join my team in London. We are about to embark on a major transformational change journey to build a global treasury function and I would like you to be part of the new team leading the change.'

I was quiet. I am generally quick on my feet – but this call, I had not seen coming. And I didn't like what I was hearing.

After stumbling a little, I replied, 'Firstly, thanks for thinking of me, Miles. I am really flattered but I love being here in Buenos Aires and I am finally settling in. So… I will pass. But thank you for the offer.'

Now, it was his turn to be quiet. With a slightly different tone, he said, 'Maybe you should think a little about it. It would be great for your career.'

'Sure…', I replied. And that was that. I put the phone down. I sat looking out into the now empty office. Move to London? Back to HQ, misty weather and fifty shades of grey skies? No, thank you!

I had been clear with the company about wanting to live in Argentina, so I was confused but also a little upset over the call. In the end, I parked my emotions and tried to take it as a compliment.

The next day, Patricia called me into her office. She smiled and asked me to close the door. She got up from behind her desk and moved over to the coffee table, which she used for informal conversations. I took a seat.

She smiled in her usual warm way and said, 'So, you said "*no*" to the Group Treasurer?' and chuckled a little.

I was a little disoriented but gathered myself and responded, 'Yes, I want to stay. I love it here. And now you have asked me to lead the Planning function and support Treasury, I am even happier to be here. I finally feel like I'm making a difference.'

She smiled and said, 'But it's not really a job for you…'.

I didn't understand.

She elaborated, 'You are *clearly* overqualified for the position you are holding and I will never be able to find a finance position in my organisation that matches your grade and salary. After three years here, then what?'

I said, 'Well, that's in two and a half years. Life and job opportunities can look different by then.'

I began to feel hemmed in. I began to realise this wasn't an offer but a request. Change was being forced upon me. Again. And I didn't like it at all.

I tried to explain why I had come to Buenos Aires in the first place. That even though it had been difficult, I had finally settled in. That I had overcome all the challenges that come with landing in a new company and country, speaking a language that I barely knew, and that I really liked it here. I told her that I had little interest in going to London to work at HQ and even less interest in taking up a position that was newly created. It didn't sound that interesting at all. Besides, it was within Treasury and wouldn't I be going backwards into a specialisation I had already mastered?

Patricia responded that she understood, but then said, 'Do you want a career in the Group or not? If you reject an offer from such a senior person, the Group would most likely write you off.' She added that I would, of course, be able to stay for another two and a half years in Argentina as the Group had promised, but what then? I would probably be out.

By this point, my smile had entirely vanished. In an attempt to make me feel better, she said, 'That someone in HQ has you in mind, even though you are on the other side of the world, is a compliment. It means that you have impressed someone.'

It didn't make me feel much better and I could no longer see the compliment for what it was. I could only see the nice life I had carved out for myself melting away. We agreed that I should think about it over the next days and I left her office.

Unhealthy Stress

The next few days were tough. I hardly slept. My mood was visibly down. I had made this big life decision to give up everything in Denmark to move to Buenos Aires. Landing here had been much tougher than I thought. Along the way, I had realised that I was not as agile as I thought in respect of moving to a different culture, country, and continent. It had required a lot more work and energy than I'd expected to build new routines and friendships.

The first four months had drained me immensely. Only in the last two months had I begun to feel more at ease and somewhat stable in my work and personal environment. Just the thought of starting all over again after such a short time was unbearable.

Eventually, I called my parents and closest friends in Denmark and spoke briefly to them. They listened and told me their views. Unsurprisingly, most really liked the idea of me moving to London, which would only be a two-hour flight from Copenhagen. I could see that as a positive as well but as for the rest of the arguments, I couldn't agree. I appreciated their thoughts but I didn't really like what they said so I thanked them but decided to park it for the moment.

The stress, however, affected me a lot. Late at night on the third day, I suddenly had unbearable pain and cramps in my stomach. I could barely stand up. I called the emergency services and went into hospital with severe peptic ulcer symptoms. The only position I could find to ease the pain was to lie curled up in a ball on the hospital bed. The doctor explained that the symptoms were likely caused by excessive stress and ordered a few days' home rest and a strict diet. I hadn't paid attention to my body. It was the first time I experienced what stress could do to me physically and it worried me.

Lucia, who was indeed a friend, helped me a lot over those days. She came to look after me every day. She shopped for my groceries and prepared the meals recommended by the hospital (various nutritional soups). But more importantly, she provided care and tenderness. Feeling alone on the other side of the world, far from family, it made the world of difference.

I wouldn't call my parents or friends. The pride and will to manage my own situation, along with them not saying what I wanted to hear about London, deterred me from reaching out. Plus, hearing about the stress I was under would only have devastated them. They could hardly pop by and help me, so I kept it to myself.

After a few days at home, I returned to work. I had made up my mind – I would accept the job in London. Although it wasn't what I wanted personally, having the company keep me in Argentina for two and a half years knowing that they believed I was overqualified for what I was doing and, in all likelihood, having nothing else to offer at the end of the period did not seem like a great alternative either.

From a personal perspective, I had really enjoyed staying in Argentina. I had been out most weekends, loved the buzzing nightlife and had made friends outside work. Then, there were my lovely colleagues. We had so much fun in the office and they had taught me a lot that I would take with me into future roles. I would definitely miss them all, but was convinced that, one way or another, I would return to Argentina at some point in the future.

To move to London would mean I'd be back in Europe and closer to family and friends but, more importantly, it was the right decision from a career perspective and ultimately, I wanted to progress professionally. So, London was my decision. And London it would be.

The following week, I called Miles. He was delighted that I'd changed my mind. Whilst he wanted me to join as soon as possible, I managed to prolong my stay in Buenos Aires for another two months. I needed the time to properly hand over my job but, more importantly, to mentally prepare for yet another new beginning in a new country. My start date in London was set for September.

Shortly after speaking with Miles, my new manager, Samir, also gave me a call. He was overjoyed that I had accepted the role and was already heaping praise on me. I don't know whether he was just trying to cheer me up or whether he really believed I would be great, but it helped improve my mood. Resolved to my decision, I soon began to prepare myself and reset my brain for wrapping up my stay in Argentina and starting afresh in London.

Over the last two months in Buenos Aires, I utilised the time as best I could – handing over work, packing up my life and saying an elongated goodbye to friends, colleagues and, not least, Lucia, who had been such a friend in my need. Luckily, our friendship would continue despite me moving back to Europe.

I had some major learnings about myself during this period. Firstly, I hadn't been as agile as I had initially thought. I had never moved to another country so I didn't know what to expect. Secondly, reflections during the difficult first months had made me realise which of my ego's core needs I had to pay special attention to – inclusion and control. My reactions to them had been deeper than I could have foreseen. In the future, I wouldn't seek to avoid these emotions, but to be more aware and anticipate them. Thirdly, I discovered that I had a certain stress tolerance and that it was important to take note of that. I was able to cope with a lot of pressure but I had not paid enough attention to my body and the stress signals that appeared before the peptic ulcer.

The stress I experienced had a major impact on my health and I realised what I was and wasn't willing to accept. No work can ever be important enough to cause your body to collapse. I promised myself that in the future, I would pay more attention to those early signals in my body and to reach out to family and friends. Not sharing with them when things were tough was an absolute no-go for me. It was one thing to live on my own on the other side of the world, but to also refuse the support they could still have provided long distance regardless of the cost was, in hindsight, stupid. I should also only have asked them for advice *if* I was open to receiving their frank input. They were free to give their advice, but I was also free to weigh it and ultimately make up my own mind.

To help me make the decision to move back to London, I used two basic exercises. The first one was simply to jot down a list of pros and cons on a single sheet of paper. I revisited the list daily and added to it. Initially, I didn't see many positives to moving to London. However, on paper, the pros list grew gradually longer as I was able to see the options more objectively after the initial fear of losing control. My brain began to factor the pros into my overall thinking and I began to appreciate them more. In the end, I had an extensive list of pros and cons, from minor to major factors. I assigned each factor a weighting of 1-10, which helped me to prioritise the most important factors from unhelpful noise. I focused on those.

While the exercise is simple, it is tried and tested. When many thoughts are rushing around in your brain all the time, this busy activity absorbs most of your capacity to critically analyse and make decisions. There are too many factors. If you combine this with the negative emotions triggered by your ego when confronted with a sudden forced change, it becomes difficult to see the real options and opportunities objectively. When you put pen to paper, you relieve your brain of some of the energy-consuming analysis work (a part of the brain that operates with a fairly limited bandwidth) and the conclusion can suddenly become obvious.

The other activity I carried out was the post-mortem exercise. I imagined myself three years down the line looking back. How would my life have unfolded if I'd rejected the offer and stayed in Buenos Aires? How would it look if I'd accepted the offer and moved to London? Looking at something from different angles and focusing on those values that are important to you will help you to figure out what is actually important in the medium term.

For me, the choice was between becoming fluent in Spanish, meeting a Latin partner (given my family, I felt more affinity to the Latin culture than the Danish), and potentially growing old in Argentina, versus a successful international career, continuing with my bachelor lifestyle, experiencing more cultures, and growing in new and unexpected ways personally and professionally. Many of my future decisions would be based on these imagined ideal futures.

Food for Thought

☞ Have you ever been given an ultimatum in this way?

☞ How did it make you feel?

☞ What did you learn from that experience that has been useful?

☞ How do you manage stress?

☞ Can you tell the difference between healthy and unhealthy stress?

☞ Are there any big decisions you could use the 'pen and paper' or 'post-mortem' exercises on?

☞ What are some possible imagined futures for your life?

Part 2

Culture

Chapter 7: The Treasury Transformers

I landed in London on the morning flight from Buenos Aires, together with the other long-haul flights returning from all over the world into the British capital. The diversity and busyness fuelled me with energy. There was a familiarity to the city for me. I was back in business.

I had been to London many times over the years for work and pleasure, and had always loved it. I already had a few good friends in the city and, having come to terms with my Argentinian adventure being over (at least for the time being), I had even begun to look forward to setting up life in London. I would be closer to family and friends in Denmark and it would be an easier start to Buenos Aires, especially since I now knew what to look out for emotionally.

The first and most important task upon arriving in London was to start my second flat search of the year. I was dreading it. The experience in Buenos Aires had been a nightmare. This time, I braced myself and filled out the lengthy relocation forms even more meticulously, attaching photos of my previous homes and specifying exactly what I wanted in minute detail.

I already knew London well so I had clear ideas of where I did and did not want to live. Margaret, the agent assigned to me, wanted me to live in the posh parts of the city – areas that were already filled with expatriates such as Kensington and Knightsbridge. However, given the inflated prices, I would only get a tiny flat – the furniture I'd shipped over from Buenos Aires would barely fit!

I wanted to live centrally and suggested Kennington, an area many of my friends were living in. Margaret responded with, 'Kennington? You'll find nothing there. It's *south* of the river'. Clearly, she could have found *something* there, but it's much easier for agents to drive around showing you ten flats in buildings and streets they are already familiar with. Many properties will not even be close to what you asked for. Of course, Margaret was right – *she* couldn't find anything there. I doubt she even tried. She continued to drag me around flats the 'better' side of the river.

Needless to say, the chemistry between us just wasn't working. My blunt feedback was not fit for this British lady and I was stubbornly not conforming to her ideal of expat life. She clearly preferred to operate in certain circles of the British capital and I reckon I was in one of the lower tiers when it came to budget for a flat.

Luckily, one of my closest friends, Henry, lived in Kennington and suggested we meet after work to go flat-hunting together. He left the office early and we went into all of the local real estate brokers in the area. There were some potential properties but none were a perfect match.

At ten minutes to closing time, we went into the last estate agent on Kennington High Street and again explained what I was looking for – a bright spacious two bedroom with a modern kitchen and bath.

The agent instantly smiled and said, 'I have exactly what you are looking for. We got the flat in earlier today. It's a converted pub – one big open space with combined kitchen and living area on the ground floor, high ceilings and loft-style. Plus, two bedrooms and two bathrooms in the basement.' My face lit up like a Christmas tree. He continued, 'In addition, the flat has access to a large private patio in the back and is located on one of the best streets in Vauxhall, close to Kennington.'

It was within my budget and I couldn't wait to see it. Henry and I went over immediately and peered in from the outside. We even looked through the letterbox until a neighbour asked what we were doing! Today, Vauxhall is being rejuvenated to an extent that you would not have thought possible ten years ago. Back in 2009, it had a lot of edge (although some would call it rough!). It had a diverse ethnic mix of Latino, black and white people. Centred around the railway, there were streets of old and worn-out industrial buildings. Many of these transformed into a wild party scene at night. I loved it.

The next morning, I went back to officially view the flat with Margaret. It was perfect. She was visibly surprised. Twenty minutes walk to the London Eye and, even better for a Dane, I would be able to cycle again. The ride from the flat to the office would only take 15 minutes. It was the perfect location and I was filled with energy. I signed up on the spot.

Now, I knew London was going to be a great experience despite my lack of understanding of what job I was exactly there to do. Whilst it would take a couple of months to ship my furniture over from Argentina, the flat was taken care of within days. The company rented furniture in the meantime and I moved in immediately. Undoubtedly, this made the transition to London much easier. I had done my stint of short-term accommodation in Buenos Aires and although it sounds great on the paper, I wouldn't recommend it for extended periods. Start making your home as soon as you can – that's my advice.

KEEP CALM and Enjoy Your First Day

My first day of work at the Group's headquarters was interesting. Within seconds of arriving in the lobby, I understood I was just another employee. My seniority counted for nothing. Like most HQs, it was crowded with even more senior people and the sooner you realised that you are neither senior nor special, the better!

I took the lift up to the third floor where Finance was based. I was met by my new manager, Samir. They say that a person evaluates another in less than 15 seconds. Have you heard of the once-over? Upon meeting someone, we read micro signals in each other's faces, body language, voice, attitude, etc. It sounds scary when I put it like that, but we all do it.

Of course, we can revise our initial views as we get to know each other better, positively or negatively, but the first impression is vital and can be hard to shake off. Luckily, my 15-

second impression of Samir was positive, and I sensed it was reciprocal. He was around six feet tall (like me), well-dressed (like me!), had dark hair, dark skin and a big smile with shiny white teeth – a contagious cheeky smile you could see from a long distance away.

I quickly noticed that Samir was the type of manager that sets high standards for himself and his team. If you deliver, you will get along well with Samir. If you do not, it can turn out to be hell on earth for you. Luckily, I was not dissimilar in my own personality and approach, and it worked well for me.

We sat in his office and spoke for a while. I asked Samir, 'What do you actually want me to do? I still have no clue. I understand that you want me to take on the role of Transformation Change Manager, but what exactly is that?' He replied, grinning, 'I want you to make the change happen!'

Smiling back, I asked, 'What change?' His next answer was even less illuminating: 'The treasury transformation!' I decided to leave it for now. Clearly, it was a work-in-progress.

Over the following weeks, I read endless reports, notes, and presentations. It seemed to be all over the place. They wanted to change many things within the treasury space – systems, processes, ways of working, behaviours, team structure, and so on. Basically everything!

The vision was to be 'world-class' – a nonsensical phrase I have always disliked. What is 'the best in the world' and who is judging this? Plus, the Group was operating in more than 200 countries and each subsidiary was doing treasury in their own way – it seemed like an unmanageable task.

To give a bit more background, the company had successfully grown over many years both organically and through acquisitions. Indeed, the latter was how I joined the Group. This expansion strategy meant that the organisation was run like a federation of kingdoms. All kingdoms (subsidiaries, regions or areas) had to follow some universal guidelines, but overall, most were left to manage their activities themselves as long as results carried on being delivered. This set-up is highly inefficient for a global company, hence the Group had kicked off a major project to streamline and standardise across the organisation.

Within Finance, Treasury would be one of the first departments to kick off the transformation journey. Corporate Treasury, which covers areas like banking, foreign currency exposure, funding, and risk management, is best led as a centralised function, so it made perfect sense to start with us. Nonetheless, such a change on a global scale was a major task.

The team I joined, led by Samir, consisted of six managers. Each of us would focus on a different area like systems, processes, banking, and so on. My focus was on the broad topic of 'change'. We were truly an international team consisting of a Brit, Canadian, Indian, Irish, Russian, and me, a Dane. This would be my first time working with such a diverse bunch of people and without doubt I thought that it would bring new cultural challenges and opportunities.

Our team was embedded in the wider Treasury team, which was doing business-as-usual treasury activities. The rest of the team enjoyed making fun of us. As it was around the same time that the new version of The Transformers movie was released, it didn't take them long to ask us what we had transformed ourselves into and if Optimus Prime was around today. Thus, we were known as 'The Treasury Transformers'. We laughed along but to be honest, it got a bit tiresome after the tenth joke.

Over time, I realised that change and leading change is a funny area and many people don't really acknowledge the challenges that come with implementing change or the skills it requires. Perhaps it's their own ego issues that are triggered. It began to teach me why so many change initiatives fail. Many come to change management focusing on all the tasks that need to be carried out. They think it's obvious that change needs to happen, so end up telling (read 'dictating') what will change, how it should happen and to what timeline. Many forget the softer aspects of leading change such as addressing people's mindsets, behaviour, and culture. Change requires buy-in from all parties, otherwise it is an uphill battle.

To its credit, the Group had foreseen this and appointed six people dedicated full-time to leading the change journey in Treasury. There were many more in the wider Finance Transformation team. It seemed to be overkill to me but I was oblivious to how much effort it takes to drive a global transformation.

> *'Just take any step, whether small or large.*
> *And then another and repeat day after day. It*
> *may take months, maybe years, but the path to*
> *success will become clear' Aaron Ross*

As I began to understand the magnitude of the transformation the Group was after, I still struggled to understand what my own precise role was. Yes, I had worked on change in previous roles. I had also been involved in integrating the former Nordic part of the organisation with the Group, but a full-time transformation change manager? What was I actually supposed to do?

My ego issues around competence had been activated. I had never studied change management as a topic before. I had implemented it to the best of my ability, using knowledge, logic and empathy to manage different situations. That wouldn't do here. I printed hundreds of pages from the internet and read them in the evenings. When I'd exhausted the internet, I bought books. The topic was bigger than I had imagined!

Within change management, there many roles. There is the change process leader who keeps track of all the projects. The change initiative leaders execute different sub-projects. The change manager is responsible for the change journey (e.g. building awareness, planning communications, ensuring the change is embedded through company culture and so on). It can be a small and defined role but also a large and broad role, depending on how the rest of the change team is set up and how large the change is.

Still confused? First question is what type of transformation is it – a development, transitional or transformational change?[3] Based on what I had read, it seemed to be a transformational change, not least because the end game was not set but would be determined as we progressed. This is the most complex type of change and requires effort and skills exceeding what is normally captured under the umbrella of 'change management'. For simplicity, I use change management as a catch-all term throughout the book despite most of the challenges I refer to falling under transformational change.

I found more things to search on Google and gradually began to see the silhouette of what my role would encompass. As I had been given free rein to define my job, I began to build a plan that included all things 'engagement' – from presentations, town hall meetings and newsletters, to electronic learning zones and global roll-out plans.

I presented my initial ideas to the other five change managers. They provided helpful input which I took onboard and a more concrete strategy began to take form. Then it was time to share my grand plan with Samir. I presented it at the next team meeting, setting the scene and walking through the various steps.

Samir stopped me. I looked puzzled. He said, 'This seems vague and- '. Before I could respond, a colleague interrupted and said, 'Give him a chance – it gets much better.' Samir let me continue. I ran through the rest of the presentation and before I even got to the last slide, he stopped me again but this time, he burst out with, '*This is great.* I *really* love it. It's just what we need.'

Phew.

He told me I should present it to the Finance Transformation Board as soon as possible and ask for the funds to start. That was always Samir's approach. He could have presented it to the Board himself but he liked those who'd actually done the work to have exposure to top management. This was a feature I always appreciated and something I tried to apply as a leader myself.

The Board signed it off. We could start on the journey right away. I was excited. I had made sure to include several streams that really fascinated me. I was beginning to learn about leading change in a more structured way and I was being backed by my leaders around me. The energy was back and now I felt it was the right decision to be in London. I had a role I had basically designed myself and set the parameters to which I would be measured on, and now, I was about to embark on implementing it.

Still, I had a lot to learn about this new Group, and this takes me to the Group culture.

The Group Culture

All companies have a culture, not least of all long-standing companies with a strong cultural inheritance. The culture is not typically written down in manuals or listed on the company's website. No – it is subtle and intangible, and it is the unspoken behaviour that drives how the company operates as an organism. It will be reflected in who gets promoted and what behaviours are and are not acceptable.

When companies hire new people, the hiring managers will make unconscious choices around who they hire. Many corporates even have cultural tests that you are asked to complete and they will tell the hiring manager how aligned you are to the underlying DNA of the company. And once you are in, companies will seek to mould and form you further into their DNA via shared corporate values and behaviours.

I will share a personal experience I had with this. After Samir signed off on the strategy, he asked me to present it to his manager. I told you it was a hierarchical organisation! It didn't stop there. I also had to present it to other very senior finance managers before taking it to the Board. Yes, even people I didn't know, need to know or who should have any interest in what I was saying. But guess what? They did and they had plenty of feedback.

My own cultural background is a consensus-seeking one. The concept is in no way alien to me. However, seeking agreement from unrelated senior persons for how *I* would carry out *my* newly-created role was. As I was still relatively new to the company, I did as I was advised.

Many of the managers gave good feedback and helped to improve the approach I had come up with. Others gave weak feedback and I struggled to see the point of making any of their proposed changes. However, speaking to Samir, with his many more years of experience, I learnt something valuable. He taught me how to incorporate a little feedback from everyone into the strategy. It didn't have to be a big thing and I only took the most relevant points, but enough to demonstrate that I had listened, reflected on and appreciated their views. I could also see that it helped me to build relationships across HQ and start to build a name for myself in the organisation.

Although I couldn't see it at the time, as my understanding of the company grew, I realised that one of the strongest DNA features in this Group was consensus-building and inclusion. Without this realisation, you would be doomed in the company. Even if you had good ideas, you wouldn't be able to get the buy-in for them and this was a company in which you needed broad buy-in.

Over the years, I would see this numerous times. I would also adapt my approach to seeking input and providing input when asked, even into areas I had little interest in. The beauty of this *shared ownership* DNA is that a large group will visibly support the project and provide back-up should you need it, even sometimes with resources. They do this because they feel it is also their project and they have a share in its success or failure. Clever, isn't it?

Basically, I learnt that you do not always get exactly what you want, but you can get close, and that is much better than getting nowhere at all.

Food for Thought

☞ How quickly do you form impressions of new people?

☞ What features or personality traits are you drawn to or put off by?

☞ How much does it take for you to change your initial opinion?

☞ Have you ever created your own position?

☞ In what ways can you do that in your role now?

☞ What three characteristics define the culture in the company you work in (or companies you have worked in)?

Chapter 8: Let's do Lunch…

As part of my move to London, the company offered me half a day of cultural training. Coming from Denmark, I thought it wouldn't be needed, but I could not have been more wrong.

We met in the office and Alice, the trainer, began running through some of the key differences between Danes and Brits. She had a beautiful, well-articulated English accent, and was suitably tactful in her explanations of the main cultural differences between the two nations. She didn't just talk about what characterises the Brits, but focused on where there were distinct differences to the Danes. I began to understand that working and living in the UK was going to be quite different to visiting for a week's holiday or work conference.

Until the session with Alice, I had observed some differences but I hadn't really grasped that all countries are characterised by a distinct set of cultural features, wrapped up in the country's history, geography, politics and so on. Whilst not everyone will behave in the same way, if you take a large enough group, then this is the behaviour that the majority will exhibit, albeit to different extents. That is the nature of culture.

I started to learn with fascination. What makes a Dane recognisably a Dane, and a Brit characteristically a Brit? A book that really helped me was *The Culture Map* by Erin Mayer. Mayer is a professor at INSEAD and researches cross-cultural differences. Through the rest of this book, when reflecting on my experiences working with cultures from all over the world, I will refer regularly back to her cultural scales. Whilst my own experiences taught me a lot about different cultures, Mayer helped me to understand them in a more structured way.

Mayer describes different cultures according to eight scales:

- Communication
- Evaluation
- Leading
- Deciding
- Disagreeing
- Trusting
- Persuading
- Scheduling

I will cover the first four here and the remaining four in later chapters.

Communication

Mayer categorises different cultures according to their communication approach – from low-context to high-context. This was also one of the first areas that Alice brought to my attention through the half-day cultural training.

On one end, you will find the US amongst the lowest context in communication, while Japan and Korea are amongst the highest context. Think of a marriage. If you have been married for 50 years, you do not need to use many words to communicate with your spouse. Your methods of communication will be nuanced, multi-layered, and much will be expressed by tone and body language alone. This is possible because of your shared history and deep knowledge of each other. This is how high context cultures work. You will typically find this in Asian, African, and Middle Eastern cultures.

On the other end, you have Americans acting more like newlywed couples. The US was essentially founded on immigration. It is a nation of immigrants who brought their own languages and cultures, so it makes sense that messages are conveyed in a direct and often basic way. Nuance hasn't had a chance to develop over many years of shared history. The communication style is precise, simple and clear. Repetition is appreciated. Messages are taken at face value. This is what Mayer would call a low-context culture on the communication scale. Other countries in this camp would be Australia, Canada, Germany and the Netherlands.

Denmark and the UK would still be considered low-context, but less so. If you included humour into the equation, the Brits would score higher given their love of irony and sarcasm. In the middle of the range, you find many Latin cultures across Europe and Latin America, and Russia.

While the exact reasons for the evolution of a country's communication style is complex (it's a mixture of many factors), one factor that may play a major role is how isolated or closed-off a country has historically been. Japan would be a prime example of a country on the high end of the context scale and even today, 98% of its population is of Japanese descent. The important thing to remember is that there are many different methods and modes of communication. One isn't necessarily better than another but different approaches will be appropriate for different situations. It's good to know where you and your counterpart are likely to be on the scale.

Evaluation

When it comes to evaluation, Denmark is characterised by having a direct negative feedback culture, together with countries like the Netherlands, Germany, France, Italy, Spain and Russia. The UK, like much of Latin America, favours more indirect feedback. Middle Eastern, African and Asian cultures are the most indirect in their feedback, with some Asian cultures feeling extremely uncomfortable to give or receive direct feedback.

As I would come to learn, in practice, this meant that my culture was much blunter in delivering feedback than the Brits were used to. Often, I would unconsciously use so-called up-graders such as 'that is *absolutely* inappropriate', 'how *totally* unprofessional' or 'I *strongly* disagree' when providing feedback. This was normal in Denmark but didn't fit in with the UK working practice.

In Denmark, it wouldn't be unusual to present something during a meeting and have the other team members openly express their strong disagreement. You would take time to clarify and justify your points. At times, your team mates would change their minds and come to your point of view. At other times, they would not. For Danes, disagreement and debate is a highly effective way to test a point of view. For some cultures, such as the British, open debate can feel highly uncomfortable, confrontational and even rude.

This isn't confined to professional contexts. You can find the same dynamic at social events. With my friends and family, the discussion can touch on almost any topic and a heated discussion will often take place over the dinner table. Even if it leaves the impression that people are arguing strongly and emotionally engaged, it won't negatively impact the relationship afterwards. It's part of the fun and part of expanding our viewpoints. Of course, people can always step over the line but then you or someone else would usually jump in to say, 'let's focus on the ball, no need to get personal, it's only a discussion'. When you are accustomed to such a culture, direct feedback is perceived to be authentic and honest.

Brits, on the other hand, are far less confrontational and often make use of so-called down-graders. They soften criticism, e.g. 'I think that is *somewhat* inappropriate', 'that may be *a little* unprofessional' and 'I'm sorry, I *kind of* disagree'. Seen from a Danish angle, Brits do their utmost to avoid bluntly saying that something is bad or not up to their expectations. Instead, they embark on long-winded speeches that frankly confuse other cultures like mine. What may be based off the best intentions not to offend someone else, actually results in them not actually landing their message.

It took me a while to get this.

Let me share a few examples. To me, 'quite good' means 'quite good'. For Brits, 'quite good' means 'that's a bit disappointing' or, in the best case scenario, 'that's OK, but not great'. The phrase 'I hear what you say' would mean to me 'I buy your arguments and I will take that into account', whereas what Brits are actually saying is 'I disagree with you and let's not discuss it further'. When Brits end a conversation with 'Oh, by the way…', I hear 'this is not really important but now that we're talking, …'. What they are actually saying is 'what I've been meaning to say this whole conversation and why I set up this meeting up in the first place is…' and deliver a criticism. Furthermore, a word like 'interesting' for Brits means 'this is clearly nonsense'.

I definitely needed the half-day cultural training just to learn this lesson! Alice provided some lively examples and explained that most British people are brought up from childhood to avoid putting other people into an uncomfortable situation or intentionally hurting them. Thus, when a Brit is chit-chatting with a new colleague at work, many would ask 'do you have a long commute?' rather than 'where do you live?' The latter may make the other person feel uncomfortable because they will feel compelled to answer you and they may be private or live in a bad neighbourhood. By asking the length of the commute, the other person can volunteer extra information or give a safe answer that doesn't reveal too much and doesn't make anyone feel uncomfortable.

Another example would be when you bump into someone you are not that fond of on the street. It could go like this.

> A: *Oh* it's been *ages*, how are you doing?
> B: I'm doing very well, thanks. And you?
> A: I'm doing *very* well too, thanks. Well, I'm in a hurry but let's do lunch one day.
> B: That sounds great. That would be lovely indeed.
> A: Well, take care.
> B: Thanks and you too!

Coming from a direct culture, I would be expecting an invite by email or text soon, before realising that we don't actually have each other's contact details and so, clearly, the Brit did not want to have lunch but was being polite. And that we would both know this.

Alice certainly raised my awareness in this area but I also had to learn it through experience. Shortly after I designed the new change management strategy, I was asked to present it to Miles. I ran through the whole presentation and at the end, he was a little quiet but remarked in his posh British: 'interesting'. Prior to my cultural training, I would have heard that as him being impressed with my work, but now I had my doubts.

The combination of my Danish bluntness and being alert to his response made me burst out, 'OK, so you don't like it?' As Miles raised his eyebrows, he responded, 'What do you mean?'

I explained – I had just received some cultural training and had understood that 'interesting' usually means the opposite in the UK. He laughed gently and explained that it is true but there are two versions of 'interesting'. To know which one, you needed to pay attention to the intonation. One would mean 'this is clearly nonsense' and the other would mean 'this is interesting'. What a minefield.

We laughed and as I left the office, the only thing I was thinking was that not only do I have to be aware of the dual meaning of sentences in Britain, but also be alert to the intonation and facial expressions. I would have to decode every sentence like Sherlock Homes!

Generally, Danes make much more use of *facial* up- and down-graders when speaking and use them to emphasise what we feel and mean. Brits excel in the opposite. As ones preoccupied with not offending others, they use facial expressions to dampen what they mean. A neutral facial expression or overly smiling one may be particularly used in situations where they are disagreeing with you. In Denmark, this is also called two-faced but in the UK, to not do so would be insensitive! The truth is that even in Danish, 'interesting' can have two meanings. However, when 'interesting' is negatively meant, it would be delivered with a clear sarcastic tone and with exaggerated facial disapproval.

It would surely be easier with written communication, or so I thought. I was asked to draft a note for the Management Board of Directors. I took lots of time to carefully construct it. For people not used to writing board notes, I can tell you it can be a complex and lengthy task. You have to include all the relevant information without surplus details (without knowing necessarily what the Board will find surplus), and it needs to be well-written, concise, easily understood yet highly informative. Regardless of the complexity or scope of the project, the note cannot exceed a handful of pages. The shorter the better. These guys do not have long to spare and they receive a lot of information all day long. They are expected to make incredibly difficult decisions on limited information, and the buck ultimately falls with them.

I had written many board notes in the past in my other companies but this was the first time I was writing for this Board and this was a much larger company than any I'd worked in before. I read some notes that others in the team had written and got a good idea of what was expected. I put pen to paper and gave it my best go. After working on it for many days, I sent it to the wider Treasury team and waited for their feedback.

It went like this: 'great draft' and 'the first is always difficult to write and I only have minor corrections, which I will send through later today'. I was relieved. Maybe I have a natural talent for this!

I couldn't have been more wrong. When I received the marked up document, there wasn't a *single* sentence that had not been altered. It was a full rewrite. I could barely recognise it. I ended the day annoyed and demotivated.

Over the following weeks, the note was rewritten many times over by many different people. This was when I began to understand that when Brits say 'great, we're almost there' or 'I would suggest...', we are nowhere near and I would need to take their 'suggestion' into account or justify myself.

Leading

Alice's cultural training helped me understand some of the experiences I'd encountered in previous years. Denmark is amongst the most egalitarian countries in the world, together with the rest of the Nordics and the Netherlands, and this is what Danes take into their leadership style. Australia and Canada are also in this bracket, but to a lesser degree. On the opposite end of the spectrum, you have hierarchical cultures such as those found in large parts of Asia, Africa, the Middle East, India and Russia. The US, UK and many Latin countries fall in between.

It is relative. If you are from a more hierarchical culture like the UK, you may find Brits egalitarian but when you come across Danes, you will find the Brits *more* hierarchical on a relative basis.

You can see this reflected in different ways. For example, many Danish senior managers and politicians cycle to work and often also dress casually, to match their employees or voters. They may have a nice company car but they may not use it that often (their spouse may end up mostly using it). In Denmark, I also had a company car (an Alfa Romeo 159) but I mostly cycled the 6km to work in my suit – always worn without a tie. Delegating the ownership of tasks and decisions is also common. It is seen to motivate people to take ownership and grow as individuals. In hierarchical countries, this can be perceived as an outright lack of leadership and that you are not able to make decisions.

Deciding

When it comes to making decisions, Danish culture is consensus-based. On the Mayer's scale, Japan has the most consensus-based culture, followed by the Nordic and North European countries like Germany and Netherlands. On the other end of the scale, you will find countries like Russia, India, China and Nigeria, who have a top-down approach to decision-making. In the middle of the range, you will again find the UK, US and the Latin world.

Again, it is relative. Even though Denmark is a consensus-driven culture, we, Danes, would consider our neighbouring countrymen, the Swedes, much more so and likewise, they would consider us as more top-down driven.

During the integration of the Danish subsidiary with the Group, the British team struggled with the endless discussions that we had on any decisions. That even personal assistants and newly hired graduates would air their views during the meetings did not make it easier for them to accept. My role increasingly became centred around managing the discussions among the Danish employees in Danish, gathering the consensus view and then sharing it with the UK team. Often, the UK team would support the decisions but they found things moved slower.

In my experience, there are clear advantages to consensus-based decision-making. It may take more time but once a decision has been reached, implementation is carried out pretty quickly and you avoid the political hiccups that come with top-down decision-making. People feel like they have been consulted and their opinions taken into account. I believe this work upfront is worth it and gives people time to adjust to the new direction. However, there is also a disadvantage - it makes it difficult to make course corrections at short notice, which are often necessary somewhere down the line.

As the Danish subsidiary inevitably took on more of the Group's UK-based culture, many employees did not feel heard and this was frustrating. During the days of the integration, I didn't fully comprehend how much cultural differences impacted the working relationship between the two organisations. You'll rarely see a Danish employee treating a senior director with more respect or gratitude than to a security guard or the receptionist. All are treated with equal respect. In the new organisation, this was no longer the case. With hindsight, it explains many of the tensions and incidences we experienced at the time. Although it sounds obvious now, back then, we did our best and learnt whilst going, often through mistakes.

Back in the UK, despite my cultural and on-the-job training, I never adjusted fully to the British culture. I still believe that bluntness saves time and effort. Things are done faster and there are fewer opportunities for misunderstanding. I recognise I may be biased here and it continued to cause me occasional trouble. Samir often laughed at me and would then coach me to soften my communication style. Gradually, I learnt to add more down-graders into my sentences.

I didn't truly appreciate what my bluntness must have felt to Brits until I worked with the Germans and Dutch. They are more direct than most Danes. They are also lower context in their communication style and really spelled things out. When I experienced this for myself, it gave me some insight into how Brits must have viewed me! That was some raw unfiltered critique! Even for me, their approach felt a bit harsh and provocative. I softened my own approach further after that! Still, I think some would still have considered me too blunt, rude or direct. What can I say? They should be happy they didn't experience me before I received the cultural training!

Food for Thought

☞ Would you consider yourself low or high context when communicating?

☞ Would you consider yourself direct or indirect when evaluating?

☞ Would you consider yourself egalitarian or hierarchical when leading?

☞ Would you consider yourself consensus or top-down when making decisions?

☞ Can you identify someone different from you in each of these areas?

☞ How does this impact your interactions with them?

Chapter 9: Simon Says

My change management strategy consisted of several strands. One of those involved a complete revamp of the internal intranet site. We would over-communicate in order to make sure that some of the messaging got through.

I had to work with the IT department to put it into place. It was a lengthy process. Some of the IT functions had been outsourced to India, so I worked with contractors in Bangalore. Here, I soon realised that when I suggested something specific and with a strict deadline, I would normally get a 'yes, we can deliver this' response. To me, this meant that the activity would be carried out in good time. To the other party, this meant that the deadline would be a rough aim and that, if there were delays (of which there always were), the timeline would be renegotiated again. It caused a lot of frustration on my side.

The Indian culture is a very high-context culture. Communication is less explicit than my culture. I also communicated directly with the individual at the call centre appointed to help me rather than going through the coordinator as information was often lost when my messages were passed on. This approach works well in egalitarian societies like Denmark's, but it was not well received by the manager in India. I was oblivious to this, however, and ended up unintentionally upsetting the manager and putting his employee in an uncomfortable position. Thankfully, there was an Indian lady working in the IT department in London who was amazing and helped me to understand where I was going wrong culturally. She eventually took over the communication with the call centre and that made my life a lot easier. The simple fact that two IT people were now speaking directly to each other made everything work much smoother.

Within the treasury department, all of the functions were involved in some way with the transformation project. After all, they would be the ones whose ways of working (hilariously shortened to 'the WOWs') would be impacted. However, they also had full-time day jobs (their business-as-usual work), so the change project was at the bottom of most people's to-do lists. It caused a lot of frustration on my part. Often, I wanted to do everything myself but they were supposed to be the subject matter experts and, in any case, they needed to take ownership. It was my first real experience of leading change among people from so many different cultures and people who had little interest in the change.

The idea was that the finance community across the globe would understand and buy-in to the overall vision – where we were going, why we were embarking on the journey, what exactly would happen and when. But some of the changes meant that control and responsibility was being taken away from the local markets and concentrated at HQ. Understandably, people don't like having their power and responsibility reduced. You're fighting an uphill battle before you've even started.

To address this, we needed to seek buy-in into the broader picture. A lot of engagement across multiple levels was required. Promotional videos were recorded with the main sponsor of the change, the Group FD. Other more targeted presentations were made to different senior finance employees across the globe.

One major project initiative was around the process for forecasting cash flows in different currencies. When you operate in around 200 countries, the daily movements in currencies can have a large impact on the company. Managing currency movements is vital for international companies. To manage this, the Group needed an integrated reporting tool and standardised process across the globe. Initially, my role was to cover the communications and planning of the rollout of the new forecasting process and system, but this soon grew to leading all aspects of the project, from design to implementation. This was a meaty task that I would relish.

Having worked with cash flows and forecasting for over ten years, I had a profound understanding of what was needed. I tried to strike the right balance between simple and sophisticated in order to ensure the change would be manageable. However, it didn't take long before my approach was questioned. Several senior finance managers across the operating markets began to ask what I knew about the Group and how it operated.

I was a little put out by the question and puzzled by all the noise, which didn't seem justified. I spoke to Samir, who asked, 'Which pilot markets have you included in your trial?' 'Pilot markets?', I said. 'Yes, have you not planned for some piloting to be done in certain markets? Markets who can test out and feedback on what you've designed? To act as a sounding board to ensure you've catered for different needs?'

'No...', I responded. He looked at me disappointed. I realised I had not understood the dynamics of this Group or my audience well enough. I had only seen the task from the HQ side. We needed the information, so we could centralise and make decisions based on it. But where were the operating markets in this discussion?

The Group's culture overall was a consensus-building one, but it wasn't as clear cut as the theory suggests. This Group had a consensus-building culture, yet was also hierarchical in its approach. Therefore, consensus was typically sought among senior managers and stakeholders, and not typically those who would be personally impacted. I wouldn't be able to do much without broad support, but I needed broad support amongst the senior managers first. I couldn't just come from HQ with a 'Simon says jump' attitude and expect everyone to jump.

I asked Samir which countries to include for the pilot and together we selected a group of markets with different business models and varying degrees of complexity. We also chose markets that were benchmark markets in their respective regions. This meant that if we had their support and buy-in, it was more likely that other markets would follow suit. Another key learning.

Initial progress was slow. Several of the pilot markets did not show their support. I decided to invite them to London on an all expenses paid workshop. This called for some personal engagement skills. A month later, seven treasury colleagues from seven operating markets came to London to attend a three-day workshop.

They stayed in boutique hotels in the centre of the city and I took them out for dinners each night, not just to woo them but to get to know them on a personal level. As the days went on, we progressed well. Engagement rose substantially. I began to appreciate how relationships-based this Group was. Even more so, I began to appreciate the benefits of managing your stakeholders. This had been less important in Denmark, not because stakeholder management is not important, but because this was on another scale. It's one thing working with and convincing others who are similar to you. It's another thing to work with and convince people who were culturally entirely different from you, long-timers in the Group and from a global organisation of lots of local kingdoms. It required a wider stakeholder understanding than I had been used to.

After three great days of work (and pleasure) in London, the seven said goodbye with a hug and travelled home, now far more committed to the project. Over the following weeks, we made progress and we had setbacks. Compromises had to be made on both sides but we were all broadly happy with the final product.

Wiser from my earlier mistake, I actively involved the pilot markets in the rest of the global roll-out. In fact, we brought representatives from the pilot markets with us as we travelled around the world holding workshops with the local markets. It was helpful to be able to demonstrate that key peer markets were happy and I believe we were met with less resistance because of this strategy.

The learning is clear. Always ensure you include the influential opinion-makers in your rollout strategy. They may not always agree with you and it will take longer to win them over, but in a smaller forum, you can work with them individually and reach mutually agreeable solutions that everyone can live with. This will ensure a more successful rollout and implementation and save you time overall. Thereafter, thorough planning and ensuring you have invited the right stakeholders is key.

'The world is a book and those who do not travel read only one page' Saint Augustine

We kicked off the first round of workshops in Europe. As travelling around Europe is relatively cheap, we held three meetings in three different locations – London, Copenhagen and Amsterdam. Markets were invited strategically to one of the meetings.

The first workshop, held in London, included only the UK, Ireland, and several HQ functions. Given my cultural training and experience in the UK, I adjusted my speech and approach (e.g. shaved off some of the bluntness). Discussions were balanced and no one rocked the boat too much. Typical of the Brits, the overall feedback was that the workshop was 'not too bad'.

The second workshop, held in Copenhagen, was for the Nordic and Baltic countries. The Nordic countries are culturally similar and at the least, they are all familiar with each others' differences. Denmark, who was the leading operating market in the region and one of the pilot markets, already felt a sense of ownership of the new design, so it was a joint effort to bring the other markets onboard. The Scandinavian audience appreciated the egalitarian and consensus-building approach that was taken and, after a few days and lots of debate, ownership was established amongst the other markets as well.

The final workshop covered the remaining 30 European markets. This would be more of a challenge. Participants congregated in the Group's offices in Amsterdam. It was a mixture of mega markets like Germany and much smaller ones like Belgium and Switzerland. Given Germany had been a pilot market and had been intimately involved in the design and testing, it was difficult for the other European countries to raise many concerns. Everyone knew that what came from the successful German operating market would have been thoroughly thought through and tested – like a German premium car.

As the workshop was hosted in the Netherlands, the Dutch team was richly represented. They were a loud and blunt crowd. Their questions and challenges were fierce but it didn't put me off. I enjoyed the challenge. As the Dutch team unleashed their blunt and direct feedback, I took onboard their views and knew that, despite the hard tone, the critique was directed at the change, not at me as a person. Still, it left most other participants quiet for a while. The southern Europeans were more accommodating. Having lived in Argentina, I had a few tricks as to how to win them over. I knew the social and relational aspect was key so I took care to connect with them on a bilateral basis, especially in the break and meal times. The eastern Europeans were mostly silent during the workshop sessions, but they approached me off stage and raised their questions and concerns in smaller groups. All in all, it was a successful workshop, with many different cultures and demands managed. European engagement – done.

We tackled Africa, the Middle East and Russia next. We met in Istanbul. I sensed this was going to be the toughest one yet, not least because of the breadth of cultures and opportunities for cultural missteps! This was the first time I had worked closely with people from these regions, so it was a huge eye opener for me. Was I up to the challenge?

Like Germany, Russia was a mega operating market in the Group and they had been one of the pilot markets. Through the piloting, I had already learnt a lot more about the Russian culture and way of working. Again, very different to my own. In many of Mayer's cultural scales, the Russians are almost the exact opposite to the Danes. The Russians are high context communicators, extremely hierarchical and top-down decision-makers. It made for some frustrating situations in the early days of the pilot stage. Whilst I sought input from all parties in my typical egalitarian and consensus-seeking way, the Russians almost saw this as weak. Had I understood their respect of strong and firm leadership, I would have been far more direct and authoritative.

The local Turkish team were brilliant hosts and Istanbul was breathtakingly beautiful – a vibrant city full of history and culture spread across two continents. At this point, in 2010, Turkey was fairly open and liberal. All of my preconceived ideas of what it would be like there were corrected. As the Group had recently acquired a large local company, there were some of the same challenges that we'd seen during the integration of the Danish subsidiary some years before. However, what really surprised me was that nearly all of the local finance team and *all* of the managers, very competent managers, were women. It was refreshing to observe what we mostly seem unable to achieve in the West.

Other countries included Egypt, Nigeria, South Africa, Saudi Arabia, and many more. Many Middle Eastern and African cultures are similar on the cultural scales, but they are all on the opposite end to the Danish. Despite this, the three-day workshop went very well and there was a friendly and collaborative atmosphere. I could see that trust was built during more informal settings such as at dinners where people could relax and get to know each other on a more social level.

Three regions down and onto Asia Pacific next, but first, a few further observations on three more of the cultural scales.

Disagreeing

Another of Mayer's eight scales focuses on disagreeing. From my observations, the Russians are even more confrontational than the Danes but only when not limited by hierarchy. In the workshop, the Russians typically did not question or disagree with their managers, but they absolutely did when they were amongst peers. Other high scoring disagreeing countries include Germany and the Netherlands, as I had well experienced first hand. In the middle, you'll find Australia, the US, the UK and Latin American countries. Amongst the least confrontational, you'll find the Asian and some African and Middle Eastern countries.

Trusting

Today, I know that when it comes to trusting, the Russians have a relationships-based culture. Respect only comes after you have gotten to know each other on a more personal level. Before working on the cashflow forecasting project, my initial perception was the opposite. This was partly based on how I'd seen Russians often portrayed in movies, but also because of the heated debates I'd personally been in over the months of the pilot phase. In Denmark, trust is built over time and based on your track record. Mayer calls this a tasks-based culture. Hence, if you are going to work with someone who is known for being talented and delivering, you will logically trust them to be trustworthy and deliver for you too. With the Russians, trust was built through relationships and over vodka shots in the evening. Whilst I recognise this confirms another stereotype portrayed in movies, things did go a lot smoother after those evenings!

Persuading

When it comes to persuading, the Russians, Germans and Latin Americans have what you would call 'principles-first' or 'why' cultures. These cultures build up the 'why' based on theory before moving onto the practical. Take foreign language learning, for example. Such cultures are taught languages with a focus on learning the grammar rules first. Only when there's a good grasp of this do they move onto speaking and applying that knowledge.

The Danish and British cultures are more 'application-first' or 'how' cultures. The US is the same. Real-life examples are showcased first, with less effort initially placed on the theoretical or philosophical underpinnings of the language. In Denmark, English teachers will start speaking the language to you from day one and gradually teach you the grammar and structure as you go along.

As we had a combination of 'why' markets (Russia, Germany and Argentina) and 'how' markets (Denmark, UK, Canada and Australia) in the pilot, we ended up needing a good balance between principles and application when it came to persuading the markets.

Looking back, I could understand why Samir, who had lived in Canada for most of his adult life, had stopped me after only ten minutes of my change management presentation. He came from a 'how' culture and found my 'why' introduction far too long and boring. I needed to have captured him with a story or built up an image of what the change would practically mean. Luckily, I had learnt this lesson in time to apply it in the implementation of the project itself.

Food for Thought

☞ How comfortable are you with confrontation and disagreeing with others?

☞ Do you consider yourself task-based or relationships-based when building trust?

☞ What works better on persuading you – 'why' or 'how' arguments?

☞ Can you identify someone very different to you in these areas?

☞ Would you change your approach when engaging with people culturally different than you in the various areas?

Chapter 10: Making a Fool of Yourself Can Build Trust

We had two more regions to tackle – Asia Pacific and Latin America. The next workshop was to take place over three days in Singapore. We had participants coming from all over the region, including Japan, Australia, Malaysia, Korea, Indonesia, Pakistan, Sri Lanka, Bangladesh and, of course, Singapore.

It was my first time in Singapore and although tiny, it is a fascinating country. I loved its futuristic architecture and I would say for that alone, it is worth a visit. It's a highly controlled society, with people behaving orderly and politely. You might know it for its cleanliness and for having banned chewing gum. However, it is also a mix of cultures itself, with language, food and people from its neighbouring countries. Whilst the national language is Malay, most people speak English or rather Singaporean English (affectionately known as *Singlish*). You should listen to it. It has a rhythm and melody that I found very soothing to the ear!

Perhaps I should have done more research given the mix of cultures culminating in the one place, but hindsight is a brilliant thing. What I had picked up from previous travels and colleagues was that many Asian cultures were known for keeping up appearances, not sharing their emotions and definitely not losing face in public.

I had planned the workshop in my typical egalitarian style. I was looking forward to great discussions with the participants. Unsurprisingly, this wasn't how it turned out. Out of 25 participants, there were only a few comments made here or there, and barely any questions raised. Only the Australian team were sharing their views and I already knew theirs before arriving given they were a pilot market. The Singaporean team had some comments too but apart from that, nothing. As the first day came to an end, I was exhausted even though we'd finished an hour earlier than planned.

When I got back to the hotel to freshen up before dinner, I had little energy for the rest of the night. I was frustrated and slightly disappointed. I felt I had given 110% of myself in energy and charisma, yet I had received nothing back. I was dreading the next few days. One of my colleagues from Romania was accompanying me on all the workshops and felt the same way. We were able to laugh a little about it. I took a quick shower and had a strong drink to pep up my mood before making my way to dinner.

On arrival at the restaurant, I could already feel a shift in the atmosphere and a buzz I was surprised about. People were smiling and laughing. A lot! I sat down and soon had a glass of wine in my hand. A group surrounded me immediately and said how they had loved the day and found it really interesting, but now they wanted to know more about me. I talked about my background and they were eager to know more about Denmark. I was the first Dane many of them had met.

What followed was an amazing meal including the delicious Hainanese chicken rice and the less appealing dessert fruit, *durian* (only to be eaten whilst not inhaling through your nose). Absolutely stuffed, we moved onto a bar – a karaoke bar to be precise. Now, anyone who knows me knows I hate karaoke. I have absolutely no tone to my voice. Even when intoxicated. Soon though, I found myself in full X-factor style standing on the stage screaming into the microphone to the tune of *Don't Stop Believin'* by Journey. Had Simon Cowell been there, I would definitely have been buzzed off and derided for even trying. But he wasn't, so I survived an entire song, to everyone's amusement.

Thankfully, the laughter from the crowd was sincere and warm. It didn't seem to matter that I sounded awful, I had given my all and was fine making a fool of myself. For some reason, karaoke is a game changer in Asia! Singing terribly at high volumes into a microphone with others somehow bonds you together. It ended up being a fun night and I found out that some of my colleagues even had a decent singing voice! After many drinks and many more songs, it was time to call it a night. I went back to the hotel a bit baffled about how the day had ended so well! I had been completely unaware of how relationships-based most Asian cultures are. And how warm, funny and engaging many are when they're outside the office. In my culture, people are more or less the same at work as they are outside work but in Asian cultures, there are specific rules around how you should act whilst at work, and those are only relaxed when you're outside the office. This can make sense too.

The next morning, the atmosphere at the workshop was entirely different. People seemed more engaged and, even though the discussions never reached the level of debate of their European counterparts, it grew day after day.

This left only the last workshop, which we held in Costa Rica a few weeks later. It covered the entire Americas, North and South. And what a difference there was between the northerners and the southerners. It gives me the opportunity to bring in the last of Mayer's cultural scales – scheduling.

Scheduling

Latinos are very social and communicative. They operate on the 'more is better' mantra. Stories are rarely kept short and time is flexible. Whilst we had kept pretty well to the schedule in the workshops, it was clear that time and agenda were only regarded as a guide to the Latin Americans.

In her book, Mayer differentiates between cultures that operate on linear-time and those that operate on flexible-time. As with all the scales, it is a continuum. Along with most Northern European and North American countries, the Danes operate on linear-time. This means that everything is measured in time. Meetings are planned to a pre-agreed agenda, with time slots allocated for each point. To keep to the timing schedule, including arriving and departing on time, equals respect for each other. And this isn't just in the work context. If you are running more than five or ten minutes late to meet a friend in Denmark, you will send a text or make a call. You do this as soon as you know you will be late. Time has a high value.

In flexible-time cultures, agendas are more indicative. It is less important to start and end meetings on time. It is acceptable to interrupt a meeting to take a phone call or to take toilet breaks even during a one hour meeting. When someone realises they missed something important because they weren't paying attention, it isn't rude to ask people to repeat themselves. Everyone who paid attention the first time will now hear the same points being repeated, but they won't be offended. In my culture, this would be outright disrespectful to another person's time.

Outside the work context, arriving on time may not actually be regarded positively. Do you not have other things to do? Being late, on the other hand, is acceptable and even expected. Others won't be there if you turn up on time even if you arrive half an hour or an hour after the agreed time. This even happens at weddings in some flexible time cultures.

This was what I'd experienced during my nine months in Argentina. It was an unwritten rule – 7 p.m. means 8.30 p.m. at the earliest. After sitting on your own in a bar for an hour, you end up adjusting pretty quickly to this new rhythm. I hate waiting alone in a bar. People would be late for good reasons. When you commute in a city like Buenos Aires, your journey could take an hour on a good day or four hours on a bad day. In light of this, it's entirely understandable that time is a flexible concept. However, it was challenging to manage the agenda of the workshop in Costa Rica, not least because the Canadians and Americans turned up on time! This final three-day workshop had the longest working days of them all but they were also the funniest.

One Size Fits None
The global rollout of the new cashflow forecasting system taught me a lot about leading change globally. Specifically, how leading change in different cultures requires sometimes radically

different approaches and a lot of extra sensitivity and skill. Whilst my descriptions above are based on what I felt, your experiences will differ because we have different cultural DNA. As I've said, it is all relative. If you come from Brazil, you may well perceive the British as direct and even confrontational, but to a Dane, Dutch or German audience, they are frustratingly the opposite.

When we left London for our global tour, we had designed a three-day programme that would be identical for all of the markets. On day one, we would introduce everyone and cover the 'whys', i.e. why we're doing this, why it had been designed as it had, and so on. We would give real-life recent examples or forecasting errors that had resulted in extra cost and risk for the Group. We would build the clear case for change. We would then cover the 'whats', i.e. what would change now and what other changes were still to come.

We would only lightly touch on the people implications of the changes. In other words, the potential redundancies or role changes (without using these exact words). Coming from a low-context culture, I would have preferred to have such important topics out in the open with no second-guessing or potential for misunderstanding. If this isn't done, in my experience, people gossip amongst themselves, and typically guess the worst anyway. So, this is what I did – I opened the floor for people to raise their questions.

Again, hindsight is a brilliant thing.

Immediately, the cultural differences were visible. In Europe and the Americas (low-context cultures), most people jumped in. Our openness was appreciated and it led to some hectic discussions. In Asia, Africa and the Middle East, it was met with silence. It was not the right forum for such a discussion and had I known what I do today, I would not have included it in the session.

All of the participants appreciated the dinners as a time to get to know each other and build relationships. However, again you could sense that for some, those times were more important than for others. In Costa Rica, the American and Canadian teams where the first to call it a night. They needed to be fresh for the next morning. After all, on a cultural scale, the US and Canada are among the most task-oriented cultures.

In some Western cultures, losing control and saying something stupid when you're drunk could result in trust being broken and a loss of respect, whereas for Asian and Latin American cultures, almost the opposite is true – you come across as more authentic. The more you reveal of yourself, or the more you make a fool of yourself (*Don't Stop Believin'*) the more others will begin to trust you. You're not trying to hide your real self, so others can take you and what you're saying at face value. I wish I had swotted up on this more prior to the workshops.

Over the course of the global tour, we learnt a lot more about how the new system would practically work in different contexts and for different needs. Based on participants' feedback, we tried to adjust certain elements, but we would never be able to satisfy everyone. The input gained from the Russians wouldn't have addressed the concerns of the Canadians. Subsequently, I learnt that to design a global rollout required pragmatic terms. One size fits none. You need to take into consideration the local needs, culture and mentality, but you also need to know what is set and where there is room for flexibility.

Culture is a vital element that is often forgotten in business. When you understand that other cultures are different from yours, you generally tend to accept more. Why? Because you now understand that their behaviour is culturally driven and not rude or deliberately difficult.

Despite my unpreparedness, we managed to get the majority of the approximately 100 operating markets onboard that we initially focused on, and overall, the feedback was positive. Empathy and smiling a lot seemed to help! Soon after, the entire Group began to report in a common and structured way and my mission was accomplished. What a tour!

Food for Thought

☞ How good are you at building others' trust?

☞ Would you feel comfortable making a fool of yourself if it serves a larger purpose?

☞ Do you consider yourself linear-time or flexible-time in scheduling?

☞ How culturally aware are you and is it something you think about when interacting with others?

☞ Have you seen people from other cultures through the lens of your own culture?

Chapter 11: The Two Minds

The last challenge of the global rollout was to ensure that it was embedded into the everyday workings of the local treasury teams – a vital stage when implementing any change. Here, some understanding of the two systems of the brain is helpful.

Psychologist Daniel Kahneman talks about it in his book *Thinking, Fast and Slow*. The first system, System 1, is the fast, automated part of the brain. It operates in an unconscious, involuntary, and intuitive way. According to scientists, this part of the brain makes use of pictures and reacts to them without using a lot of energy or time. It is the part of the brain that accesses the enormous amount of data stored in our unconscious.

The other system, System 2, operates more slowly and consciously. It is the part of the brain that is used when we reflect on things. It requires much more energy to operate (sugar and oxygen) than System 1[4]. It was the system I used when thinking though the difficult decision of whether to leave Argentina for the UK or not. It was also the reason why writing the pros and cons down helped me. It relieved my System 2, which can only process so much at a time.

Our ego operates from our fast-working System 1. The core issues of safety, inclusion, power, control, competence, and justice are triggered by memories of similar situations in our past. A negative memory is automatically brought up and a response is triggered to protect us against the repeated threat to our ego. Only when we consciously work through our automatic thought patterns and behaviour do we begin to understand our unconscious mindset and think how we can avoid being misled by System 1's autopilot.

I'll give you an example. System 1 automatically concluded, on my behalf, that I was being excluded by the management team in Argentina. I now know that this was triggered by previous experiences of being excluded from certain groups. It started as an uncomfortable thought and grew in system 1 when I couldn't speak to others about it. Why am I being excluded? Could it be because of this or because of that? I'm on my own in this and I don't know what to do. When I finally spoke to others, I realised that in that situation, it was not related to me but more about them. They were suspicious of me and saw me as an outsider. Perhaps they were worried because they were aware of the poor results of the company and didn't want anything to change their comfortable set-up. Only when I employed my System 2 did I understand the more likely reason for their unpleasant behaviour towards me and the stress that I felt started to calm down. My System 2 was taking control of the situation, reflecting, and calming the emotions triggered by System 1.

The two systems are at play and interacting constantly. They have an impact on most things. Another example is when you drive a car and your mind starts to wander. You suddenly realise you haven't been paying much attention to the traffic so, while your System 2 was busy thinking and analysing some thought, your System 1 was driving the car. It would have reacted instantly if a danger were to arise and then your System 2 would have to take over to manage the longer term consequences.

Our external environment also impacts the two systems. Experiments have shown that the brain will build a connection between a certain learning and the place it was learned. One of the main reasons for this is that System 1 operates with pictures. Your unconscious mind reacts to pictures that are fairly similar to other pictures it has stored in the unconscious part of the brain. It may not be exactly the same picture, but the brain will still make the connection as it is operating at an extremely fast speed and the slower analytical System 2 hasn't kicked into gear yet.

For that reason, you may also hear a song on the radio while driving under a bridge and think 'I need to download that song when I get home', but then you forget and only when you drive under the same bridge three days later do you remember the thought again. Your brain stored the memory of the song and attached it to the memory of the bridge.

Understanding the dynamics of the two-system brain is really helpful when working with change. When we were carrying out the workshops, I wasn't aware that participants would primarily be employing their System 2s. Luckily, they were also being fed plenty of coffee and snacks to fuel their brains as they burnt energy reflecting, analysing and learning. However, it would take longer for them to incorporate the learnings into their day jobs, especially as they had learnt them in an environment different to the one where they would subsequently be putting them into practice.

When they first got back to their own offices, they probably felt energised and had great intentions to implement the changes, but then the daily workload would hit them. All the tasks and emails that had been piling up in their absence, waiting for their attention. All the visuals (i.e. pictures) in their surroundings reminded them of their old ways of doing things. Deadlines were coming thick and fast, and so it was much easier to revert to whatever they'd always done. That is typically how it goes. Their days are mostly driven by their System 1 brain, used for executing daily routine tasks without excessive use of energy. There are no visual triggers in their office reminding them of their recent learnings.

For that exact reason, learning and training in your daily environment, especially in the form of 'at-the-desk training' is very powerful. We tend to do the opposite – hold workshops elsewhere. Whilst that has its advantages in terms of fewer distractions, we also lose the ability to use the environment to re-enforce learnings. I wasn't aware of the two-systems brain until a few years later but had I been then, I would have constructed the workshops in such a way to also appeal to people's System 1.

For example, we could have given participants longer to plan how they would implement the changes in their own specific contexts. They would visually have built up new ways of working in their imaginary usual business environment. If we got them to design their new routines with clear trigger points at the workshops rather than wait until they returned home, there would have been less of a disconnect between the workshop ideal and business-as-usual life. System 1 requires pathways to be recoded and this can be done through repetition. The likelihood that you will recode your autopilot increases if you start to think of them in the present form (i.e. I do) rather than as a future event (i.e. I will do) and apply the new changes immediately. It would also have been good to get them to identify some helpful triggers in their work environments that would remind them regularly of the new ways of working and why they're a great idea. However, as we hadn't sufficiently thought this through, the embedding of new routines was not a smooth journey. Other measures therefore had to be taken and this leads me to reflect on carrots and sticks.

Carrots and sticks

Another key learning I had about embedding change was the importance of leaders leading by example. The senior managers (typically local FDs) rarely attended our workshops so they didn't have an active stake in the change. They weren't always ensuring that there was sufficient focus from their teams on implementing the changes.

We tried to establish buy-in via endorsement from the very top (the Group FD), promotional campaigns, etc. Still, it was inherently challenging due to the fact that the centralisation and standardisation project would inevitably lead to a leaner finance function in the local subsidiaries. Local FDs knew this and many were understandably resistant.

A few initiatives were employed to try and improve their commitment. One initiative was to include the forecasting accuracy metric into the bonus metrics for treasury and associated functions. One of the problems with forecasting real cash flows is that the treasury team is reliant on many other functions (e.g. procurement, marketing, HR, etc.) to accurately forecast their cash flows. Treasury can assist in this but ultimately the quality of what comes out of the forecasting process depends on the quality of what goes in. Consequently, the support from those most senior in finance, typically the local FD, was vital. This initiative was what I would call a carrot approach to incentivising behaviour among employees.

Another initiative was to name and shame those countries who weren't complying with the new process. This was the stick approach. The reporting would be shared on a dashboard that all FDs globally could see. Local FDs are typically ultra competitive creatures. When something gets measured and reported, they want to rank better than their peers.

The first initiative mostly addressed the motivation among the doers, whereas the second initiative ensured the interest of the senior directors who were in charge.

One of my main learnings from this time was that our stakeholder engagement had to be much stronger and broader. This isn't unique to the Group because of its consensus-building culture. Rather, it is key to the success of any transformation project. If senior managers are not leading by 'walking the walk', any initiatives will lack staying power. I subsequently learnt much more about senior stakeholder engagement in later roles and will touch further on this in later chapters.

Food for Thought

☞ Recall three things you tried but didn't manage to change in the past?

☞ Similarly, recall three things you succeeded in changing?

☞ How do you think the two systems were engaged in these situations?

☞ What else could you have done to engage System 1 more?

☞ Do you respond better to carrots or sticks?

☞ Why do you think this is the case?

Chapter 12: How Much do You Want to Stretch Yourself?

It was never boring in the transformation team but after two years, most of the initiatives had been completed. My knowledge around cultural differences, transformation and working with global project teams had been substantially lifted. The cash flow project was one of the most visible as it impacted all of the markets across the globe, but there were many other initiatives that we implemented that laid the foundation for continued centralisation for years to come.

It was time for me to move on. The team of transformers would eventually be absorbed into the rest of the treasury team. My new role was to be the Regional Treasurer of the Americas. I would be London-based but travel a lot to the region.

After two years working primarily in transformation, it was good to be back in commercial treasury, getting a sense of the business and helping to drive business results more directly. Although there were still some treasury staff in the local subsidiaries, much of the decision-making was now centralised into HQ. The regional treasurers essentially owned the treasury activities for their region and were tasked with ensuring that decisions were aligned with Group policy and strategy.

It was still early days in implementing the new operating model and there were plenty of teething issues. It required a lot of stakeholder management to hold the Group position and not unravel the good standardisation work. In a technical field like treasury, and with plenty of local regulatory rules restricting and allowing certain activities, this was not easy!

The role deepened my ability to lead indirectly. Local treasury staff reported to their FD, not to me. I therefore learnt to lead through communicating a strong vision, motivating the staff by involving them in regional initiatives and supporting their development. My peers were a broad group of senior partners and stakeholders at HQ, ten cluster and local FDs, and the rest of the central treasury team. I also managed many international and local banking partners across the ten clusters and countries. It was not an easy task. On those rare occasions when you were able to orchestrate the right solution where all parties won... well, it was extremely satisfying.

It was also exciting to travel so much, not least because many of the countries went through periods of stable growth and improving living conditions for its populations. During each of my visits, I got a better sense of the particular culture and pride of that country. It was a privilege to have this opportunity and to work with so many talented people.

Some people who travel frequently for business get into the routine of flying in for their meeting and leaving again without seeing the country or spending time with locals. Given travel from London to anywhere in the Americas was long distance, I always tried to extend my business trips to include some time for pleasure and exploring (at my own cost). I would add two or three days to see more of the country. I found this invaluable for my understanding of the country and culture, and it was invaluable from a professional perspective as well. You get a wider impression of a country than you do living a day or two in an international hotel, eating with your colleagues in an expensive restaurant filled with expats and only taking taxis to and from the office. I believe it helped me to understand the local operating market and its people better. It always awoke a curiosity in me to imagine what their daily lives must be like and the challenges they might have to cope with.

After two great years as Regional Treasurer, I began to feel under-stimulated again. When I am under-stimulated, my energy level drops and I am not my best self. I will take care to do my job well, but it'll only be good, not excellent.

I know the signs. I begin to lose the drive to push new initiatives. Activities that used to excite me just don't anymore. It feels like fatigue. Of course, when new projects are birthed, I'll feel a burst of energy but it won't last. In any case, most changes in the region had already been implemented and it was time for a period of stability. We weren't going to change again for the sake of keeping my job interesting! This is when I know it's time to move on.

For the same reason, I think it is healthy for corporates to require a change in senior management after a certain number of years. Fresh energy and fresh ideas are needed not just for the company but also for the manager to keep growing. The tendency to comfort and complacency is stronger when the company is in a relatively stable business environment. It is much easier to coast when there isn't a stick. We all know this. Newcomers, however, are able see the landscape with a new pair of eyes and not only spot new opportunities but also to pre-empt problems.

The Group had given me a mentor a few years back. Although many companies have mentoring programmes in place, not all companies have successful mentoring programmes. One reason for this is they don't pay enough attention to matching the mentor with the mentee. It's like any other relationship – there needs to be trust, respect, and chemistry. There may be two great individuals but if they're not a good match, nothing fruitful will come out of it. Sometimes there is absolutely no chemistry between the two parties. At other times, the two are almost like friends. This isn't good either as they become too familiar with each other and what you talk to a friend about is different from what you go to a mentor for.

On occasions, I have seen that some mentors are too senior or junior for their mentees. If there is too great a gap, the mentor may struggle to understand the mentee at the level at which they operate. If the mentor is at a similar career stage or level themselves, they will have limited additional experience to share. This is what peer relationships are for, not mentors. There are many things to think about, but when it's a successful match, it can be a powerful tool to get the best out of your people.

I hadn't utilised my mentor, David, much at all. He was a senior guy with a lot of varied experience in the Group. He wasn't the most talkative person. He would make himself available when I reached out to him, but otherwise we would have no contact. The mentoring was exclusively based on my need.

In the first few years in the Group, I hadn't felt I needed David much. But now was different. I needed some advice from someone who knew the inner workings of the Group much better than I. I reached out to him and we talked about where I was in my career. I shared that I had reached a plateau and that I wasn't feeling challenged and therefore not giving my best.

David listened and asked, 'Why only treasury?'. I began with my usual speech about being an economist and having a long background in treasury. David looked at me and said, 'So? Why not something different? Maybe FD in an operating market?'.

I looked confused at him, 'I have absolutely no experience in that field and in any case, I don't have an accounting qualification'. He smiled, 'You're around 40 years old, you have more than ten years of management experience and have already held several senior roles. Do you use your economist training in your current position?'

After reflecting, I responded, 'Well, no. But I use my experience from other roles on a daily basis.'

'Experience in finance or management?', he asked.

After another short pause to think, I responded, 'Both... but mostly management' and it was at that point that I had a realisation.

David continued, sharing his own career journey and describing the many varied roles he had held. He explained that what had made him strong in each of them was not his technical knowledge but his ability to lead. His strength was to see solutions for problems and to take tough decisions.

I left the mentoring session with my head spinning. All these years, I'd been working in Treasury but I'd been building up my management and stakeholder engagement skills, plus an ability to understand and work with different cultures. I hadn't been to a school of management. I had picked up the skills on the job. Also, why do I still call myself an economist when I don't really do anything economics-related in my day job? As I said, I had many thoughts.

I reached out to my network of colleagues and friends who were, as usual, ready to coach me. They all asked the same question, 'Why not?'.

Yes, why not?

I gradually started to see that it was my own fear of failure that was preventing me from taking a chance and doing something new. I had taken the plunge in previous years, moving from Denmark to Buenos Aires and then to London. But I'd had four years of relative stability and I'd gotten out of the habit of taking risks. As the day job for the last four years had been sufficiently challenging, I hadn't quite realised this. But it had been challenging in a different way and challenging *within* my comfort zone.

What was the worst that could happen? I wouldn't die. It wouldn't cause me physical pain. It would hurt my pride and damage my self-esteem if I didn't do well, but on the flipside, what would happen if I stayed in my role for the next two, four, or ten years? Stalemate. Boredom. Despair. That's how much I dislike not being challenged!

Some old ego issues were beginning to surface again – my all too familiar competence and inclusion issues. Over the years, I had realised just how important feeling both were for me. But I had learnt that the best way to address these ego issues would be to challenge them. To take chances and demonstrate to myself that I could overcome them. Instead of holding me back, I would use my ego issues to accelerate my personal development.

Overcoming Fear and Taking Chances

A career move towards FD would mean moving away from the UK. Over the four years, I had grown attached to London. A city I wasn't that keen on moving to originally, I now had an amazing flat in central London and wonderful friends. I still hadn't quite gotten used to the British culture or the HQ stiffness, but my private life was thriving and I lived a rich bachelor life in every sense. My friends and family from Denmark loved that they could come and visit me at short notice and have somewhere to stay where there was always something happening.

I had fallen in love with the diversity that I think can only be found in major cities like London and New York – diversity in all its forms. I had built friendships with people from all over the world. It had really expanded my cultural awareness, but also appreciation of different ways of living. In London, you can be yourself and no one really bats an eyelid. There isn't the same social cohesion as you find in a place like Denmark, but that was exactly what challenged and developed me. It forced me to see things in a larger context than I had ever done before. It was so enriching.

It was 2013 and London had just hosted a standout Olympic Games. The city was blooming as never before and a sense of pride and unity was felt across the capital. This was years before the word Brexit had even been invented. Was I really ready to give it all up for my professional development?

When I made the decision to move to Argentina, it was something that I had already decided for myself. The job opportunity was a bonus. When it came to the move to London, it wasn't so much a suggestion as a strong encouragement from the company. This time, there were no obligations connected to the idea. Only me thinking about my current life and how I wanted it to develop.

So, how exactly did I want it to develop? I imagined myself five years down the line – still in London, not having developed much and having turned cynical in my comfort. Definitely not. I want to continually grow. To be challenged. Not end like another corporate HQ body waiting to collect my pension.

*'You Can't Make Decisions Based on Fear and
the Possibility of What Might
Happen.' Michelle Obama*

Back in the office, I asked for a meeting with my manager, Nick. He'd been in the Group for over 20 years but was fairly new in the position of Group Treasurer and new to the world of treasury. By then, Miles had rotated out into another senior role as part of his development. I didn't know Nick that well.

After the obligatory five minutes of British informal chat that starts every meeting, I shared my thoughts about wanting to continue developing and move onto the next thing. Nick was surprisingly supportive and promised to bring it up at the finance top team's next talent meeting.

Less than a month later, he called me into his office and as I sat down, he smiled in a cheeky way, saying, 'I have good news for you'.

Immediately smiling back, I responded, 'Ohh?'

'Yesterday, we talked about you and your next move in the global talent meeting. There was broad support for you to try your hand at your first FD role.'

'Amazing!' I said intrigued, 'Where?'

Nick paused and said, 'Well that depends… How much do you want to stretch yourself?' and smiled again.

I looked at him a little confused, 'What do you mean?'.

He replied, 'Well, there's a smaller FD role in Europe… and a larger one in the Americas region'. As I had worked with the Americas region for two years now and really loved the people, I asked him to tell me more about the Americas role. Nick responded, 'It's Venezuela'.

My face stiffened and I felt my stomach tighten in knots. I knew it – it was too good to be true. I had visited Venezuela as Regional Treasurer. It was one of the most dangerous countries in the world. There was security everywhere – armoured cars, restrictions on every movement. But also, a great and competent team.

I asked him to explain a bit more about the two roles. The one in Europe would be a lateral move – a safe choice with limited stretch opportunities. Venezuela, on the other hand, was a full-blown market with its own factory, sales and distribution. The country was going through a lot of financial distress so my economist background would serve me and the company well.

I asked if I could think about it. He confirmed I could but asked me to respond after the weekend. I left his office equally excited and worried.

Venezuela.

I had been told I could call the two former FDs who were already in new roles in other countries. As I already knew them, I gave them a call straight away. They both spoke warmly about their experiences there. They mentioned the obvious challenges but also talked about how great the team was and that it had been one of their best experiences in the Group. It really helped talking to them, but I also knew that they'd been there many years before and the security situation had since worsened a lot. If they felt it was difficult then, what would it be like now?!

Over the weekend, I spoke to the usual suspects - my parents and friends in Copenhagen, and my friends in London. Suddenly, my concerns were less around whether I would be successful and excel in the role of FD, but how I would live in such a restrictive environment. It would be an experience like no other. My family and friends were supportive but also expressed concerns with the security situation in the country. One thing was moving to Argentina, which was far away but still relatively safe. Venezuela, on the other hand... I assured them that security would be provided by the company. Still, most expressed that I should not expect them to visit me.

I returned to the office after the weekend and went straight to see Nick. I told him I was interested in the role in Venezuela. He was delighted and said that he would come back with an indication of timings. Either way, it was going to be soon. I couldn't help but feel excited. This was really happening! I felt the energy I'd missed coming back to me.

I had another catch up with Nick a few weeks later. This time, he told me there was a slight delay. 'It's still yours', he said, 'But it will take another seven or eight months before you can move'. The energy drained out.

Despite having lived in the UK for four years now and been taught that appearance is everything, I couldn't hide my disappointment. Having seen my reaction all over my face, Nick once again assured me that the role would be mine, I just had to wait a little longer. I left the office early that afternoon.

My newly found motivation had evaporated in an instant. I'd had a single weekend to make a very difficult decision. I had made that decision and now, the position wasn't even available for another seven or eight months. It felt like standing in the queue to the world's biggest rollercoaster. You know you will love it when it when you get on but you feel tense and nervous while waiting.

Getting Your Story Right

Over the following weeks, I thought about what I could do and it suddenly hit me – could I perform my current role as Regional Treasurer of the Americas out of the Americas? I was traveling back and forth frequently anyway. Surely it would be easier just to be based there.

I spoke with Peter, a close friend in London. One of my few English friends. He had been perfect for giving me guidance on how to engage with the British culture and especially senior English managers. He said the idea was good, but questioned why the company would support it. Because my motivation was low? That's hardly the mentality of high performing talent, is it? He had a good point. What did the company have to benefit from my brilliant suggestion?

We decided that rather than talking about being disappointed and demotivated now that I'd been mentally preparing for my next role, I would rephrase it more positively. The more direct approach would have worked in Denmark but in the UK, it would sound immature and egocentric. I would most likely be met with 'Dry your eyes, eat your cookie and move on mate!' and I would have gained nothing.

We rephrased my suggestion as the following: What if I performed my current role out of Buenos Aires over the next six months? I'd be able to study and practice my Spanish and being in an operating market (which is very different from HQ) would give me a better feel for how one operates. It would be great to shadow Patricia (the local FD), who I already knew well, and could learn a lot on the ground. In addition, working and travelling around the region would be much cheaper than travelling long haul back and forth from the UK and... not to mention that the Group would get the best and most motivated Kim as I'd be stimulated by all the changes and challenges around me.

It sounded like a good story to me and Nick was positive about the idea! He said he would investigate it and came back a few days later to confirm that the Group supported the approach too. We should go ahead with the planning. I was delighted! I would be returning to Buenos Aires, a city I felt I had left way too early. It was perfect. I was to wrap up everything and move just two months later in September – exactly four years since I'd arrived in London.

Reflecting on those four years, I had made substantial learnings both professionally and personally. London had been good to me. From a work perspective, I had learned a lot about transformation, but I had also been lucky enough to work with many senior and inspiring managers like Samir and Miles. They operated at a level I had never personally observed before. Each had, in their own way, nurtured and inspired me to become a better leader myself.

Both taught me about effective communication, and the power of stakeholder management and vision creation. If I could go back and start my transformation role again, I would do many things differently, especially around managing stakeholders more effectively and developing my own way of leading and engaging others.

Working in the London HQ with 65-plus different nationalities had been mind-blowing. Being in such an international environment, with all the value that such diversity brings, had been a blessing. In addition, the roles that I held had granted me the opportunity to visit so many parts of the world. I had built a strong network across the HQ and now I could say I understood the Group's culture much better than when I arrived.

The Treasury team in London was a great department to work in – lots of brilliant people. I always looked forward to coming into the office and have fun with my colleagues. I had even started to master the important British office banter! Many colleagues had become personal friends and we would frequently go for a pint after work on a Thursday or Friday, along with the rest of London. Being right in the city centre really helped with that. Covent Garden and Soho were just on our doorstep. Imagine what I would have missed out on had I rejected the offer four years earlier? Up until then, the Group's intentions for my development had been right – and I trusted that this next move would also prove to be a good call.

Living in a city like London had taught me so much more about tolerance and respect for people different to myself. I don't think that's possible in many places in the world. Just travelling on the Tube (the metro system) in London and visiting different parts of the city was itself a testimony to what diversity, tolerance and inclusion is.

It wasn't all positive though. At times, I felt immense frustration. In all companies, you'll find some politics, but at HQ, this was amplified many times over. It took some time for me to see this as an opportunity for growth rather than an obstacle. That said, I can also say that it taught me what sort of leader I didn't want to be and what games I was and wasn't willing to participate in.

With all these learnings, I couldn't stop reflecting on my earlier career and wondering how I would have managed different situations with this new mindset. For example, the situation with Elisabeth around the controversial office furniture. Would I have been more curious as to why she approached me in the way that she did? Sought more insight before reacting and essentially giving her an ultimatum? Would I have sought wider support for my choice among other executive managers in her absence? Would the outcome have been much different? Maybe not, but at least I would have understood her position better. If I had gained support from the other executives, I could have dealt with some of the noise before her return. Perhaps she hadn't had an issue with my choice herself but felt she needed to say something because of the other senior executives.

At the time, I basically tried to mimic a leadership style that I thought was appropriate for the situation. I thought I needed to stand up, without compromise, for my values and beliefs. Today, I would look with more curiosity at people and first try to understand their position. Growth. Self-reflection is a brilliant and necessary exercise, but also sometimes uncomfortable!

Reflecting on my time working in the Argentinian office, if I had applied my more rounded and curious approach to understanding my fellow senior peers, I wonder if I could have bypassed the problems of trust. Could I have more explicitly shown my support? Been more tactful and built up trust before sharing my observations as a newcomer? I will never know, but I was looking forward to seeing what my new mindset could bring me in the future.

It was now time for fresh adventures. For the first six months, I would be in the same role, but I would be in Argentina. And then I would start my first FD role. Just thinking about it filled my stomach with butterflies. It was a big step up. Whilst I looked forward to the challenge, I was also nervous. Plus, what was life going to be like in Venezuela? Still, I knew I couldn't stay in London and plateau, so I didn't really have a choice and that was helpful to know. New opportunities would surely arise out of this risky move.

Food for Thought

☞ How long does it typically take you to start to feel under-stimulated in a job?

☞ How important is it for you to have new challenges?

☞ Do you have a mentor (official or unofficial) who you could turn to?

☞ Are you getting the most out of the relationship?

☞ When persuading, how much effort do you put into the framing of your message rather than just the content?

☞ What are your limits in terms of geographical relocation?

☞ Think back to an important episode or event in your life in the last decade. With the mindset and experience you have today, would you have handled it differently?

☞ In what way?

Buenos Aires, Argentina

Chapter 13: Lucky to Have Been Born in Denmark

It was late September 2013 when I landed back in the southern hemisphere. Springtime. To me, Buenos Aires is to Latin America, what London is to Europe, and what New York is to the US – the most multicultural city on that continent. It is a truly amazing city. Full of energy and diversity. It was great to be back.

The Argentinian subsidiary had arranged a desk for me on a different floor from Finance. My role of Regional Treasurer was not specific to Argentina, so it didn't really matter where I was parked. It worked well. I travelled a lot around the region and I felt more connected to the underlying business. Patricia generously shared her experience and coached me in the role of local FD. A lot had changed in the company since I'd left four years ago. It no longer felt like a sinking ship. Many of the issues had been addressed. The company was now smaller and leaner, with more agile and engaged staff. Most of the senior management team had been replaced and the new team was aware of the challenges, acted promptly and changed tact when things weren't working. It was great to see it flourish.

Having grown in my understanding of different cultures, I was able to look at my own cultural background and reflect on where some of my personal unconscious biases and ego core issues had come from.

I believe we are all a product of what has happened in our lives. No person sees a given situation completely objectively. We see and understand the 'truth' through the lens of our own lives and experiences. We apply assumptions built up over a lifetime on reality and morality, and put together our own version what is actually happening.

'We don't see things as they are; we see them as we are' Anaïs Nin

For an individual, perception is reality, but perception is easily coloured by your internal state of mind. If you are feeling upbeat, you will tend to perceive a situation (e.g. a challenge or someone else's behaviour) more positively than if you're feeling upset or agitated. This doesn't mean that our lens cannot be adjusted. It definitely can, but it requires more effort. It requires us to be conscious of our personal biases and our automatic thoughts, and to see how our mindset is impacted by our ego.

In many ways, I would consider being Danish an asset. To a lot of people I met in Latin America, Denmark is a relatively unknown country so I rarely came across any negative feelings when I introduced myself as Danish. If known at all, Denmark would be lumped in with the other Nordic countries, all of whom are recognised for their long and stable democracies, high living standards, a clear focus on sustainability, efficiency, and human rights.

People in Denmark have very high levels of trust in others. There is little corruption in the country. People are, in general, open-minded and perceive other people as being equal human beings with equal worth. Regardless of whether you are born rich or poor, from one of the high or low classes in society, your gender, sexuality, or religion, Danes strive for and take pride in an equal society.

If I look at my own friends and family in Denmark, some earn a lot of money, while others earn less, but this doesn't really impact people's views of each other. The same applies to people's educational attainment. I am good friends with people from my childhood irrespective of the fact that we are on completely different income scales, have had different education and career histories. Friendships are based on what the other can bring to the table as an individual rather than wealth and prestige.

That most things are free and managed by the Danish state has a major role to play. While there are some private schools, most children will still attend state-funded primary and secondary schools. Boarding schools are rare. There are no private universities or business schools. They are all state-funded and free to all students. People from different backgrounds will study together and build important relationships. Your effort and hard work will determine if you succeed, rather than how much money you or your family has.

Of course, as always, there are exceptions. Some people will care a lot about your background or earnings bracket, but this group is in the minority. Most Danes hold the value that everyone has the same fundamental rights and value in society. As this value is deeply ingrained in people, official minimum salaries do not exist in Denmark. For certain sectors, salaries are negotiated between employers and workers' unions. The beauty of this is that the salaries of typically lower paying jobs are much higher in Denmark than in other countries, and income inequality is less of a problem. It is no coincidence that many other governments have tried to understand our secret.

The generally accepted view is that if you have a job that doesn't require many years of higher education or training, such as a cashier in a supermarket, cleaner, or bus driver, you should still be able to have a good life. One where you can afford to buy your own home, provide your kids with a comfortable upbringing, travel and generally enjoy life. You may live in an area of the country that is less expensive and you may not buy the designer brands, but you will not be poor. To give you an idea, the average monthly salary after tax in Denmark is roughly £2,600, compared to just under £2,000 in the UK and £300 in Argentina (or local currency equivalents)[5]. A bus driver in Denmark gets nearly £3,500 a month before tax, compared to roughly £2,400 in the UK and £300 in Argentina[6]. US post-tax salaries appear similar to Denmark, but most Americans pay a lot of money for health insurance, whereas healthcare is freely available in countries like Denmark and the UK, and also largely in Argentina.

The entire set-up in Denmark is based on everyone contributing what they can based on their income. Unemployment is relatively low compared to most other countries and the majority (around 80% according to a 2010 survey) fall in the middle-income group. This is why it is able to fund such an extensive social system. Housing, healthcare, benefits for food and clothes, pensions, etc are provided to all Danish citizens as needed. Such a system like this would be found in a socialist country, but Denmark is a mature capitalist country led by a strong market economy that is considered the engine of the society.

The state doesn't own industries or intervene by dictating prices, etc. It legislates to secure the safety and sustainability of society as a whole. The overall role of the state is to provide the backbone needed for companies and their employees to thrive. This includes kindergartens, day-care, schools, high schools, universities, healthcare, care for the elderly, security, justice and so forth. All of the support is targeted at releasing labour to the market economy (albeit a certain proportion of those re-entering the workforce will be heading into the public sector that provides these services). This is perceived to create more value for society that a mum is guaranteed state-subsidised kindergarten in the city she lives in so that she can return to work and create value for society after her maternity leave.

Basically, every person is expected to be productive. By the state providing access to social services for free, even the poorest are able to receive support so that they can work and work up the ladder. And if they succeed, they are expected to pay society back through taxes. Trying to avoid paying taxes is considered anti-social in Danish society.

The Danish system works as long as the majority of citizens buy into this collectivistic model. It creates a safe country, with among the lowest income inequality between the rich and poor, and amongst one of the best work-life balances in the world. This type of society is not everyone's cup of tea (not even for all Danes) but for me, it provides a good balance between ensuring that everyone is able to have a decent life and still provide many opportunities for individuals who strive for more in life to make their own fortune. It no doubt had a stabilising impact on my core ego issues around justice and fairness.

Inequality

Some countries are known for the opposite. India is such an example. Their caste system ensures that a small privileged group, born into certain rights and privileges, will continue to get access to the best opportunities. However, the majority of Indians are born with less or very little. In other countries, family wealth, history and political influence hugely define who you are and who you will become. It keeps you in a bubble where most people around you are like yourself. It can be difficult to appreciate other ways of living unless you possess a lot of empathy to understand the challenges that other people face outside your circle.

As I travelled extensively around Latin America, I could see with my own eyes how unequal lives are. Many of the big cities had zones of *favelas* or *barrios* (slum areas). Some were as big as most small to medium-sized European cities. Many living in these slum areas worked day and night in the city serving the wealthy and middle classes. The slum areas were usually so dangerous that often even police and official authorities would not enter them.

Then, you would see another group – the super-rich. People who lived in a bubble of wealth and security, shielded and protected from the poorer parts. The middle class was small compared to European countries, but an important group for driving innovation and transformation in society.

Trip after trip, I began to realise what a privilege it was to have been born in Denmark. In Latin America, children often have access to free education, but in many countries, the good schools and universities are still largely filled with the middle or upper classes. Many would subsequently work for international companies and be paid very well. In many of the countries I visited, a large group of these companies belonged to a closed network – either you had access to it (typically through connections or going to the right schools) or you do not.

Over the years, I connected with many people across the region. Mostly, I met people who were part of the elite group, but I also met those who weren't financially well off. I sensed differences between the groups but I always felt accepted by those I met. I think it helped that I was an outsider and foreigner, which meant it wasn't easy to place me in any local bracket. Instead, I was rated on my behaviour, personality, and country of origin.

Nevertheless, I recognised that my life has been very different to the lives of most of the people I met and worked with in the region. Being aware of the beliefs and values that my background had fostered in me helped me navigate these often very different cultures.

The Value of Trust

I was born in Copenhagen in 1972. Mum was only 18 years old when she had my older brother and, a few years later, me. Dad was equally young and this meant I was raised by young parents by Danish standards, even at that time.

My parents bought a small plot of land to build a house from scratch. My grandfather (my mum's dad) was a carpenter and had built many houses. He came down from the Faroe Islands to join my dad in building a brick house on the plot. My dad worked in the metals industry and my mum in healthcare. They were educated but not what you would label as white collar professionals.

We considered ourselves middle class and probably the lower end of it. We lived in a sleepy suburban part of the city. The school we went to was only two streets down from the house. As my parents both had to be at work by 7 a.m., my mum would typically wake us up before leaving in a rush at 6.45 a.m. We got up, showered, ate breakfast, prepared our own open sandwiches for lunch and walked to school by ourselves.

There are only a few years between my brother and I. He took on the typical role of older brother, taking care of me in our early years. Typically, after school, we would go to a youth club before heading home. My parents would be back from work around 3 or 4 p.m. In 1980, around 85% of men and nearly 70% of women worked in Denmark. Almost all of my friends' parents both worked as well. It was a simple lifestyle and one that was typically Danish in those days.

The Danish society was, and still is, an incredible safe and trust-based society. My parents had no worries with us walking to school on our own at seven and ten years old. We lived in a quiet housing area so there wasn't much traffic. Crime rates were, and still are, incredibly low. Kidnappings are not an issue. Despite what you might think from Scandi noir dramas like *The Killing*, *The Bridge*, or *Wallander*, killings and other serious crimes are not common. We would happily play with other children out on the street, sometimes until sunset (after 10 p.m. in the summer). Nothing was going to happen and nothing did happen.

Having been brought up in this strong trust-based culture, I always assumed that others had the best intentions towards me. That people weren't out to harm or hurt me on purpose. That when someone said something, it was true and I could trust them.

There were no mobile phones in those days. Only in my teenage years did the first personal computer reach the Danish market.

Those were the days when we used our imagination to entertain ourselves. And if we ran out of ideas, I would ask my mum, 'What should I do? I'm bored...' and she would normally respond, 'Intelligent children are never bored!' I quickly stopped asking her for ideas.

It was a different childhood than many will be experiencing today in the western world. Like all families, there were ups and downs, but in the 1980s, Denmark suffered a major financial crisis that led to tough austerity measures that impacted most families. I remember frequent conversations between my parents about money and not having enough of it. However, whilst we couldn't afford many toys and we chose non-branded supermarket items and clothes, we were never short of love and I didn't feel like I lacked too much. I had a good childhood - a childhood where the small things and simple events left a lasting impression for my brother and I.

Food for Thought

☞ Do you primarily surround yourself with people who are similar to or different to you?

☞ What are the positives and negatives of this approach?

☞ What core values and beliefs did your upbringing foster in you?

☞ How do you think a very different upbringing would have impacted you, your core values and beliefs, and what you are doing today?

☞ How easily do you trust others?

☞ How has your cultural environment shaped this?

Chapter 14: What Does an Economist Actually Do?

My brother and I were strongly encouraged by our parents to work and earn a living for ourselves from a young age. They were blue-collar workers and believed that by working alongside school, we would learn the right behaviours. We would not end up being lazy. We would be too busy to cause any trouble for society.

My first job was putting flyers into people's letterboxes once a week. At the age of 12, I did this with my brother. We did it all afternoon and we got paid a little for it. Then I started distributing newspapers on my bicycle during the weekends. As they had to be delivered before 6 a.m., I started my round at 2 a.m. I have never been a morning person and I was definitely not a middle-of-the-night type of person. I handed in my notice on the third weekend.

We then got a job in a large conference hotel in the city. I was 13 years old and it was great fun working in the hospitality industry. We helped the waiters arrange tables for different types of conferences. In the breaks, we went in to refresh the rooms, clear up drinks and bring in new pastries. It was a great job. We even got to stay overnight in the hotel if it was an evening event on the weekend. We loved it. My parents couldn't really afford to take us to hotels so this was the first time we had experienced this luxury.

A few years later, I got a job in a larger hotel in central Copenhagen. I worked as a bell-boy helping guests with their suitcases and doing chores for the reception. When I wasn't doing that, I was on the information desk giving tourists recommendations on restaurants and booking excursions, etc. I loved meeting people from other countries. I got to practice my English and helped people enjoy their stay in Copenhagen. I typically worked two days a week from 3 to 9 p.m. Even then, I knew how much I enjoyed interacting with other cultures.

When I turned 18, I was too old for the hotel job so I found a job in one of the country's largest supermarket chains. I worked there from the early afternoon to 8 p.m. on some weekdays and each Saturday. It was a hypermarket located in one the most ethnically diverse areas of south Copenhagen. It was somewhat like a ghetto. Unemployment was quite high by Danish terms and a parallel society had arisen.

One of the beauties of Denmark's free education system is that they actively try to promote children from working class family's like mine to pursue higher education. I recall one brilliant teacher, Mr Larsen, who I had for social studies. It was one of my favourite subjects and focused on things like societal demographics, government finances, monetary policy, the healthcare system, the political system, etc. He was also my careers counsellor, so he was advising me on what to do after high school.

All I knew was that I wanted to study more. I enjoyed learning. I was alright in mathematics and saw myself as an accountant. My cousin and her boyfriend both worked in that area so it was one of the few professional jobs I knew a bit about. I would have to attend a business school in Copenhagen, before training as an accountant.

Mr Larsson asked me why I didn't consider becoming an economist. I looked at him with doubt. I said something like, 'But that's at university right? What does an economist actually do?'

He confirmed that yes, it would be at university and explained that it was more in-line with the topics he had taught me, which he knew I enjoyed. He also added that economics was often an entry ticket into certain jobs. Many politicians and senior executives in Denmark have a masters in economics, for example. Ultimately, it would be up to me to decide in what direction I would take my career.

In those days, going to university was not a given. These days, it seems you have to have at least a Masters degree to get an entry-level job, but back then, there were many more ways to start working.

I spoke with my parents and then with friends, fellow students and my wider family. My grandfather (dad's dad) was especially supportive. He had a university degree himself and, as a land surveyor, had started his own company. He was thrilled by the idea that I would potentially attend university. Most people were supportive, although a few said, 'You... at university? Really?' with a cheeky smile.

I filled in the application form and listed Accountant as my first option and Economist as my second. The Danish higher education system is free but you need to get good enough grades. Each year, the education department sets minimum levels for entrance to various subjects. That year, I just missed the minimum metrics by 0.1 points. I wouldn't be going to business school. But my second choice, university, was granted.

At first, I was disappointed. I didn't see myself at university. I had this perception that it was for children of parents who had university degrees themselves. Not people like me. Even knowing the meritocratic society I was brought up in, I still couldn't shake my social heritage – child of blue-collar workers.

Regardless, missing my grades by 0.1 points had made my decision for me. I would be heading to the University of Copenhagen at the end of the summer. My grandfather was so proud of me. He would be helping me financially and paying half of my rent during the five years at university. I would top it up with a sort of student salary paid by the government to all students, plus a student loan provided by the state. On top of this, I got a job at a petrol station and a cleaning job at a doctor's clinic. I was working all the hours of the week (20 hours on top of the 50 hours I spent on my studies), but I was blessed. It was the first time in life when I felt financially privileged.

The university year kicked off with a freshers' trip. It was here where I first met my fellow students. Out of 450 students, there were only a few with a similar background to mine. Most students had parents with jobs in senior management or holding other influential positions in politics, academia, etc. This was the first time I came across some of the true elite – the less than 1% of the population born into ultra wealth.

At first, I felt intimidated by them and it definitely triggered some ego issues around inclusion. Our worlds were so different. However, over the course of the first few years, many students dropped out. It was a course that was known for having a high dropout rate and there were times when I struggled too. The group gradually diminished to about half its original size. As this happened, people from all different backgrounds merged. People either matured or they knew that those who were left were dedicated to finishing the degree. Succeeding didn't depend on background or class, but your determination, effort and skill. And we needed each other. Needless to say, I enjoyed the latter period of my studies much more. Still, my best friends today are those who came from a similar background to mine.

So, why have I shared so much of my background and upbringing with you? Well, for you to understand where my values around equality, justice and trust comes from. But also to help you understand where some of my unconscious biases come from. At times, I found myself full of prejudice and assumptions about others without even realising it. How often have my assumptions been wrong? My next chapter in life, and in this book, takes me to Venezuela. This would be the period where I would be forced to reflect a lot on my own values and beliefs, and to be mindful not to let my unconscious biases about groups or individuals lead me to decisions and views not fitting for my new role as FD. It would turn out to be a period in my life where I became more conscious; where I started to seeing the world more clearly for what it is and not for who I am.

Food for Thought

☞ What did you want to be when you were younger and how have you found yourself doing what you do now?

☞ Who had the largest influence on what subject you studied or what career you pursued?

☞ Are you living your own dream or conforming to others' expectations?

☞ How do you think your own background and your upbringing colour your values, beliefs, and unconscious biases?

Part 3
Transformation

Caracas, Venezuela

Chapter 15: The Legacy of Chavez

I start this part of the book with a few chapters that set the scene. Venezuela was such a different environment to anything I had experienced before that it requires some explanation of its history, politics and economics to fully understand the context in which the team and I were living and working. So, what follows is about transformation, but is also about the descent of a country and the resilience of its citizens.

It was March 2014. I had arrived in Caracas Simon Bolivar international airport just seven hours after taking off from Buenos Aires. As I walked on the airlift from the plane to the terminal building, the humidity and heat hit me like a hammer.

I had barely reached the terminal before I noticed several young Venezuelan guys in military outfit with machine guns. They were standing in a line patrolling the gate area. It seemed excessive given weapons aren't allowed onto planes, but I sensed that their main or sole purpose was to remind people who was in power.

After making it through immigration, I waited for my five suitcases to appear on the conveyer belt. The humidity was still high and I hadn't stopped sweating since I'd gotten off the plane. Nothing prepared me for the noise of the crowd. Although the luggage pick-up area was only a fifth full, they were all shouting non-stop.

I searched for a luggage cart. There were none to be found. Without a cart, I found myself pushing the five suitcases in train style towards the customs line. It wasn't the expat welcome I was used to!

In many Latin countries, if they see anything they believe should be taxed or confiscated, they will take you to the side. In Europe, this scanning takes place in huge scanners before your bags are released onto the conveyor belt. In Caracas airport, I needed to load my suitcases onto the large scanners myself. The customs staff stood observing, loving the power.

I had packed my suitcases well. Most of my belongings and furniture had been stored in London whilst I was in Argentina and would only be shipped once I had found a permanent flat. What I had brought in my suitcases was a fraction of what I owned, but they were the most important things that I couldn't be eight months or longer without.

It was my turn to load my suitcases onto the scanner. Unsurprisingly, I was taken to the side for inspection and asked to open all of my bags. Suddenly, I couldn't find the key for one of them. I was already sweating profusely, managing the five heavy suitcases without a luggage cart and desperately trying to find a key in my man bag – I didn't look suspicious at all (British sarcasm).

I searched and searched, increasingly panicked. Eventually, I had to tell them in my poor Spanish that I couldn't find the key. One of the staff immediately called another guy over their walkie talkie. Before I knew it, another guy came with heavy duty bolt cutters and destroyed both the lock and a chunk of my suitcase where the lock had been. It was clear it was not the first time they had gladly destroyed someone's suitcase.

Trying to stay composed and without provoking anymore unnecessary drama, I smiled while the two customs guys now ran through all of my precious belongings, from shirts to underwear, in front of everyone in the queue. It was disgusting to see the joy they had in this task, but there was little could I do. Having found nothing illegal, they dragged the suitcases to the side and I was left on the floor trying to gather all my things. I shoved everything back into the suitcases in any way that I could to just close them and get out of there. Welcome to Venezuela.

Leaving the customs area, the sliding doors opened and I stood in the middle of the arrivals hall in a fresh inferno of noise and people. I was supposed to look for a particular security guy. I had received a small picture of him on my Blackberry. The quality was so poor that I couldn't be sure who I was exactly looking for.

A guy looking completely different to the one I recalled from the photo approached me, '*Señor Kim?*'.

'*Si*', I responded. Before I could say anything else, he and another guy took my suitcases and began to walk away. I frantically open my phone to check the photo one more time. Although it was highly fuzzy, I could tell it was definitely neither of the guys who had just taken my bags and were now gesturing at me to follow them.

As we reached the exit and stepped out onto the pavement, two armoured cars drove up right in front of us. To my relief, a guy who resembled the picture on my Blackberry stepped out of one of the vehicles, welcomed me in Spanish and asked me to get into the car. I got in with him. My five suitcases went into the other car. We set off towards Caracas city centre and I allowed myself to relax a little.

I had been to Caracas twice for work, but it had visibly changed over the last eight months. Hugo Chavez, long-standing president of Venezuela, had died of cancer the year before. After a quick election, Nicolás Maduro, acting president and former bus driver, assumed power having won a narrow majority.

It probably helped Maduro that he had received the late president Chavez's blessing to run for president through a little bird that sung to him. Apparently, the bird appeared, circled him three times and whistled to him. It was at that point that Maduro knew it was the spirit and blessing of the late Venezuelan leader.

Despite widespread accusations of fraud from both local and international observers, the election result was not investigated. He had since managed to withstand the pressure and stay in power. However, the Venezuelan people's discontent with him had led to major demonstrations across the country. Chavez was an old military general. He had always kept the military close and on-side during his presidency. As he had appointed Maduro, from the grave as his replacement, the military continued to fully support Maduro and his party.

Over the months since my last visit, the demonstrations had grown in strength, size and violence. The military had reacted with force to stop them and many people had already been killed.

The route to and from the airport was notorious for being dangerous. You pass through several slum areas on the way. As we approached downtown Caracas, it became evident that right now, the centre was one of the least safe parts of the city. The hotel I was supposed to stay in was a block away from the main square, where most of the demonstrations had started. These normally ended with fights between demonstrators and the police and military. I was therefore moved to another hotel further out of the centre and closer to the office. As I was dropped off at my new hotel, I was instructed to stay indoors and not go out at night. The next morning, I would be picked up and driven straight to the office.

As instructed, I stayed in the hotel. I had no desire to go out. I stayed on the 22nd floor and could still hear sirens all through the night. I went to bed with many thoughts. What on earth had I signed up for? The country had worsened so much in just eight months – what would it be like in a year or two's time?

Keep Calm – and Good Luck in the New Job

The next morning, I was picked up and driven to the office. As we drove the short way there, we passed several areas where there had been riots during the night. Now, the city was being cleaned by the garbage teams that removed burned out cars, tyres, and waste containers on the streets. I arrived at the office. Everyone was talking about the security situation and the 17 people who had been killed in the riots the week before. The tension was clear.

I was greeted by the current FD, Joao, and my new team. Joao was packing up and about to leave Venezuela to take up a new role in another country. He showed me around and introduced me to the other directors and various people in the organisation.

Over the next week, I was officially handed over the responsibility of FD. As it was my first role as FD and I would be in charge of an 80-person team, it felt daunting and exciting at the same time. How would I manage it? I calmed some of my ego concerns about being competent with the advice of my mentor – focus on what you're good at (leadership and decision-making) and not on what you're not (accounting and book-keeping). That and reminding myself that whilst I'd never been an FD, I had started from scratch many times before and I was good at that. I would be fine.

As the security situation had worsened so drastically over the last year, the budget I had been given for housing had been increased to cater for a more secure home. Caracas had not seen that many investments in new buildings since Chavez took over around 1999. Many flats were old and not maintained.

Over the next few days, I visited several flats. I was used to the routine now. There weren't many available that were suitable but eventually, one came onto the market that looked promising. It was in a brand-new block and probably one of the most beautiful ones in the capital city.

Caracas is situated in a valley up in the mountains about 1 km above sea level. This location makes the city more temperate (in the high 20-degrees Celsius) than the coast and Caribbean Sea where temperatures would often be near 40-degrees Celsius.

The flat was on the Avila, Caracas' most famous mountain. It was on one of the highest streets overlooking the city and it had a breath-taking view. From the balcony, there was a 180-degree view over the city. Petare (one of the largest slum areas in Latin America) was on one side and the high rises of downtown Caracas were on the other. The slum areas looked pretty from a distance with their self-built, colourful houses. When you got closer though, it was a different view.

The flat was in a safe building where several guards provided security around the clock. The building itself was surrounded by high walls with high-voltage fences on top. Inside the area, there was a little park with palm trees around a large swimming pool and an exclusive terrace area where you could host events if you wanted to. It was peaceful. You could only hear the sound of parrots, the circulation of the pool water and, in the distance, the eternal din from downtown Caracas.

This would become my golden cage over the following years – a little paradise I would live in when not working. The owner of the flat, a young widow in her forties had, like so many other Venezuelans, activated her Plan B and was moving to Miami with her mum and children.

It was sad to see. She, like so many other Venezuelans, felt she had no choice but to flee her own country. And she was one of the lucky ones. Many others didn't have a choice but to stay. On my part, I was delighted that I could rent her beautiful flat. It would take a couple of months for her to move and it would take time for my furniture to arrive in Venezuela (and make its way through the ineffective and corrupt customs system), so it was a good fit timing-wise. In the meantime, I would stay in the hotel. I had never stayed in a hotel that long but thought it would make it easier to focus on the new job.

Chapter 16: Understanding the recent history of Venezuela

All companies in Venezuela were struggling to keep their production lines running. Ours was no exception. Soon after arriving, I met some FDs from other local and international corporates. I wanted to better understand how they were managing the mass scarcity of raw and packing materials.

Venezuela should be an incredibly rich country. It has the world's largest proven oil reserves. Indeed, through the twentieth century, the country was one of the richest Latin countries, with close ties to the US. Its massive oil revenues paid for much of the infrastructure that's still around today, like hospitals and schools. PDVSA, the state-owned oil company in Venezuela, generated much of the revenue and this meant that the rest of the population and other industries did not have to contribute much in taxes compared to most other countries.

Up through the 1980s and early '90s, most people in Venezuela got richer, especially those who were already rich. However, disaster struck in the late '90s when the price of oil fell to its lowest level since 1973. State revenue from taxes dried up. The price of crude oil fell so low that it barely covered the costs of extraction. The government had to reduce spending. Everyone in Venezuela felt the pain, especially those from the poorer parts of the country.

On top of this, there had been a large influx of migrants – especially Colombians - into the country. Some were guest workers moving to the much richer Venezuela during the 1970s and '80s. Others had fled the guerrilla war that was devastating Colombia and had killed many people over the decades. Many Colombians had settled in the bigger slum areas (or *barrios*, as Venezuelans call them) in the cities.

In the presidential election of 1999, Chavez, a charismatic leader, promised a better life for the working-class and the poor and was elected. He also delivered – with help from the oil price.

It sky-rocketed from an all-time low (around US dollar 20 a barrel) to more than US dollar 50 a barrel only one year after coming to power. Rapidly, government funds were re-channelled into massive social housing schemes, passive benefits to the poor, the building of more and better schools, healthcare, and so on.

Gradually, the oil company, PDVSA, was nationalised so that Chavez's government could control it more directly. Foreign companies were beginning to be taken over or removed. Every time a company or industry did not do what the Chavez-led government wanted, it was expropriated or legislation was passed that meant the company either had to comply or leave the country.

Industry after industry was put under price control mechanisms to cope with the inflation that the government's expansive fiscal policy had fuelled. Gradually, various industries began to struggle to survive. The companies taken over by Chavez were now led by faithful party soldiers. Often, they had little to no knowledge around how to run a company. Others were led by family members or friends of senior people in government and the military. As Chavez had come from the military, they held a central position in his government.

Gradually, more and more industries went under. Milk, for example, was under strict price controls. Unfortunately, high inflation meant that the costs of producing the milk were higher than the revenues received, so dairy farmers slaughtered their cows. They sold the meat and stopped dairy farming. Local milk production in Venezuela basically dried up and was replaced with long-life milk imported from countries like Chile. This sad story repeated itself across many industries. Gradually, Venezuela became more and more dependent on imports for most of its finished goods.

In the case of milk, imported milk was bought in directly by the government with US dollars and sold to the Venezuelans at the lower price-controlled price. This birthed a new industry of resellers. They were called *bachaqueros*. The name came from the Spanish word *bachaco*, which is a big voracious ant, usually red, which tirelessly carries things on its back. The *bachaqueros* would predominantly be poorer people buying up large stocks of price-controlled goods and reselling them in the black market for ten to twenty times the cost.

This hoarding of goods then led to frequent stock shortages in shops and supermarkets. Some resellers would even cross the border to Colombia and other neighbouring countries to sell these scarce goods at a huge profit. The *bachaqueros* were essentially gaining from the government subsidies on certain products, which led to a major distortion of the market and a breaking down of normal demand-supply dynamics.

Slowly, the shelves of even the largest supermarkets emptied out. Certain goods such as toilet paper, sugar, bottled water and milk could often only be sourced from the black market. The quality of many goods also visibly fell, as most manufacturers were unable to source the right raw materials to produce the finished goods or the right packing materials to securely wrap their goods. Gradually, more and more local producers shut down their plants and large factories remained empty like ghost towns.

At this time, the high oil price (which peaked at a whopping USD 165 per barrel in 2008) masked the brewing problems in the broader economy. Given the decline of general industry, soon more than 90% of export revenues came from oil alone. However, as everyone knows, oil prices fluctuate. In addition, the government had taken over daily control of PDSVA. Chavez had placed his party loyalists in management positions in the company, which meant poor management and little capital expenditure and investment. Socialist regimes are notorious for not investing in the longer term. They don't have the same incentives as competitive markets to remain productive, relevant and, well, competitive.

There is a reason why companies use a lot of funds to maintain their fixed assets such as updating parts of their vital machinery and carrying out maintenance checks on their plants. It is cheaper to look after what you have rather than to constantly repair damaged machines or buying new ones. And lack of maintenance can lead to fatal accidents, which are damaging as well as costly. And so went the now state-owned oil company.

Instead of investing in the company, the government extracted as much cash as possible from the company to fund social benefits and build houses for the poorer population. They wanted to secure votes for another few years in power. And they also pulled millions of US dollars out for themselves and placed them in secret bank accounts around the world for a rainy day!

This wasn't sustainable. After many years of poor maintenance, issues began to arise. More and more fatal accidents were occurring in the refineries. Oil production began to fall. Foreign oil companies had already been thrown out of the country. Many of the excellent oil engineers that Venezuela once had now worked and lived abroad. On top of this, Chavez built friendships with Cuba and other Latin countries by providing them with free oil. Lastly, petrol in Venezuela was de facto free for Venezuelans. As the local mantra says: 'the oil belongs to the people'.

The net outcome of this was that less and less crude oil was available for exporting. Combined with falling oil prices, this decimated the government's income sources. To keep the country running, they began to issue bonds in PDVSA and sold oil futures (i.e. oil contracts to be delivered in the future), especially to China. Essentially, the government used PDVSA to borrow to fund the government's spiralling expenditure. Consequently, the country now owed a part of its diminishing oil reserves and production to China every year, and the PDVSA needed even more US dollars to pay interest costs to its foreign bondholders.

It was a lethal cocktail that eventually caught up with the country. Infrastructure started falling apart. The electricity sector had not been well managed over many years, despite a growing local need. Rolling power outages were common. It was a similar story with the water supply, with frequent burst pipes and water outages. Water was rationed in many parts of the country. In many areas, you only had access to water for a few hours each day. The best internet connection allowed for only 1-2MB of download and less than 1MB of upload capacity, even for large corporates.

Most Venezuelan newspapers and TV channels had already been taken over by the government or closed, especially those that were not friendly in their coverage of the government. The country was falling apart. And this was to be my new home for the next couple of years.

Everyday Life in Caracas

In the office, life was very different. It almost felt like a bubble of happiness. Venezuelans are, by and large, happy and incredibly generous.

The main office site in Caracas included a factory, a warehouse and the head office. This meant that blue-collar workers (mostly people from the poorer areas of the city) and engineers, managers and other office staff were together on the one site. However, I'd never experienced such a strong divide between different groups.

The factory workers belonged to unions and the unions were very close to the government. Most workers were therefore called Chavisters. On the other side, the office workers would mostly be supporting the opposition party. Often the division between the two groups was so strong and emotionally charged that they would avoid talking about anything political together. I had never experienced such a strong division in a country before. Sadly, this has become more common in recent years across many countries, including the US, Poland, Hungary and Brexit in the UK, to mention only a few.

Despite this, the overall atmosphere at work was positive. Most people were grateful to have such a good job and our industry was one of the few the government was not thinking of taking over.

I continued to struggle with my Spanish on a daily basis, so I was given a private assistant, Estrella, who would help me with my language challenges and general chores. Estrella isn't her real name but I have named her so because to me, she was an absolute star. Estrella was in her forties, tall, coloured her hair red and either dressed completely in black or in full colour. She had been an English teacher previously and would turn out to be my saviour during my two and a half years in Venezuela.

There was not one thing she would not try to do for me, but she also had a strong will of her own. She could be incredibly loud. An energiser and party creator, which was a breath of fresh air in the typically conservative and calmer finance function. She was an open book. We soon established a good chemistry and she knew when I had time for fun and chit chat, and when I did not.

Estrella was a single mum and had elderly parents and siblings who relied on her for support, so she had a lot of things going on besides work. Still, she rode around on her scooter across all of Caracas and made things happen - arranging work events, team-building, buying things for me or assisting me with visits to the dentist, doctor, and so on. I don't know how she had the energy but I definitely could not have survived without her.

My furniture had finally arrived. After weeks stuck in customs, I finally managed to get my hands on my personal belongings and move into my new flat. After three months in the hotel, I cannot express how happy I felt to begin living a normal life again.

Whilst the scarcity of many things in Venezuela affected me too, I knew I was hugely privileged. I had a high income and access to hard currency (US dollars) so I could, in theory, still get most things in exclusive and expensive shops. Nonetheless, I adjusted my needs. It didn't feel right to buy salmon or fillet steak at triple the cost of Europe or the US. Someone was clearly getting extremely rich on the parallel import market. Should I branch out on a side hustle?

I generally used my local supermarket, which was only a few blocks from my flat. Even so, I had to drive in my armoured car to get there. The area was known for its wealthy inhabitants and there had been lots of kidnappings recently. Predators hung around like birds circling a fish pond. The supermarket itself was not what you would expect from a supermarket in a wealthy area. It was dirty and smelt terrible. It wasn't big but had a larger selection of goods than most of the supermarket chains. By law, supermarkets were not allowed to have empty shelves if they had stock in the warehouse. For this reason, in the larger supermarkets, you would often find an entire aisle full of Pepsi Cola, followed by a section dedicated to canned food, rice, flour and sugar four aisles down, followed by another full aisle of Pepsi Cola. It was surreal.

In my local supermarket, there was a small section where you could buy fresh meat. It was mostly chicken. When you saw that they had any meat of decent quality, you would have to stock up. I got lucky on my first shop there. I also bought large amounts of processed food and canned products whilst there was stock.

When it came to cleaning and hygiene products, there was another level of scarcity. You could rarely find toilet paper, liquid soap or body wash. It was all very cheap but you just couldn't get your hands on any. You could sometimes find some Colgate toothpaste, but most cleaning products were poor quality. I decided I would have to stock up the next time I was in Europe. The office had enough toilet paper for now.

What was never out of stock, which was great, were the locally produced fruits and vegetables. You could also buy the most impressive colourful tropical flowers at a nearby flower market, and that became my weekly treat.

Most of my evenings and weekends would be spent by myself in my flat or by the pool. I enjoyed sitting on my balcony in the evening with a glass of wine and a book, looking out onto downtown Caracas in the distance. What a view. And what a peaceful respite from the bustle of all that was going on below.

The flat itself was huge at around 300 sqm. There were others in the building complex that were much larger, including the duplex penthouse flats on the upper floors. Half of the flats were permanently empty though as most of the owners had moved to the US or Europe. Occasionally, owners came back for short visits but generally, only around four out of sixteen flats were occupied at any one time. It was a little like living in a ghost building.

The benefit of this was that the impressive park-like garden and 25-metre pool was mostly entirely mine to enjoy. For the first three months, I never saw anyone else by the pool apart from the occasional security guy checking everything was OK. It was great. I just didn't have anyone to enjoy it with. And it was unlikely I would have visitors from abroad. I kept in touch with family and friends with occasional calls over the internet but the time difference was tricky – by the time I got home from the office, it was generally well past midnight back in Copenhagen.

So here I lived in my safe little bubble – almost all by myself. Only the security guys down by the massive steel gate that safeguarded me from the dangers unfolding in the Caracas night-time reminded me that I wasn't actually free. The streets around were empty after 8 p.m. Most people in this part of the city went home and stayed home in the evening, as I did.

Food for Thought

☞ How do you think you would cope living in such an environment?

☞ What do you think you could gain from such an experience?

☞ What minimum requirements do you have in terms of living environment or support around you?

Chapter 17: The Importance of the US Dollar

The first major topic on my agenda besides landing in the new role and picking up the business-as-usual activities was to address the significant hard currency need and high inflation. Most companies were struggling with the same issues.

There was barely any access to US dollars for corporates. Most local Venezuelan subsidiaries with foreign parents were being heavily subsidised by their parent companies at HQ. Often, HQ would be paying for all of the foreign materials needed for production that could not be bought by the Venezuelan company. It was not a sustainable business model.

Many corporates had materially stripped down their product offering and compromises had also been made with product quality. If there was a product the government wanted to be freely available to its citizens, it would simply confiscate the factories. As such, some corporates had chosen to shut their production plants. Sometimes the government would try to start up production with government-appointed management and staff in place, but this rarely went well. Overall, many workers across the country were simply laid off.

In our company, most things still worked. One of the advantages of being part of a large foreign-owned multi-national corporation is that local subsidiaries can withstand pressure and challenging times for longer periods. The losses can be absorbed by the rest of the Group. The expectation is that when a country turns around, the business will once again resume normal working conditions. As long as there is hope for a turnaround and the benefits are greater than writing off the subsidiary, the Group will continue to pay up in the interim. Writing off an investment in a large country like Venezuela is not something that most corporates want to do. Nevertheless, it happened with many of the industries.

Despite the severe US dollar shortage in the country, the implications and challenges for the company were not that widely understood across the organisation and outside the finance department. According to most people, everything was working well. The imported raw materials entered Venezuela and were paid for. Plus, we were definitely in a better position than other industries, so what was the problem? With my treasury background and HQ experience fresh in mind, I knew it was unsustainable. Sooner or later, we would run out of US dollars and at that point, it would be too late.

To some extent, it reminded me of what I'd seen in the Argentinian subsidiary back in 2009. There was a fundamental problem but the vast majority in the organisation either were not very aware of it or, if they were, did not consider it a major problem. Perhaps it was safer to live in a happy bubble. To only see problems when they arose. To be fair, there were many other daily work and personal challenges they needed to attend to on a daily basis.

In the beginning, I tried to raise awareness at board meetings, especially when raw materials and imports, which were paid for in US dollars, were mentioned. There was some sympathy amongst the other Directors, but there was no sense of urgency to do anything about it. Outside the boardroom, the understanding and awareness was even weaker. It seemed, for now, that there were bigger challenges.

I believe two major factors contributed to this. Firstly, Venezuela had been an oil-producing country for more than a century. The oil reserves had historically provided enough US dollar supply to the country. And, for the last few years, when the US dollar need had exceeded the supply, the government had simply borrowed US dollars from outside to make up the shortfall. This was all about to collapse. Secondly, if you are raised in a socialist regime or are a true believer of the Chavez/Cuban socialist ideology, it can be difficult to really understand why parent companies outside Venezuela would *not* want to provided unlimited support to their subsidiaries, even if they subscribed to a capitalist ideology. They would surely support them forever and ever, in all circumstances.

This belief was more readily held by the company's blue-collar workers and their union representatives, but also by a minority of the office staff. Some of the younger generations also struggled to understand the corporate point of view as ideology is a strong force when it is indoctrinated into society.

From a professional perspective, it hugely frustrated me that people did not see what I clearly saw. Plus, I was in my first FD role and had left London with a clear mandate to address the hard currency issue. I felt that if I did not manage it well, I would have failed.

Spiralling Prices

Another big problem in Venezuela was the 25-30% official inflation rate. It was the highest inflation I had ever experienced. Apart from a brief period in the early 1980s when inflation was around 20% in Denmark, inflation had mostly been steady at or below 2%. In more recent years, it had been closer to 0%. In Venezuela, a rate of 25-30% was considered normal. Expectations were that it would reach three digits within a year.

When prices increase so quickly and expectations are all over the place, it is near impossible to price your product correctly. If you increase your prices too quickly and frequently, you'll price yourself out of the market. People won't be able to afford your products. If you don't increase your prices enough, you'll dilute your margins and, in the worst case scenario, fall into loss-making territory. It was a fine line and decisions had to be made on little concrete information.

I was really in unknown territory. I suddenly found myself in a situation where I had to convince people of things that, for me, were obvious and relatively simple. It was a healthy challenge for me but it continued to frustrate me a lot. Why did people not understand that we couldn't just sell our product at a loss so that consumers could afford to buy it?

I still had a lot to learn as FD. I felt the pressure daily. There was no let up. Luckily, I had a strong team around me. I got all the support I needed in regards to the regular FD tasks. My top team was an amazing group of talented men and women. They were hard-working, dedicated professionals and we had already got a strong team dynamic going. They were as determined as me to bring the US dollar currency and inflation challenges to the forefront of people's minds. They did their utmost to talk about it in various conversations and forums. Nonetheless, it was clear that, despite our best efforts, the message was not getting through.

We decided to go on an offsite team-building day, all arranged by Estrella. We put our heads together and came at the problem from a different angle. We realised that we were speaking a different language to the rest of the organisation. When we spoke about finance matters, we assumed everyone was on the same page and understood our rationale. However, we were communicating finance matters with predominantly non-finance people. Should we really expect them to get it?

A lot of my work experience up until that point had been in corporate treasury. My communication and engagement had mostly been with other highly skilled and technical finance professionals. People who knew more than me about specific accounting or tax rules. I had never really reflected upon the language I used or how much I assumed that everyone else understood what I was saying.

We had never had anyone opposing our messages. People said that they were onboard and expressed their respect and support of what we were saying. Still, it had resulted in little change in their behaviour or attitude.

We realised they hadn't translated our messages into actions or behaviours. They essentially trusted us and left us to manage it. The problem was that we needed their help to implement various initiatives.

Thinking about it in this way, it sounded completely obvious. When you live in an environment like the one in Venezuela, the pressure on everyone is incredibly high. Every employee had struggles of their own living in such a volatile country. For many, personal finances were tight; there were shortages of basic goods; security was a constant worry; access to basic utilities like electricity, water and the internet was unreliable.

Furthermore, they had demanding jobs with each department having their own challenges. The Legal and Corporate Affairs department struggled with working with ineffective government institutions. The Factory and Procurement teams struggled keeping normal production running smoothly. The Trade and Marketing department had challenges around security on the streets and managing the limited product portfolio. The IT team was constantly battling the unreliable data connections and trying to find basic hardware in a country where most things were out of stock. And, of course, Finance had its challenges with managing foreign currency, changes in tax laws, payment terms, and budgeting and accounting in an economy with hyperinflation.

Clearly, in an environment like this, most functions would focus on their own agenda. Only by communicating with them in a language that they understood, with clear instructions, would they have capacity and knowledge to make changes. After all, if we ran out of hard currency, it would be the end for all of us, not just Finance. We needed to approach this in another way.

We began to brainstorm. How could we communicate in a more appealing way? We found inspiration from our marketing colleagues. The entire Group was very marketing-driven. They were excellent in making spins on everything. Explaining in clear terms and in a language that appealed to the rest of the organisation. We, on the other hand, communicated in dull finance language and in a way that did not awake (positive) emotions in people.

We began to speak in much simpler language. 'Less is more' became our mantra. We used animated graphics to illustrate our points, even using cartoons like the Minions, the Smurfs and other well-known cartoon characters to make people laugh. We told engaging stories, that appealed to the brain and the heart, and this really brought the topics to life. And it worked! It was striking to see how a relatively simple change in communication form could have such a positive impact. Suddenly, people began to talk about finance and demonstrate their support through their actions. It felt good.

My team toured around the country and made presentations in Spanish to all the sales offices so that the sales teams would be able to implement pricing strategies that included inflation expectations. Essentially, we began to engage with our internal customers in a positive way. We had to be marketeers rather than pure finance people.

In addition, a culture of dollar consciousness also arose. We worked together to find alternatives to US dollar usage and initiatives that meant the US dollar need was reduced or replaced. And we celebrated even small wins together. That was important.

A Time Out

It was nearly time for a break. I could hardly wait. I was flying back to Denmark to join my parents, brother and his family for a trip to the Faroe Islands. For ages, my brother had wanted to show his family round the 18 small islands in the middle of the North Atlantic Ocean and to share our family roots with them.

In January that year, he had been diagnosed with throat cancer and had undergone three months of intensive chemo- and radiotherapy. It had made him very sick. It had been difficult to visit him from South America, but my parents had kept me updated on how he was doing. Only later when I saw him in-person did I realise how poorly he must have been. Living and working on the other side of the world comes at a price - something I was learning the hard way.

Despite still suffering side effects from the radiotherapy, he wanted to go now and I was going to join them. I looked forward to seeing them all. My niece and nephew were now five and seven years old and yet I hardly knew them. Given how close my family is, this felt strange but I had left Denmark when the eldest was two years old and only saw them a few times a year when I visited on vacation. What better way to connect with them all now than by visiting the Faroe Islands – and with my mum as our local guide!

Six months in Caracas with its frenetic rhythm of chaos, riots, shortages and work challenges, and now I was returning to a safe part of the world, at least for a short break.

Living in Caracas had been incredibly rewarding workwise but painful on a personal level. I had always been used to freedom and safety. From cycling home at 3 a.m. after a night out with friends in Copenhagen to discovering new parts of London on the weekends. Even Buenos Aires had offered the free life, although I didn't dare cycle due to the heavy traffic.

Over the last six months, I had been out a few times on work-related field trips. Otherwise, I just travelled from home to work, and back again the next day. The monotony was only broken up occasionally by an exciting trip to the supermarket. I never cycled anywhere. I never walked around in the city. Let's just say that the COVID-19 pandemic brought back some familiar memories. I missed my freedom but living under those restrictions also toughened me like never before.

Still, my life was better in so many ways than most Venezuelans. It made me grateful for my circumstances despite the many things I missed. At least I had the option *not* to walk given I had an armoured car provided by the company. At least I had work to keep me occupied. And at least I could occasionally pop away to another country and find respite from the urban prison I found myself in.

Although an independent country with its own history, language, and culture, the Faroe Islands are a part of the Danish commonwealth. The 18 islands are incredibly beautiful – its green mountains in sharp contrast to the blue Atlantic Ocean. We were lucky. The weather was amazing this time round. It gave me some time to relax and experience some peace. I hadn't noticed how stressed I had been on a constant basis in Venezuela. Being back in a safe and known environment, I could feel the difference in my body and mind. After a week on the Islands, I spent a week in Copenhagen seeing friends and other family members. Then I braced myself for returning back to Caracas.

This time, I was more prepared. I brought a third suitcase with me containing everything I thought I would need - from soap, toilet paper and cleaning products, to milk powder and cheese. I even managed to fit in a water purifier. Due to shortages of wrapping and packing materials, you could no longer find water in the supermarkets. The quality of the tap water was terrible. I had to boil it several times before drinking it. Now, I would be able to purify the water at home. Again, I was lucky. Many households only got running water through their taps for an hour a day and many of those in the slum areas only had it a few times a week. Apparently, the wealthy people living in my building had arranged for running water via some informal channels. I was part of the tiny privileged minority that had access to water all the time. It's amazing what you take for granted.

Despite the hardships of living there, it was good to be back. There were still so much to learn and accomplish at work. My next break from Caracas was to be at the end of the year, in four months' time, but I knew it would go fast.

Food for Thought

☞ Are you aware of how many technical terms you use when communicating with others outside your area of expertise?

☞ Have you been on the receiving end of this yourself and how did it make you feel about what the other person was saying?

Chapter 18: I've Never Felt Leather as Soft as this Before…

It was approaching autumn. The weekly security briefings we were getting at work had begun to get me down. Some weeks earlier, the son of another senior manager had been 'express kidnapped', a term I had only previously heard in films. He was taken when leaving a cinema in a mall on a Saturday night at 8 p.m. Luckily, the kidnapping went relatively well in the sense that the kidnappers were paid quickly and the son was released without physical injury. Still, it played on my mind.

One morning, I was driving to work in my armoured Ford Explorer. It was a sturdy marine blue car with darkened windows for security (so that potential criminals wouldn't be able to see how many people were in the car). I was driving one of the standard routes. We had been trained not to take the same route every day, so I had two or three options to pick from. Often, my System 1 brain kicked in and automatically picked the shortest route, but that morning, I took another route.

Suddenly, a white jeep stopped in front of me. I immediately braked but felt my bumper just touch the car in front. The braking distances are a little longer in armoured cars because they are heavier. The driver, a man, immediately got out of his car and started shouting aggressively at me with equally aggressive hand gestures. My immediate thought was: Shit. What do I do?

I had been instructed not to leave the car if there was an accident, but to call security straight away. I frantically tried to get hold of Estrella. The guy was not backing down. And he didn't like that I was just sitting in the car. I slowly unlocked the door and stepped onto the pavement. When I saw his car, I could understand why he was so upset. What had felt like a slight bump to me was actually my car having entirely pushed the reserve wheel on his backdoor into his car.

Understandably, he was very emotional. I tried to calm him down in my poor Spanish, and I said I would pay the charges to get his car fixed. Eventually, I got through to someone in the company. At the same time, the security department had noticed that my car had been stationary for a while. My car's GPS system was being monitored. Security had already sent someone out to check on the situation. Pretty soon, a company car arrived with two security guys.

Nothing serious had happened. We reassured the owner of the white jeep that we would cover all the repair costs. I went with one of the guards in his car and the other guard stayed with my car, waiting for the police to turn up, which is the law in Venezuela. Still, I felt shaken up that morning and realised that I had changed.

Up until moving to Venezuela, I would never have worried about a situation like this. Living in such an alien environment, under constant concerns around safety, was a challenge and it had changed me more than I thought.

Caracas was a complete change from my four years in London, living a relatively normal bachelor life. In Caracas, the upscale clubs were populated by the same crowd of people – many were loud, pretentious, and rich. Not my crowd at all. In fact, ones that I had unconscious biases around. I had only attended less than a handful of parties when invited by my colleagues. These parties were fun as I already knew many of the people there and knew I could trust them.

After six months, I was still struggling to know who to trust and how to open up. As I was born in a trust-based society and brought up to trust everyone irrespective of how different they are from me or how they appeared, I really struggled in Venezuela to make the right call. During security briefings, it was constantly reiterated that we should not share personal details with others. It made me overly cautious and I often avoided answering certain questions or even lied about what I did there.

It didn't make it easier that when I arrived at a party, I would be dropped off in my armoured car, followed by a back-up car and two additional security guards. At times, it felt like overkill. When I left the club a few hours later, I would be met by three security guys who had been waiting outside for me the whole time. Although they were dressed in civilian clothing, they were clearly security staff. If you were after attention, this would be a sure fire way of getting it.

The security guys were amazing though. Gradually, we got to trust each other, or rather I started to trust them and they looked after me. They monitored every move I made and were trained to step in if I was in any danger. It is a high ask to step into the face of danger for someone else. The automatic reflex is surely to preserve your own life. To this day, I feel immensely grateful to all of the security guys who took such good care of me.

As time went on, tensions in the country grew. The scarcity problems were worsening by the day and so were the currency and inflation issues. The government introduced new currency schemes but it was old wine in new bottles and led to no real change. The public sector continued to spend the limited US dollars available on buying new equipment for the military. A strange priority when millions of people were suffering from malnutrition and basic supplies (including medicines) were out of stock. It led to larger demonstrations that were quelled by the increasingly brazen and violent military. It was governing by fear.

The metropolitan area of Caracas has an estimated population of five million. At the time, around 140 people were murdered each weekend during the time I lived there. To get a more accurate picture, you actually needed to add the number of kidnappings. Estimates in 2014 indicated that around 50 kidnappings were happening per day (although 90% of kidnappings aren't reported).

All of these stories and statistics worked for the regime. Fear made people stay at home. People at home meant fewer riots for the government to crack down on. There was a lot of corruption in the system so you couldn't trust the authorities. The police, military and security forces were in the pockets of the criminals. Not all of them, but enough not to know who to trust. Impunity levels were around 99%, so crime was often a better option for poor people than an underpaid job.

One morning, one of my team came in and told us a harrowing story from the weekend. Her husband was a senior manager in a multi-national corporation in Venezuela. On Sunday, around 8 a.m., one of his directors had left his home (which wasn't far from mine) and driven to the Avila mountains, where he liked to go for a morning run. Two cars drove up. One blocked him from the front and the other from behind. He was in an armoured car like mine. The kidnappers got out of their cars, held up a hand grenade and flashed it in front of him. They yelled that if he didn't open the door right away, they would pull the pin and leave the grenade on his windscreen. Knowing that the armoured cars are built to protect against hand weapons but not explosives, he had no other option but to open his door.

He was taken out, blindfolded and driven away in one of their cars. They took him to a deserted place and stripped him naked. My team member told me that the thinking behind this tactic is that people who are naked feel more vulnerable and are easier to break down. They asked for the code to his mobile phone. He refused. Still blindfolded and absolutely terrified, they threatened to pass the chainsaw through his body and head. With the chainsaw still whirring by his ear, he gave them the code. Scrolling through the photos on his phone, they assessed the pictures of his family – pictures of them on vacation in Europe and pictures that confirmed his senior position and wealth. They decided the ransom should be set at USD 50,000.

His wife was contacted. She immediately called his company. Over the course of the Sunday, the company scraped together all of the US dollar cash they had. It didn't add up to the sum requested, so they threw in expensive watches, jewellery, and other valuables. Eventually, they got somewhere close to USD 50,000.

The ransom exchange took place. The kidnappers, who were in their early twenties, told him that he was lucky. There had been payment for his freedom and they would now drive him out to an area where they would let him out, still naked and blindfolded, onto the side of the road with his clothes. One of the guys said that his belongings would be found a little further up the hill. Only once they had driven off could he take off his blindfold. The guy added, with a smirk in his voice, 'You'll find the contents of your wallet, but I will keep the wallet as I've never felt leather as soft as this before.'

This is what happened. When the director took his blindfold off, he put on his clothes and ran up to found his others belongings, minus wallet, in a pile on the side of the road. He rang his company and was soon picked up. That same night, he and his family were flown out of Caracas on a private chartered jet and never returned to the country.

It was too close. A senior employee working in an international company, living in my neighbourhood. The only difference was I had no spouse for them to call. Who would they call? My parents in Denmark?

I now saw the constant security surrounding me in a different light. It took weeks before I stopped replaying it in my mind. It only added to the constant tension I held inside my body and the feeling of injustice that those around me shared as well. If there was ever a time where I wanted to follow my dad's advice around just punching someone in the face, it was then. Of course, his advice was never meant for a situation like this.

I just couldn't understand how people can make kidnapping into a 9–5 job, oblivious to how much the victims and their families will suffer for the rest of their lives. I spoke with a colleague about it and he said, 'You cannot change the security situation in this country, but you can follow the wise guidance given by the security department. And then, you can make an active choice about how much you want it to impact you emotionally.'

From that day onwards, I tried to remind myself of this valuable advice. It helped me keep my frustrations under control, not only in other situations like this, but in many other professional and personal situations. I may not be able to change the situation but I can do what is sensible and I can make an active choice about how much I'm going to let it impact me.

Food for Thought

☞ How well are you able to tolerate uncertainty and/or fear?

☞ What is your typical reaction to it?

☞ In what situations have you felt helpless to change something?

☞ How could you reframe your thinking so that you focus on what you can control (i.e. your emotions)?

Chapter 19: Can you teach an old dog new tricks?

Thora was known across the entire organisation for her terrible mood. She had been in the company for many years and her reputation had grown over that time. I assume she was softer in her younger days but I couldn't have been certain. Everyone knew who Thora was and everyone knew her as loud, rude and moody.

Nonetheless, she was excellent at supervising one of the six finance functions within my area. She took care of her area with pride. It was important to her that she was good. She also had good connections outside the company which, in a country like Venezuela, is vital for success in many different areas. Unfortunately, Thora also enjoyed shouting at more junior colleagues. She didn't listen to people she didn't respect, and she only respected more senior people and a few of her peers.

I have never liked such managers. My first job after I graduated from university was in one of the largest Danish companies at the time. The FD was kind enough as a person. At least that was my impression from the few interactions I had with him, which were primarily of him walking around at the Christmas lunch and wishing them a merry Christmas. However, the rest of the year, he was entirely unapproachable and horrible as a manager.

He followed the lead-by-fear school of thought. Even at a young age, I could see how his management style was generating all the wrong behaviours in the organisation. I promised myself that I would never lead like that and I would not tolerate managers like that. It was a style that triggered particular ego issues in me and clashed with my fundamental values around inclusion, justice, and a more sophisticated use of power in the workforce.

I knew Thora was well regarded by the other directors in the company, especially given her many years of service. And I cannot say what previous FDs had done or seen. But from what I observed, her behaviour was unacceptable, even after correcting for the more hierarchal leadership style that exists in Venezuela versus Denmark. It was a tricky one. I had only been in the company about seven months. We had a good working relationship overall. She treated me with respect, and I her. She knew her technical area well, so I had a lot of trust in her. But If I allowed her to scream in the open office at the others, I would also de facto be endorsing such leadership behaviour and culture.

I had a dilemma. Many people were fleeing Venezuela, so replacing a talented employee would not be easy. However, the latest incidence had led to an employee running out of the office in tears. I wasn't there when it happened but was infuriated when I heard. Ideally, I would have liked her to stay, but would she be able to change? As one of my first managers (and role-model) always said: You can't teach an old dog new tricks. I tend to agree but I also believe the best in people, so I wanted to give it a go. I fathered support from the other directors (including the HR director) and swotted up on the local employment laws, knowing that it would be tricky if I had gone in unsupported and blind. I asked Estrella to set up a meeting.

The fact that Estrella had set up the meeting already signalled that it was to be a serious conversation. I started by asking Thora to say how she felt she was doing on the company's eight competencies. These eight competencies (four were related to professional skills and four to managerial skills) were used by the Group to assess how a person was performing. The night before, I had decided that it would be best to take a tactical and problem-solving approach as this would match her analytical approach, rather than confront her behaviour head-on.

Overall, she underscored herself on the professional competencies but *over*scored herself in the personal skills. It surprised me to see her disbelief as I shared my perception of her capabilities. I raised that I wanted this meeting to discuss her behaviour and skills as I had observed and informed of certain situations that were not positive. I stressed that other people's stories can be biased but that their stories also fit with what *I* had observed, and that it would be those incidences that I would focus on.

I tried to make it comfortable for Thora. Several times, I stressed that I wanted her to stay but that I needed her commitment to work on some of her behaviours urgently. She was visibly thrown. We agreed that she would go home and think about it further, and come back to tell me if she would agree to a clear action plan for improving her personal skills. If not, I would be recommending that she left the company. We would, of course, pay severance payments. Again, I reinforced that I would prefer she stay. We ended the meeting there.

A few days later, we had a follow-up meeting. She came into my office and this time, with more self-confidence, informed me that she had thought about it and would work on herself. I was delighted and relieved. I offered my support and time. The following weeks, she was jovial to everyone. I was impressed at how much she had taken onboard the feedback. I commended her and she seemed happy. Now that the urgent matter had been addressed, it was time to look forward to a more cheerful matter – Christmas in Finance!

All I Want for Christmas...
It was a few weeks away from Christmas and I would soon be off to Denmark for a long holiday. I could not wait. The last nine months had really challenged me. I always tried to keep my corporate game face on regardless of what I was really thinking and feeling, but it had worn me down and I needed a break. Given how many daily struggles there were for the team on an individual and collective basis, I was surprised to see the energy and can-do attitude across the organisation. It was great to see and it lifted me too.

Christmas is a very different experience in Latin America to Denmark. At the very least, Christmas is in winter in Denmark - the days are short and the streets are filled with little ones being pulled on sledges. It matches Disney's description of Santa Claus and a white Christmas, i.e. how I think it is *supposed* to look! Or at least it did until climate change…

I absolutely love Christmas! A feeling of *hygge* is sought even more than usual.

In Venezuela, where the weather is almost the same all year round, Christmas is plastic fantastic. Clearly, most people don't have real pine trees but they do have plastic trees, plastic decorations, and basically plastic everything! The Christmas music is also more Latin (check out *Al Llegar Aquí*).

Each year, the different departments in the company would decorate their own workspaces however they wanted to. Every department except Finance, where the Grinch had stolen Christmas many years ago. So, when Estrella asked if we should have a competition for the best Christmas decorations in Finance, I was game. Did I already say that I love Christmas?!

The competition was launched and now I saw how competitive my team was. Each of the six finance teams went above and beyond themselves, adding on more and more colour, glitter and plastic. And all to win a tiny plastic trophy, some booze, and a lot of peer respect, obviously! The creativity and energy the teams put into decorating was amazing. It was like a hidden energy was released and suddenly people started talking about how Finance was the place to be! I threw myself into it as well, decorating my own office with a tiny plastic tree with multi-coloured baubles and a string of lights from London, and other decorative items from my home. And I walked around commenting on people's efforts and stoking the competitive spirit.

Seeing the team's energy and happiness, and knowing that I had made space for it, made me happy. I hadn't seen it coming. I learnt that it often takes little to generate a big impact in people. You just have to say yes to your inner child and make room for the unexpected!

The Operations Finance team won. It was close but they had filled their walls and ceiling and recreated Santa's workshop. All of the Directors' names were listed at the top of the 'Good children list'. It was brilliant. The day after the prize giving ceremony, I headed to the airport for my flight to Copenhagen.

I had never really felt lonely before but being isolated, not having the freedom to do what I wanted and having a limited network (predominantly of work colleagues) had triggered this feeling in me. I couldn't wait to see my friends and family. The constant tension from the danger everywhere had put my normally strong intuition out of whack and I felt physically and mentally exhausted.

I always flew to Copenhagen via Frankfurt with Lufthansa airlines. It was the shortest route back and one of the few airlines still operating routes between Venezuela and Europe. After the usual hassle through airport security, I was met outside the plane by a 17-year-old boy in military uniform. It was far too big for him, as he nervously gripped his machine gun. I avoided eye contact and made it into the cabin without being taken aside. To my misfortune, I saw that I would be sat next to a mum with a small screaming baby.

The kind flight attendant sensed my disappointment and, once boarding was complete, she asked if I wanted to move further down the cabin and take any seat available. I had barely settled in before three young, loud *bolibourguesa* (or boliboys in English) came and sat next to me. *Bolibourgeoisa* is a Venezuelan term used to describe a small group of people who became ultra rich during the Chavez regime, primarily through their connections to senior government officials in the regime. It was essentially a new wealth class that was created out of corruption. They became more powerful and held even greater influence during Maduro's presidency. The term comes from *bolivar* (the local currency) and the French word *bourgeoisie* (the upper middle class). They represent all the values that I do not share and that go against my own fundamental beliefs.

Clearly, the three men also wanted to avoid the screaming baby, but they brought with them their own loud noise and worse, arrogance. I already knew the flight was going to be much longer than the scheduled ten hours. As we were about to take off, everyone had to turn off their phones. One of the guys next to me, only in his late twenties, ignored the air hostess and continued on his important call while we were taking off.

For someone who flies a lot, I'm not actually that fond of flying. I know that an airplane costing USD 300 million is not going to fall from the skies because an idiot is speaking on his phone but still, he was annoying me tremendously. I firmly asked him to turn off his phone and shut up. It quickly escalated into an argument. I wasn't going to back down though and eventually, he and his friends moved to another part of the cabin.

This was the first time I'd noticed that the pressure of Venezuela had done something to my psyche and behaviour. I was absolutely boiling with anger. The lack of fundamental rights, the feeling of injustice, the lack of freedom, and the clear impunity that I observed everywhere in the country – eventually, I unleashed my anger and acted in a way I had never done before. Like Thora. Was it a build-up of pressure that had led to her bad mood? No, I didn't think so. Her reputation went much further back in time. Still, I was shocked by myself and a little disappointed. This trip could not have come at a more needed time. All I wanted for Christmas was peace and relaxation in a safe environment.

Arriving in Copenhagen, I was greeted by my parents and I could feel the tension leave my body. Denmark. Home. It would be a very merry Christmas with family, followed by a fun New Year's Eve celebration with a dear friend in San Francisco. There was much to look forward to.

Just as I started to feel like myself again, it was time to fly back to Caracas. Still energised from my break, it was good to be back. As I got some distance, I could reflect that I had achieved a lot during my first year in Venezuela. I knew there were exciting challenges ahead that would require a lot of focus and energy from my side. And despite the hardship of living there, I enjoyed the challenges.

When I got back to office, Thora was still on holiday. When she came back a few weeks later, on a day I was out of the office, she handed in her resignation to the HR director. She had found another job. She wished to use up the rest of her holiday allowance, so this would be her last day in the office. I never saw Thora again.

It was a shame. I had been faithful to the commitment I'd made many years back about standing up for good leadership behaviours. In this particular case, the saying 'you can't teach an old dog new tricks' turned out to be true.

It took us many months to find a replacement. Still, the outcome was welcomed across the Finance community. Many felt that it signalled that good leadership was essential to a career in Finance. It would no longer be sufficient just to be technically competent, but your leadership skills and working manner had to match. This incidence, together with many other initiatives across the function, led to a gradual but consistent change in the behaviour, culture and reputation of the Finance function across the organisation.

Suddenly, we went from being seen as serious, inward-looking, conservative and old school to younger, more dynamic, engaging, and with a strong focus on respect. This was a department you wanted to be a part of if you wanted to develop your leadership skills and softer skills such as influence and communication. Together with my strong top team, I felt we had delivered outstanding results in a short period of time and under tough circumstances.

Food for Thought

☞ Do you have good leadership role-models?

☞ What characteristics do you appreciate in a leader?

☞ Has your view changed over time?

☞ How do you deal with constant pressure?

☞ How does your behaviour change when you are under pressure?

☞ What things do you need in order to function well under pressure in the long term?

Chapter 20: Getting Out of the Finance Box

Most companies manage the performance of their employees with an annual evaluation. Companies conduct them differently but the overall purpose is the same – to rate and feedback on how employees have performed during the year and, where needed, highlight improvement areas. It can be used to reward individuals but also to incentivise better future performance.

In some consultancy firms and banks, the 10% worst performing staff shouldn't feel too safe in their jobs. If you are among the 10% several years in a row, you should start updating your CV. The idea is that by forcing everyone in the lowest segment to perform better you are moving up the overall performance of the whole organisation. There are elements to this approach that work. It encourages a high-performance culture. Constant bench-marking within the company and against other similar companies ensures there is no let up.

Other corporates use the approach more flexibly. They will categorise employees under three categories – a small 'nearly there' group (i.e. you're underperforming), a large 'at level' group (i.e. you're performing as expected) and a small 'exceeds' group (i.e. you're outperforming). Essentially, there is a bell curve and you are rewarded according to where you are on the bell curve.

Often, an employee's categorisation will impact on their bonus or their salary increase for the next year. For the large 'at level' group, bonuses will be average and salary increases will fluctuate in a tight band around a median percentage. If you are awarded the coveted 'exceeds', you may get the same bonus as the 'at level' group but you'll receive a higher salary increase and it will look great on your employee record, which can help with future career progression. Those who receive a 'nearly there' may not receive a bonus or a much smaller bonus.

There are a few shortcomings with performance rating systems like this. There will always be an element of subjectivity. Chemistry between a given manager and employee, political agendas in the organisation, likelihood of employees questioning the rating, and so on, can all have an impact. For the same reason, many companies will calibrate performance ratings across teams and functions to ensure that ratings are given as consistently as possible.

Another challenge is the lack of expectations set around performance. Managers can limit the noise from this if they set clear expectations, agree them with the employee and document them. Even better is if they provide insight into what it will take to 'exceed' these expectations. If this isn't done, and there are a lot of managers who don't do this, the field is wide open for disappointment.

I have had many of these performance conversations over the years, both as a manager and employee. I know the challenges they bring. I have had employees who had misaligned or unrealistic expectations. Over the years, I became better at managing and communicating expectations.

In a perfect working relationship between manager and employee, the annual performance review should just be a tick box exercise. It should take no more than five minutes to sum up and agree – nothing new should arise in this review. Performance and improvement areas should be clear for both parties before the meeting takes place because more informal conversations have taken place over the year. Both parties know where they stand. The employee should know if they are delivering as expected and if they're not, the manager should have been helping them to improve over the year. If no progress is made, the poor performer may already have been asked to leave before the year is gone.

In reality, many managers don't communicate well with their employees. They may have their favourites. There may be situations where managers air good intentions around rewarding an 'exceeds' throughout the year, dangling the juicy carrot, only to have reality hit at the end of the year and too many people have delivered outstanding results. According to the bell curve, only a limited number can get an 'exceeds'. Not only do you have to exceed the expectations agreed between you and your manager, you also have to exceed them by more than others in your team.

'No one remembers who came in second'
Walter Hagen

The 'at level' group is so large that there is no differentiation between those who narrowly avoided a 'nearly there' and those who almost got an 'exceeds'. It's frustrating. You and your manager may know, but according to the rest of the organization, you are simply average.

Some companies have a lot of rotation in management. This isn't always bad. It could be due to changes in the organisation but also internal rotation for employees to gain experience in different positions, teams and countries. It was an annoying but common event to find that managers who knew they would not be staying for long enough to live with the consequences to not manage expectations well. They would rather leave on a high note with the individual or team than to be the bearer of bad news. On several occasions, I had taken over new teams and had to manage disappointed employees. Still, I was about to realise how poorly I had managed my own expectations.

At Level

Over the years, I had been rated 'at level' in some years and 'exceeds' in others. I'd had all the above types of managers - the ones who were excellent and set clear expectations, and the ones who did not. The ones who would fight for your performance rating and the ones who wouldn't bother. In some of those years, I felt I had really made a valuable difference to the overall performance of the whole team. In other years, I knew I had just delivered as expected and didn't expect anything more than an 'at level'.

The most disappointing year, however, was at the end of my first year as FD in Venezuela. Reflecting on it now, I think there were three main factors - expectations management, cultural differences, and personal development.

Before Venezuela, I had largely worked in stable environments. The challenges were clear and predictable. Everyone knew that doing your 9-5 job would not result in an 'exceeds'. You needed to bring something that was unexpected. Something that preferably contributed to additional income or cost savings for the Group.

Now I was in Venezuela. Delivering on the day job was challenging enough. I had landed in the middle of some of the largest riots the country had seen for decades. I won't rehash the challenges again but needless to say it was intense on a professional and personal level. Nonetheless, I felt I had managed well and led my team of 80 employees well. I came to work positive and gave all I had every day.

My mandate from HQ had been clear – manage the US dollar dependence away from the mothership. I had already made substantial progress and more promising initiatives were in the works. I was a new FD in a very challenging market. I had injected energy into the Finance function and spurred a fresh understanding and appreciation of finance across the whole organisation. I felt I had delivered an outstanding performance. Holding it up against previous roles I had held, none of them could compare.

I went in to see my manager, Gabriel, expectant and hopeful for a clear 'exceeds' and a pat on the back. It wasn't to be. It was a plain average 'at level'. I felt like I'd been punched.

Seriously??

I wasn't disappointed. I was infuriated. And it was painted all over my face. According to Gabriel, I had delivered 'great' but I was 'too finance oriented'. I would need to be 'more holistic' in my approach, not just bringing the finance agenda to the table but also the overall business agenda of the company.

Whilst I accepted his feedback, I still felt it was incredibly unfair. I had taken up my first FD role, achieved great results and the feedback was that I was too finance focused – sorry, what?

Over the following days, I couldn't get out of this negative spiral. I felt agitated. In general, I am an emotional person. I am very expressive and usually bring a lot of positive energy to work. So it was felt when I did not, so much so that people across the organisation asked if I was OK.

The lack of access to friends and family didn't help. Given the time difference, I could only call them in between meetings during office hours. And that was only when the phone lines were actually working. I really needed to get my emotions under control. I wasn't happy with myself or my reaction.

But I couldn't find the door out. Had I overseen something? Was I too self-absorbed? Was I not actually as good as I thought? Eventually, I got to speak to family and friends. This time, everyone unconditionally supported me. They understood my frustration and the demotivation I felt. Did I want to stay in Venezuela and live through the hardship for just an 'at level'? Was it really worth it?

After thinking more about it, I decided to talk to Gabriel again. I'd tried to imagine how it looked from his side and sensed that maybe he'd not fully understood what I'd delivered and gone through these last nine months. I came well prepared. I didn't know if it would change anything but I needed Gabriel to understand how the picture looked from my side. I had written it all down. Three full written pages of performance deliveries that I ran through with him. In the end, he only remarked, 'Yes, I agree, you have delivered remarkable results, but my overall rating of you will not change'.

The Complexity of Matrix Leadership Structures

Many companies operate a matrix structure. This means that while you report to a manager on daily matters (in my case,

Gabriel, the GM), I also had a functional head (in my case, the Regional Head of Finance based in London). They play different roles but it is often helpful to have both for coordination across complex company structures.

Your daily manager is your line manager. They evaluate your behaviour, interactions, engagement and deliverables against the local (Venezuelan) agenda. This person will make the first recommendation for your performance rating.

Your functional manager is typically located in another location. This person may have a bigger say in your career progression but less on your current role. You are ultimately owned by your function (Finance) so your functional manager, as the one who put you in your job in the first place, will be the one deciding where you'll go next.

Both matter – how you deliver locally and functionally. But the two may not always be aligned. Your functional agenda will typically be broader based and overall Group-focused, whilst your local agenda will solely be focused on your single market. You must balance your performance against both managers' needs and expectations.

Mostly, they are aligned but in this case, I struggled to see that they were and I hadn't realised early enough. This was the first job I'd had where my line manager was outside of my functional area. My finance deliverables were only a part of his overall deliverables. This also meant it was the first time I had a daily manager, Gabriel, who was not a finance manager. And he had the biggest say on my performance evaluation.

The second factor was cultural differences. For some reason, over the one year that I had been in Venezuela, I had not really connected closely with Gabriel. My mistake, when moving to such a relationships-based culture. I hadn't been particularly close with my previous managers either (when you are senior, you often only need clarity around the high-level deliverables). I would keep them updated on progress but besides that, I would largely manage myself and my team.

I think that approach works well in a task-based, egalitarian culture, like the Danish culture. Trust is earned based on your past track record, even in other positions in the Group. You would have come highly recommended, otherwise you wouldn't have gotten the job. I think it also works well when you and your manager work within the same functional area as there is a familiarity about what is expected and what constitutes an 'exceeds' in delivery.

Here, I had a Latin manager. He came from a more relationships-based and hierarchical culture. And he was more of a business generalist. I had used most of my time to connect with my team. Of course, I interacted with Gabriel and other senior managers in weekly board meetings, various other monthly top team meetings and at social and work events. Still, I also encouraged my direct reports to interact frequently with senior directors without me, as Samir had always let me do in the past. For me, that was good leadership – to raise their profile, receive praise and correction where it was due, and to grow as managers themselves.

However, our offices were in the basement. The workload was high. Often, I didn't take the time to walk around and chat more informally with the other senior executives. The egalitarian leadership style from Denmark also meant that I would be one with my team. It wouldn't matter if it was a junior colleague or fresh graduate. Over lunch, conversations would cover all sorts, from our private lives to various political and economic debates. My team felt like they could be open with me and I had spent a lot of effort cultivating this culture.

This connection with people from different layers of the organisation provided me with vital insights into what was actually going on on-the-ground. My team shared with me their frustrations around initiatives that they felt weren't working. They fed back on what they thought was good. I got to know the joys and challenges of their daily lives. This was all vital information for me to be an effective leader. To correct myself when I was going down the wrong path. Fostering trust and connection really facilitated that. It also provided interesting social interactions, which I didn't really have outside the office as I didn't know many people.

I had worked in companies where managers never had lunch with their employees or chatted about normal non-work topics. I'd never understood the approach. For me, the informal connection is vital for creating a more effective team that understands each other. It had worked well for me up until then.

Suddenly, I began to wonder whether I should have taken more time to connect with Gabriel. Most of the other directors were Venezuelan and I found it natural that they would have a closer bond with him. But now I wasn't so sure that I shouldn't also have spent more time getting to know him on a personal level too. Was I paying the price now for exclusively focussing on my team? Not applying my past cultural learnings about the Latin culture? Had I connected better with him, maybe I could have read him better. To know his expectations of me. It was too late now. It couldn't be changed.

What Time is it? Time to Get Over Yourself

It was a week later and my meeting with Gabriel was still nagging me. Why was it so important to get the approval of my manager? I knew it wasn't about the bonus, but was it a matter of justice? Or did it relate more to my own self-acceptance? That I was good enough? That I was worthy? Everywhere I went in the office building, I was met by smiling faces, positive energy and appreciation. Still, why did I crave his? I'd have to think more about that.

'Anger is never without a reason, but seldom with a good one' Benjamin Franklin

---

For now though, I had to make a call. I said out loud to myself: Come on – it's only a performance rating. It's not a critique that you haven't done a good enough job. On the contrary. Look around you! Either you accept it for what it is or you move on and find another job.

It helped. I am a reflective person. I would say that I normally have a realistic view about my own performance and behaviour. I have participated in many 360-degree surveys in my managerial career (I'll return to this topic later). They have helped me calibrate my self-understanding.

The feeling of injustice in this incredibly hostile environment was difficult for me to cope with but now I tried to reframe it. I told myself that it was OK that I felt this way, that it was a just a feeling and the more I accepted the feeling, the less it would control me. And it worked. The feeling weakened and I could focus on moving forward.

A combination of factors really helped me. Firstly, having a great team around me on a daily basis really helped. Secondly, upon reflection, I honestly felt that Gabriel's evaluation was not correct. I had tried to see it from his perspective but I just didn't agree with it. And that was OK. He might have rated me an 'at level', but I knew I had done better than the rating implied. I regained my self-confidence.

Still, they say perception is reality, so if Gabriel believed I didn't operate sufficiently as an FD yet, I would have to address it. I could address it by changing my behaviour and/or by making it clearer to him what I actually did.

I then tried to see it from a more neutral perspective. How would it look from the outside? If, for example, I disregarded my own view and feelings, and also Gabriel's, recognising that both of our views are coloured by the need to deliver our own key performance objectives. Then, I could probably benefit from having a more holistic approach to my job. The more I thought about it, the more I realised that I should see my role in its widest context.

Having worked in Corporate Treasury most of my adult life, I was still wearing my treasury and finance hat. I needed to cast that off and put on a new hat – one that was befitting of a senior manager of the company, not only of the finance department. I basically had to step out of the finance box that I was so comfortable in. I had to engage with the other areas and be more like a GM. I had to network and step up on a broader scale.

It wasn't that I had forgotten the advice I had been given from Samir at HQ years back - he had tried to teach me that wider networking was imperative for my success in this company, especially as a senior manager – but up until that point, I had only understood it from the narrow perspective of my own area. Now, I understood that stakeholder management and the ability to see things in a much wider context go hand in hand for those operating successfully at senior levels. Again, I learnt that lesson the hard way.

Over the following year, I took on various assignments in the company that weren't directly relevant to my area. I applied a more pragmatic way of thinking and often took off my finance hat to do so. I was curious when others had different perspectives and sought to understand why rather than just disagreeing. Based on that, I sought to influence areas and projects where I didn't have direct technical expertise, but still I felt I could contribute.

Consequently, I managed to raise my profile in the company and this naturally led to other functions listening to me and taking my views onboard more. It was a quick route to impacting multiple areas across the organisation and strengthened my leadership skills. I began to communicate more as a GM at meetings and people saw that what I had to say had some weight. I advocated for agenda items amongst my own finance team that were good for the overall company, even if they weren't necessarily the best thing for the finance department.

Suddenly, the job also seemed to be more exciting. The reframing I'd done around my own way of thinking had unlocked a new way of working. This is when I realised I wouldn't be returning to Treasury. I loved the breadth of general management and getting stuck into areas I could only really learn on the job. I wouldn't take up a specialised role like Treasury again. It wouldn't give me the same energy and excitement that I now felt.

Today, I should thank Gabriel for opening my eyes even though it may not have been his intention.

Over this time, I also realised how much being around family and friends meant to me. And how much they helped me to feel valued as an individual and affirmed my worth. With hindsight, it felt like I had been seeking appreciation and recognition via a performance review as compensation for the appreciation I would normally get from my family and friends.

As I write this book, the COVID-19 epidemic is raging in waves across the world. The whole world has experienced some level of restriction of personal freedom and of the frustration that generates. Being deprived the right to walk down the street, go out for dinner or hug a friend. Not being able to travel and enjoy life as you wished to.

There are many things we take for granted until we lose them. Only then we realise they matter. Or we remember that they have always mattered. Here in Venezuela, I had managed on my own for almost a year with all the above limitations. And I would have to manage for at least one more year – that was the agreement with the company. Now that I was conscious of what such restrictions did to me, I knew I would deal with it better. Because I knew what to look out for. Perhaps you felt the same in the second or third lockdowns. I had learnt some techniques to partially compensate for the limitations and anyway, I had managed for a year and boy was it a tough year, so I knew I could survive another.

The following year, I managed Gabriel better and regularly asked what his expectations were and where he saw I was performing and where I wasn't. Needless to say, the performance evaluation at the end of the second year was much smoother and didn't lead to any frustration on any side. However, I also thankfully noticed that my need for his approval had also diminished. Personal growth.

Food for Thought

☞ How much do you look for approval or affirmation from other people?

☞ What about other things, e.g. respect, appreciation, admiration, etc?

☞ Have you had any pivotal experiences or learnings that have changed your way of thinking, behaving or working?

☞ What have the benefits been?

☞ Have they led to other changes in your life?

Chapter 21: Exodus

A big summit in Rio de Janeiro was approaching. Once a year, all of the senior directors from across the Americas region would meet together for a few days. It was expensive but the Group felt it was worth it because it was one of very few opportunities to gather the whole region in one place.

At this meeting, the region's direction and priorities for the following year would be established. It was also a great opportunity to network and build relationships that would prove valuable when working with similar challenges across different markets. I looked forward to it a lot.

Still a relatively new FD, it was a great opportunity to seek advice from other more experienced FDs. I already knew most of them from my regional treasurer days, but my challenges were vastly different now and it would be invaluable to pick their brains.

I had a flight out booked for the Friday afternoon so I would have a long weekend in Rio catching up with some old treasury colleagues who were flying in from London early as well.

I had been lucky to secure the airplane ticket. The government had recently retracted US dollar (USD) currency access to the airlines. Up until this point, airlines had sold tickets in VEB (the Venezuelan currency) based off one of the government's three official exchange rates. For years, the government had enabled the travel industry to exchange all of their VEB-denominated sales into USD at the artificially low exchange rate. Now, they were suddenly told they would no longer be able to convert any VEB to USD at all. This meant several years' of sales in VEB (equivalent to several USD 100,000,000) were now useless. Without access to conversion into USD, the international airlines wouldn't be able to get the funds out of the country. The same challenge our and many other companies had struggled with for years.

The reaction from the international airlines came promptly. Several airlines announced they would stop or materially reduce flights to and from Venezuela with immediate effect. All of the international airlines refused to sell any more tickets in local currency (VEB). Luckily, we had managed to buy the tickets shortly before the government made the change.

I had promised to bring some *arrepa flour* to a Venezuelan girl who lived with her husband in Rio. It is a local cornflour that most Venezuelans miss when abroad. I had managed to pack 3 kilograms into my bag. Other than that, my suitcase was half empty. I wanted to leave space for stocking up on products that I needed myself and couldn't find in Venezuela. I also had a long list of items to pick up for colleagues.

I arrived at the airport, keen to get going. Caracas international airport is not a nice experience. Every time I went there, it felt worse. The atmosphere was of tense chaos and the presence of the military everywhere was a bit intimidating.

I had a business class ticket. I checked-in and walked past the 17-year-old guys and girls with machine guns pretending to care about your security. I knew it was all a show. You can take in almost anything you like in your handbags – they won't say anything when you scan your luggage. Often they just chatted to each other or looked in any direction apart from the x-ray screen. For the same reason, the US had put the airport on an alert list of unsafe departure airports.

After an hour in the lounge, I arrived at the gate 45 minutes before departure. Passengers had just started boarding the plane. I entered the business class boarding line but when I walked up and showed my passport, I was told to stand aside.

'Excuse me, but what is happening?' I enquired.

The lady at the counter answered, 'We called you 20 minutes ago before we began boarding and you didn't approach us. Your luggage has been removed from the plane for manual inspection and as you were not here by then, you will now not be allowed to board the plane.'

I began to explain that I had been in the lounge and had not heard any announcements. She didn't care. As my agitation rose, my willingness and ability to try to speak Spanish diminished. I started to raise my voice and, in English, asked to speak with whoever was in charge. Reluctantly, they made a call on the walkie talkie and eventually, two people from the airline approached the counter.

They tried to explain to me again, in their poor English, that I could not board the plane. Again, I explained that I had been at the gate a full 45 minutes before take-off. No one had informed me that I needed to be there 60 minutes before and, as they were still boarding passengers, could I not just go and open my suitcase for inspection right away?

No. It was too late.

I was fuming and, by now, gesturing with frustration. Now, the military came. They asked me to put on a yellow high visibility vest and follow them down the stairs to the runway area. My suitcase was already on the side and the military guys asked me to unlock it. They found the three packs of cornflour and began to laugh. They told me I could lock the suitcase again. I didn't find it amusing. I asked if I could now board the flight and they said I had to ask the airline.

Walking quickly back up to the gate, I urgently asked if I could board the plane now. I received an adamant 'NO. Boarding is complete'. I can't even express how I felt at that time. I didn't know I could feel so strongly about something. I had so looked forward to having a weekend in freedom and having fun with my old friends from London. Now that opportunity had vanished.

I was escorted by two of the military guys through the airport into the arrivals area. I had to go through immigration to officially re-enter Venezuela. Yes, I even had to wait for my suitcase to come out on the conveyer belt and to get it scanned through customs.

There I was, all dressed and packed up with nowhere to go. I rang Estrella, who was in disbelief about what had happened. She quickly got the security department to redirect the two cars that had dropped me off back to the airport, but as they had almost reached downtown Caracas and it was now rush hour, it would take them several hours to arrive. I was told to enter a travel agency in the airport to not draw attention to myself.

I asked Estrella to book a new flight ticket as soon as possible. This turned out to be impossible. Irrespective of which airline she tried, there were no available flights, especially not if we only had local currency.

The situation was further exacerbated by the high demand for one-way tickets out of Venezuela. This had increased since the latest restrictions on airlines. I sent details of my private Danish and British visa cards and all other credit cards I had to Estrella. Each time she tried to make a booking, it was rejected. It turned out that you couldn't book and pay for tickets in US dollars from an IP address in Venezuela. The government had made it illegal.

To make matters even worse, that weekend, my flat was being fumigated, so I couldn't return to my own place. I'd found insects in some of the wooden furniture and thought that was weekend was perfect to get it sorted. I was driven to a hotel in the city. All through Saturday, Estrella and I tried to buy a new plane ticket but it wasn't until Sunday that we succeeded. I had spoken with my functional manager in London and he had asked the Brazilian subsidiary to buy a ticket for me. Thankfully, not with the same airline.

Departing…..again….

I returned to the airport Sunday night and went directly to the gate. I wasn't taking any chances. I waited in front of the counter until they began boarding, keeping an eye and ear out for any announcements. I arrived in Rio on Monday afternoon and, even though I had missed the first day of the conference (and my weekend of freedom), it was still so good to be there.

I caught up with old colleagues and picked the brains of the more seasoned FDs about the challenges I faced in Venezuela. I appreciated their advice. Several provided me with ideas and new ways of approaching problems that meant that I had some great new tools to take back with me to Venezuela. Several also said I should reach out to them in the future.

After three days, it was time to go back. I said goodbye to my colleagues from the region and from London, and we agreed we'd keep more in touch. I felt strengthened by their support and it was good to share in-jokes and not feel so alone in the challenges.

As I arrived back at Caracas international airport and walked through the near-empty arrivals hall, it struck me how life in Venezuela had become so much more difficult in such a short period of time. It had taken me getting away for a few days to fully realise how much things had deteriorated. The tension that was part of my everyday life in Venezuela returned to my body. I reminded myself that my contracted term, initially set for two years, would eventually come to an end and this calmed my emotions.

I had grown fond of the place, even with its broken systems and difficulties. The people had a different spirit. Most Danes I knew had relatively comfortable lives and it felt like an odd privilege to be able to view Venezuela up close as a local resident. I didn't see how the situation would improve though. It was a natural consequence that many highly skilled people were leaving and seeking a better future abroad. Those who could afford it or those with dual passports anyway. Up until the changes in ticket prices, many middle income and poorer Venezuelans could still afford to make it abroad, but that was increasingly difficult.

The wealthier Venezuelans and those with higher education had good chance for employment in other countries. Attrition was a permanent topic on management's agenda. I had six direct reports in my top team (three women and three men), representing the different finance areas – accounting, planning, treasury, tax, marketing, and operations finance. We were a strong, well balanced and experienced team. Most of them had been in the company for many years. They had grown with the company. Some had even joined as graduates. And we worked really well together.

However, it was not unusual for staff to talk about their Plan B. It was a concept I hadn't heard of before Venezuela. Basically, what is your plan for when conditions get too bad for you and your family? Which country will you move to and what will you do there? I understood how they felt and why they wanted to leave. Favouring direct communication, I preferred to speak with each of them openly about it. I frequently asked them: Where are you and your family with Plan B? What can we, as a company, do to make you stay longer? And so on.

Where possible, we tried to help. Sometimes this meant helping them to find another job in the Group in another country. This was attractive to employees because visas and the relocation would be managed by the company. Our company therefore became very attractive to many highly educated Venezuelans. Even if we couldn't find them a role somewhere else in the Group, it would undeniably be better for their job prospects that they had worked in a large multinational company than a small local Venezuelan one. Their chances of finding work in another multinational were much greater.

It was a tension we had to manage. We had to plan for higher levels of attrition, whilst working hard to develop the internal talent. We had to ensure employees had broad knowledge and develop their leadership skills so that any one of them could backfill sudden vacancies. However, we also knew that the more skilled people were, the more likely they would be able to find a job outside the Group or country. In the end, we needed to look after our employees and do the best for them, whether that was staying in the company or moving away. You had to create a win-win situation.

The Regrettable Loss

One day, one of my top team members came to me and said her Plan B had been activated. She would have to leave soon. There had been an incident in her family. Her husband worked in his fathers' company, a successful family business selling raw materials to other companies. One morning, her husband and his sister were in the warehouse with a few other employees when the warehouse was stormed by thieves. The parents were away.

When the thieves realised that there was no cash stored in the warehouse, they kidnapped the sister. They didn't report the incident to the police but the kidnappers were driving so hazardously through the city that the police ended up chasing them. It ended in a firearms shootout where several of the thieves were killed. Luckily, the sister wasn't severely harmed but the whole family was in intense shock. As the episode was so violent, the family wanted to leave the country urgently. The plan was to head to the US and claim asylum. In the end, we agreed that she would stay a few months to help the company. She would do this because we had built a strong relationship and there was a strong sense of loyalty but also duty. Today, she has a new job in the US, and she and her family have built a new life there.

This was an everyday occurrence in Venezuela. By 2017, more than 4 million Venezuelans (around 13% of the population) had already fled the country. There continues to be an exodus. Today, in 2021, about 50% of young adults would like to leave the country. By the time I left Venezuela in 2016, two of my six direct reports had moved abroad and the remaining four would eventually leave too. Today, they live in five different countries.

This sort of attrition cannot be battled in a country like this. You can implement as many good company initiatives as you wish. You can pay employees better than other companies. You can seek to develop your employees and offer great development opportunities, but you cannot compensate for the shortages, violence, insecurity, injustice, and the many other external factors that influence people's decisions in life.

This experience led me to reflect a lot on my own biases around refugees and foreigners. On how it contrasted with what I had observed in my younger years in Denmark seeing many immigrants not really making an effort (at least visibly) to integrate or find jobs. I had developed a worldview that was often negative, viewing many of them as having just entered

Denmark for the financial benefits, but never having tried to understand why they had immigrated and what environments they had left behind. When you are brought up in a stable environment, it can be difficult to understand the drivers of migration until you get to personally know the people who migrate and start to see them as individuals. No two migrants will have the same story, but the experience made me think twice about judging. And from that day on, I applied a more holistic and open view in regards to this topic, both on a leadership level but equally on a personal one.

Food for Thought

☞ Do you hold unconscious biases around certain groups of people such as migrants?

☞ Are your views positive or negative?

☞ Are your views aligned with your political beliefs system?

☞ How objectively do you think news channels portray the situations?

☞ Do you watch many different local and international news channels to get a broader perspective?

☞ May your unconscious biases in other areas of life be equally aligned or influenced by the view of your favourite politicians and news channels?

☞ How developed is your ability to empathise (putting yourself in other people's shoes)?

☞ Does doing so make you question your unconscious biases?

Chapter 22: Angels Falling

After a year in Caracas, I had settled into my role and acclimated to the new way of living – one with limited freedom and private life. A lifestyle so alien to my former bachelor self. I dedicated all my energy to work, but I was about to experience something unexpected.

One Saturday, I went to the gym in the hotel where I had stayed the first three months when I first arrived in Venezuela. As I left the gym and paid the parking in the reception the receptionist asked me if I would join their cocktail event that evening. She told me it was an event mostly for other foreigners, but that there also would be some locals.

That evening, I decided to go. It wasn't like I had any other plans. The hotel was very safe and I felt comfortable there. I arrived and mingled around. After a few hours, I was introduced to Fran. Fran was tall for a Venezuelan and had a dark complexion and a lovely smile, but spoke very little English. I still struggled with my Spanish, but we got chatting relatively easily. We exchanged phone numbers and agreed it would be good to meet up again. It had been nice to go out (for a change) and meet new people not linked to work.

Over the following days and weeks, we messaged and met up with each other a lot. Soon enough, I realised I was developing strong feelings for Fran and luckily it was mutual. Before I knew it, I had a partner. Although we were very different, it felt so nice to have someone enjoy the weekends at home with. It definitely made my life richer on a personal level.

Besides the limited access to flight tickets, it also became increasingly difficult to make telephone calls abroad. Due to the US dollar shortage, the phone providers were unable to pay third party foreign phone companies to use their networks. There was a list of ten countries you could call, but calls to all the other countries were suddenly blocked. Denmark and the UK were not on the list.

I was more than delighted therefore when my parents bravely announced that they would be paying me a visit! Just seeing the pictures of my flat and the pool had tempted them, plus the temperate weather. They knew that my company would take care of their security and ultimately, I believe they wanted to come as they knew how badly the isolation had impacted me earlier in the year. My parents had been some of my most faithful visitors up until now. They had visited me twice in Argentina and countless times in London.

The day came when they arrived and I went to pick them up with the whole security entourage. It was so good to see their faces and hug them. I could see that they were already delighted they had come. I was too. I felt like a little boy in Disneyland. There was so much I wanted to show them! I could hardly wait.

Over the first days, I had to work, so my parents stayed in the flat and enjoyed the garden and pool area. I tried to get home early each day to spend the evening with them. I could see that they were thoroughly enjoying their time. I hadn't taken any days off because I was saving it for holiday travels out of Venezuela, but I had planned a long weekend away from Caracas to see other parts of Venezuela.

We had planned a visit to Canaima National Park, a UNESCO World Heritage Site the size of Belgium. Canaima is located in the state of Bolivar in south-eastern Venezuela. Estrella, my octopus of many talents, had arranged it all.

The area is managed by local tribes. The tribes live in villages but run a few hotels and amazing resorts across the massive park. We stayed in one of these resorts. Over three days we walked, sailed and even flew around the park in a tiny four-seater light aircraft. We flew over the astonishing Angel Falls (the world's tallest waterfall) and swam in lagunes under waterfalls. The tribes people did their utmost to make us feel at home and welcomed in their part of the country.

Back in Caracas, Estrella had arranged for a private tour of the capital with an English-speaking guide. We drove around in my armoured car with two guards in the car and one on a motorcycle.

At this point, the tourism industry of Venezuela had all but ceased to exist. It was the first time I got to see some of the landmarks of Venezuela. It was amazing to learn more the country's history.

One day, we drove up Avila mountain to have lunch at the top. The view was amazing – Caracas on one side and the Caribbean Ocean on the other. My parents absolutely loved it. They would never have chosen to visit Venezuela if I hadn't have been there. I introduced them to Fran and they were happy to see that I had someone close around me. They couldn't communicate much as they didn't speak Spanish, but it was fun nonetheless and it felt lovely to have both my old and new worlds together in one place.

The following week, the holiday was over and my parents had to head home. They were both still working full-time and had taken two weeks off to visit me. As I waved them goodbye and returned to my empty flat, I was filled with a profound feeling of loneliness and sadness. I realised how much being with people I loved and shared a long history with meant to me and just how much I'd missed it.

An Angel Falling

It started like any other day in Caracas. Due to the worsening security situation, I was now being escorted to and from work. My armed motorcycle escort would arrive around 7.30 a.m. I would only come down once I saw him from my balcony in front of the gate. In the evenings, a group of armed escorts would be waiting at the company gates, ready to escort each of the directors home.

On my 4km drive to the office that morning, I saw queues everywhere in front of the supermarkets. I wasn't sure why. Perhaps there had been rumours about certain goods being in stock. Queues weren't unusual but this morning, as I neared the office, I saw the longest queue I'd ever seen outside the supermarket around the corner. It started in front of the supermarket entrance, went down the street, continued up the next street and passed the entrance of our office. It was more than 500 metres long. Our security team were asking people to move just so that cars could enter the premises.

The atmosphere was tense. You could feel it and you could see it in people's faces as they queued. It was unnerving and I was happy to be in my armoured car with my escort driving behind me. I entered the building and the day of meetings kicked off as normal.

Around midday, I went for lunch with my team in the canteen. People were gathered in huddles and watching something on their mobile phones. It was a video clip that had been sent round on WhatsApp.

WhatsApp was the most used communication tool in Venezuela. There were groups for everything – groups for sharing news, food, cleaning products, buying or selling US dollars, etc. We got our food trays and went to sit down at a table. I asked what all the groups were looking at and they explained.

In the long queue that I had passed that morning, a thief had snatched an old lady's bag. The thief ran in the direction of our office entrance, i.e. alongside the queue of people. The crowd shouted at others ahead to stop him. About 300 metres down, a group of motor taxis was parked, as usual waiting for passengers. The drivers managed to stop the man and started to beat him up. In their rage, a few of them got their spare fuel tanks, poured petrol over his body, and lit him on fire.

He was being burned alive and screaming. The people around and in the queue were filming the scene on their phones. Some tried to put the fire out. They eventually managed to and an ambulance came and took him to hospital. It was this video footage that was making its rounds on various WhatsApp groups.

I was in shock and felt a profound sadness. I asked my team to stop watching the video immediately, and refused to see it myself. I had a longer conversation with them about how dangerous it is to start street courts – courts that judge and execute verdicts 'on the streets' before any due legal process.

They agreed, but said that in their defence, there is no hopes of justice through legal means. Most had been mugged themselves and were tired of the blatant impunity. At least here, they felt there was some justice.

Whilst I could understand where they were coming from and had, at times, felt the same, I asked them not to spread the video and to ask others in the company not to do so either – they respected this.

That evening, the story took an even sadder turn. The guy who was set on fire had died in the hospital. He was a forty two year old father of two children who had been in the queue next to the old lady. And it turned out that he was not a thief. When the lady's bag was snatched, he was standing behind her and immediately ran after the thief to stop him and try to retrieve the bag for the lady.

By the time the taxi drivers, 300 metres down, heard the shouts of 'Stop the thief!', the thief had already passed them. The drivers assumed it was the guy running towards them – no one knew it wasn't him. An innocent man, an angel, had been executed by the crowd.

The following days, there were barely any queues at that particular supermarket. Many people came to mourn and left flowers. For many weeks, I felt a deep sadness too. The window in my basement office looked onto the parking lot of the supermarket. It was a constant reminder of the sad story and of how people can act when society is falling apart. The taxi drivers were interviewed and showed little remorse. They blamed the overall lack of justice in the system. Ironic, given they would likely benefit from that lack of justice now.

It left a deep impression on me. I changed my shopping behaviour. I only bought goods in supermarkets when the queues were short. If I didn't get what I needed, I would just leave without it. Sometimes I drove to supermarkets a little further away from home. If they also had long queues or large crowds, I would just drive home again. I knew it wasn't exactly logical, but it was my way of doing something. I couldn't just carry on as normal.

Estrella was a lifesaver through this time. Often, she bought goods for me when shopping for herself so I didn't have to go as frequently and use many hours in the often endless queues. The company's employees helped each other out too. When an individual received supplies of certain goods, they would post it on WhatsApp groups or company newsletters. In an environment like this, those with connections have an easier life.

The country had deteriorated to a level where it would soon be unsustainable. I appreciated the constant security I had been given and I knew that my assignment in Venezuela would come to an end at some point, but what was life going to be like for the locals?

During my time as FD, I had already bargained with the Group for better conditions for the Venezuelan local employees. As true inflation and living costs were not correctly reflected in the official statistics, the Group's policy around inflation-benchmarked salaries did not make any sense. The local team and HR Director had raised the topic with HQ several times – unsuccessfully. In a large and bureaucratic organisation such as the Group, it was an uphill battle to deviate from any policy. It didn't help that the people asking were those who would directly benefit from the deviation.

As an economist, this was my field of expertise. I offered my help to the HR Director, who happily accepted it and was out of options. I put together a briefing note with lots of tables and graphs. Together with the Marketing Director who was also an expat, I shared the recommendation with HQ – salaries needed to increase in line with the *true* rate of inflation. As FD, I committed to delivering the required business results despite the material increase in salaries. Within a week, we received approval from HQ and the regional office to increase salaries outside of Group policy. It made a huge impact on employees' pay and lifted the mood tremendously.

During the rest of my time there, I continued to work with the rest of the top team to implement better working conditions for the employees – both the factory workers and the office workers. They all deserved the best possible conditions achievable. In theory, I could have left it to the HR Director but as the FD, I now understood how much influence I had even in areas outside of finance and realised that I could make a difference to others' lives. It felt natural to 'interfere' in an area outside my own, because it was the right thing to do. Making a difference for the employees became my driver every morning when I got up.

Food for Thought

☞ What difference can you make in your position for others?

☞ What areas outside your function do you have some influence in?

☞ Are you driven by a desire to make a difference to others and do you do it?

Chapter 23: Back to the Future

The situation in Venezuela continued to deteriorate rapidly. To cope, we had a saying in the company: 'Welcome to another day in paradise!', delivered in a high-pitched voice. Everyone knew it would only get worse.

Our canteen provided free meals to employees - not gourmet food, but the cooks did well with what they could source. Some of the factory workers started bringing their families in to have lunch. This wasn't within company policy and soon enough the canteen struggled to provide enough food for the staff. Various initiatives were introduced, including controlling entry into the canteen. It was subsequently approved that workers could bring a guest in a few times a month but that a flat fee per person would be deducted from their salary.

Basic items like cutlery, toilet paper, light bulbs and other things that people needed but couldn't source or afford were stolen from the office. It was crazy. Often the queue to pick up cutlery was longer than the line to get food. The canteen staff had to wash the cutlery quickly so that they could be reused by others. Facility management created various metal contraptions around light bulbs and toilet paper holders to secure them in place. More worryingly, medicine shortages were widespread. Employees were asked to add their needs onto an internal list and our Colombian sister company would send supplies at intervals.

It was sad to witness. A visible sign that the country was crumbling. The factory workers, many of whom lived in the poorest parts or slum areas of Caracas, really struggled. The company sought to pay among the best salaries amongst corporates in Venezuela and provided many other benefits including medical support, food coupons, bonuses, large Christmas boxes filled with food, liquor and gifts to employees and their children, but there were a lot of needs that weren't met.

Prepare to lead the change

As autumn arrived in 2015, it became increasingly evident to the Board of Directors that something radical had to be done with the underlying business. We needed a more sustainable business model. The scarcity problem was hitting more and more sectors. We were running out of several raw and wrapping materials and we were still heavily dependent on our foreign parent for providing hard currency for our imports. Despite being profitable locally, the VEB could not be converted into USD for buying raw materials or expatriating dividends.

I was asked to take the lead on the strategy overhaul by Gabriel. I put my change management hat back on. One of the first change models I got to know when I was younger was Kotters' 8-step model (see Figure 2)[7].

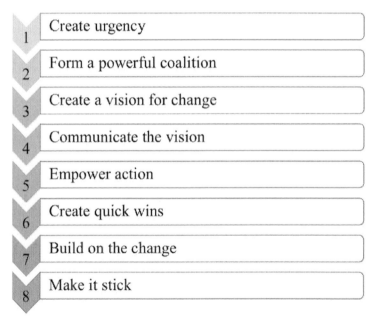

Figure 2. Kotters' 8-step model of change

There are multiple models out there and which one is most suitable for your situation depends on whether the change you're implementing is a developmental, transitional or transformational one. What I like about Kotters' model is that it focuses heavily on the people element of change – an element often overseen when implementing transformational change. As I'd learnt in previous roles, change is often less about the changes themselves as it is about how people react to changes (i.e. what ego issues are triggered) and how much they commit to the process.

I used the eight steps as a guide rather than strictly adhering to them. I found this worked well for me, especially when managing change alongside the busy day-to-day business.

The urgency was clear to all and had already been established (Step 1). I kicked off the project with a large meeting with the Board and the most senior representatives from each of the functions (Step 2). Everyone understood that this was something we needed to solve together as an organisation. Every area would be impacted and there would be no sacred cows. It helped that the Board spoke with one clear voice on this. It also helped that we were clear we wanted to keep the impact on overall employment to a minimum. The new business model was needed to address the increasing dependence on US dollar support from HQ, not to lay-off jobs in a country already suffering deeply from the crisis.

These messages effectively addressed many of the typical ego issues arising from change management such as job security, justice, and inclusion. When it came to creating a vision for change (Step 3), I thought back to my younger days at university.

The Crystal Ball

When I graduated from my bachelors degree and started my masters at university, I also finished my jobs in the department store and medical centre. I took up a more relevant job in an institute that looked at 'future studies'. It was an interesting job and completely different from those my fellow students had. Most got jobs in the Danish Central Bank or various government ministries, industry organisations, federations, unions, etc. I was often asked: 'What will the future hold?' in a sarcastic way. I didn't mind their jokes. I had a more exciting job! And one with a lot of freedom and where I felt empowered. The people I worked with at the institute were an eclectic mix of economists, political scientists, sociologists, ethnologists, etc. – all highly educated and opinionated. It made for an interesting cocktail of views and I learned a lot.

We mostly ran different future scenarios for large corporates and government ministries. I recall one project where we came up with different scenarios for what technology could lead to. At that time, in the late 1990s, we talked about a future where we would be streaming music and films on the internet, and having live video calls. Most people didn't believe it. It was too radical for them. Now, we think nothing of Netflix, Spotify, and of course, Zoom, but back then, it was unthinkable for some.

One thing I learnt from my time at the institute was how most people think linearly. We tend to think that tomorrow will be like today. We can't easily imagine a future in a year's time that doesn't look close to today's reality. This often limits our ability to prepare ourselves for the future.

As part of the study on new technology, the institute carried out a large-scale interview survey conducted in Denmark to find out how people viewed technology and change more broadly. We looked at consumer behaviours, reactions to change, adaptability to new technologies, and so on. Based on the results, we saw that people fitted into one of three groups: past-orientated, present-oriented and future-oriented.

The smallest group by far was the future-oriented group. Most of those fell under this group were young men from the bigger cities, but also young men and women who had remained in education longer. This group liked new technologies, exploring new products and travelling to exotic places. They connected less to a given home location and moved more easily to new places. Traditional family values were less important than the right to live as you wished, and so forth.

The largest group was the present-orientated. This group preferred life today and the stability it provided. The group that preferred the old good days, the second largest group, naturally included more senior people, but also tended to be those living in more rural areas. Whilst the descriptions of the three groups may have changed since and whilst I have no empirical proof, I would dare to say that the results would probably apply today. Not necessarily in regards to technology, but in regards to change in general. As human beings, we tend to prefer the stable present or the known past, rather than the future.

Personally, I have never understood the desire to go back in history. As I see it, progression mostly increases living standards and quality of life. Our brains tend to glamorise the past and dampen the negative things that happened. Perhaps it's a survival mechanism but for some, it makes them constantly think the past was better than today. I prefer tomorrow.

Because of people's preference for stability, there is an embedded resistance towards change. This bias means that we often don't see all the opportunities that arise from change. We tend to be reactive instead of proactive. In my experience, the scenarios process can help with this. It helps open our minds to the possibilities of the future.

The Scenarios Process

The process is simple. Start by defining the issue you want to address. In our case, it was to reduce our dependence on HQ for hard currency (US dollars). We created three very different scenarios. More would have been too detailed (I would suggest four at most). The idea is not to have perfect scenarios but to explore possibilities.

One of the scenarios we defined looked close to the current-day reality. The other two differed a lot. When doing this for your own issue, try to identify the key factors, trends and uncertainties that may impact your different scenarios. Include political, economic, socio-cultural, and technological factors (i.e. carry out a PEST Analysis[8]) that will influence your business environment. Also define a range of factors that affect the external environment. It becomes a little like the 'Back to the

Future II' movie, where you suddenly operate in a future period of time and all the surroundings have changed.

In our case, we had to consider that the existing Venezuelan government could become more extreme or lose its power. On the economic side, affordability among consumers could drop rapidly (resulting in a focus on price over quality) or the economy could gradually improve and consumers revert to choosing quality again. These are just some basic examples. The challenge is to identify the right factors for your scenarios so that the three or four different future scenarios are distinct from each other.

The next step is to review your assumptions about what is certain and what isn't. In a country like Venezuela, few areas were certain so it was more realistic to assume that multiple things could change. In more stable economies, people tend to assume certainties based on the past, but the scenarios process only works if you assume uncertainties in several areas.

When this is done, apply a 'weighting of likelihood' where the most likely uncertainties are more heavily weighted. You may assume that a democracy will collapse in a country that has operated with a stable democracy for centuries. Whilst this is an uncertainty, it is not very likely (i.e. it is a low uncertainty). When building your scenarios, you should focus on those factors that are uncertain and more likely.

Gradually, three future scenarios will begin to form. We ended up with a much clearer picture of the potential trajectories of the different factors (PEST analysis), but also which of the uncertainties were more likely (weighting of likelihood). Broadly speaking, we ended up with:

Scenario 1:   Most factors will look the same as today
Scenario 2:   Continued gradual economic slowdown and political unrest
Scenario 3:   The economy almost collapses and it will be very difficult to procure any resources locally

The next stage in the process was vital. We assigned each of the scenarios to a different group of people. We let each group go out and begin building a more colourful picture of their scenario. As the group built more onto the skeleton, each person began to get a real sense of what it would be to live and work in that scenario. Then the group started to build on each other's thoughts and ideas, encouraging each other to get out of their own comfort box.

When this was completed, we got the groups to answer questions such as:

- How would the company cope in this scenario?
- What would it do to the product portfolio or product quality?
- What has happened to consumer demand? What has it done to affordability?
- How does the staff react? What would the company need to do to retain people and keep production running?
- How sustainable is this scenario? If it isn't, what would the company have to do to make it more sustainable?
- How would the Group see this scenario and what support would be needed from them?

And many other questions.

Each group now refined their version of the future. They began to build a company fit for operating in that particular environment. Because each group had senior managers present from all of the functions, they held the expertise to analyse and contribute with realistic solutions.

We ended up with three very different pictures of what the company would look like and how it would be operating in the future. Each of the groups presented and shared their scenario with the executive team. The executive team came back with input and challenges, and the groups went back and made adjustments, further refining their alternative visions of the future.

It didn't always feel comfortable, but everyone, including the directors, really felt what it would be like to operate the company in the different scenarios. Based on this, we moved forward with Scenario 2 that meant substantial but not insurmountable changes.

Food for Thought

☞ Do you like changes?

☞ Are you past-, present-, or future-oriented?

☞ Have you ever employed the scenarios process?

☞ What could you try it out on (professionally or personally)?

Chapter 24: Co-creation Commits

Working with the scenarios process can be an emotional journey. No input is necessarily wrong but some may be more relevant and likely than others. As a facilitator, it is imperative that you remember your main objectives and that whilst you let people's minds wander through the process, you also steer them back when they go off on a tangent.

In the Venezuelan subsidiary, not everyone bought into the process initially. For some, it was new to look at strategy and scenarios in this way. People operated at different leadership levels. I could see this clearly as I was observing the different groups. As a facilitator, it was easier for me to take people aside for one-to-one conversations and steer them back to the topic at hand. I would do this by explaining that it was a process and talking about the rules, the mindset required and the behaviour change that would be needed for a successful outcome.

As I observed through my career, people differ in their leadership agility. This refers to their ability to be agile and apply adaptive responses given increasing levels of authority and responsibility. One of my favourite books on the topic is *Leadership Agility* by Joiner and Josephs. Leadership agility falls under the concept of vertical development[9]. It is something that people can develop through life, although some will stagnate at certain levels, whilst others will continue to gain new perspectives and leadership mindsets (i.e. develop vertically).

As people attain greater levels of understanding, they also develop more sophisticated approaches to handling different situations and to leadership. As a person develops vertically, they will have more options available to them for approaching a given problem or implementing a certain strategy. In other words, their toolbox grows. They start to appreciate that there are multiple right answers, which is especially helpful when managing complex and uncertain situations. I will come back to this topic in much more depth in later chapters.

In the beginning of the transformation process, I struggled to get everybody onboard. There were a few very vocal individuals who were not buying into the new strategy. They had a strong today or yesterday mindset and didn't like the outlook of further deterioration in the country even though it was inevitable. They found it impossible to see the bigger picture. Over many years, they had operated in highly skilled roles. They were skilled at executing the tasks at hand and had supervised their teams well, but not led them. Their approach to solving problems was typically issue-focused. They couldn't see beyond incremental improvements whereas what was needed here was a radical overhaul.

Still, we needed all participants to join and co-create the solution. It would make for a stronger and more successful implementation. Some would question others' ideas before they could even be captured on the whiteboard. It frustrated me, but I managed to keep it under wraps. I recognised they had ego issues that had been triggered. And the more I reflected on it, the more I realised that because I had worked with such scenarios in the past, it felt natural to me, but that wasn't always the case.

When I first joined the institute, I also struggled with letting go and thinking outside the box. There were suddenly no rights or wrongs! I recall thinking some of the most creative people at the institute with the wildest of ideas, were actually as nutty as fruitcake (i.e. completely insane). But they weren't. They had the capacity to think outside of the fixed boundaries that most of us operate in.

I chose to address this bilaterally, holding one-to-one coaching sessions with a few who were struggling with the process. I talked through why we were doing the scenarios process – to secure the company and ensure its future success and sustainability. I talked through the steps of the process. I mentioned how their resistance had, at times, had a counterproductive impact on others in the team and impacted the group dynamic. And I talked about how important it was that we worked together. Gradually, they started to give it a go and most even enjoyed letting go and getting into the helicopter. For many, it was a lot of change to cope with, both in their way of thinking but also with the eventual outcome of the scenarios process, which meant a lot of change for the whole organisation.

Eventually, the groups worked together more cohesively. Everyone supported the process in their own way. Some who had struggled in the beginning became some of the leading voices and forces in the subsequent implementation process. Had this challenge not been overtly addressed, it could have jeopardised the entire process.

Securing Buy-In

During the vision-building stage, it is important to let the different groups think creatively and independently. Let them *see* the future scenario and almost *feel* it inside their body - how does it actually feel to live out this scenario? It had a tremendous impact on their mindset. Only when they got to that level of almost embodying and owning their scenario did they begin to be much bolder, more constructive and more logical in their suggestions.

It is a process that takes place over many weeks (or months, in our case). It takes time for people to think through the scenarios, to let go of old ways of thinking and become bolder in addressing the potential challenges of the future. When the world looks very different, more of the same is not a solution. And for many, there can be an internal block against doing things differently, especially when you have done something successfully in the same way for many years.

Clearly, none of the scenarios will ever materialise in full. We're not in the process of foreseeing the future. However, as we know that the future will definitely not look like today, you may well end up somewhere within the spectrum of your three scenarios.

The beauty of the scenarios process is that it enables the leadership team to proactively manage an uncertain future rather than reacting, often too late, to whatever happens. As mindsets are also trained to operate in a different environment sort of in a lab, it also impacts people's behaviour and they begin to introduce new ways of doing things in the real world. The status quo has been shifted. The 'this is how we have always done it' mindset has been unlocked.

In our process, we chose to only model scenarios where things deteriorated in Venezuela over the subsequent few years. The entire foundation of the country was shaking. It wasn't realistic to argue that the short-term outcome would be better than today. We only applied a five-year horizon. As changes happen twenty times faster in Venezuela than a well functioning economy, in all likelihood, the future picture would look very different even in a few years. If I were to run scenarios in a stable economy, I would build the models out 10-20 years.

As the different outcomes were discussed over many meetings, the entire senior management reached a consensus scenario. That so many had played a vital role in designing the outcome meant that buy-in was broad and visible across all functions of the company. The teams were very creative and even designed visuals to go with the scenarios. Pictures often say more than words can. They awaken stronger emotions and therefore can also elicit stronger commitment.

Risk Aversion and Game Theory

People tend to be risk adverse. If I let you choose between two scenarios:

Scenario 1: Shrink your product portfolio voluntarily by 25%. Choose which parts of the portfolio to shrink and you retain control of the company during the entire process.

Scenario 2: There is a risk that you will have to reduce your portfolio substantially in the future. If this happens, HQ will take over and you will not have any influence over

how the portfolio will be reduced and you
will lose control of the company.

Which scenario would you chose?

Game theory was a part of the curriculum at university that I always found interesting. A lot of financial behaviour is psychological and conditioned by how we see risks and how we deal with our tendency to avoid risk. Being aware of this, you can frame situations or choices in such a way that steers people to your ideal outcome and gain more buy-in. For example, assume that you are negotiating your salary. You hope for a 5% increase but only get 2.5%. You are disappointed. You expected an increase, but it was a smaller increase than you hoped for.

Now, you have the option to renegotiate it and the maximum possible increase rises from 5% to 10%. However, opening up renegotiations means you risk turning your current 2.5% increase into a 2.5% reduction in salary. Your playing field of possibilities expands to a range of -2.5% to +10%. The gain you could achieve by taking a risk is much greater, but that opportunity comes at a risk of taking a salary cut. Would you enter the renegotiation?

Whilst the potential win is greater than the potential loss, most will not take the risk. The pain of losing 2.5% is perceived by many to be greater than the value of gaining 2.5%. Just being given the option to renegotiate, with the potential risk of loss, may actually make you more satisfied with your original 2.5% increase. The feeling of having *choices* satisfies your ego's need for control.

Being mindful of this is helpful when managing change. It can help to pave the way for change in people's minds. Each of our three scenarios were painful, in one way or another, but some were *less* painful than others. Just being aware of the spectrum of negative outcomes, including the impact of doing nothing, helped convince everyone that *some* difficult and tough decisions had to be made to prevent the materialisation of even worse outcomes. The risk awareness also brought focus to the task at hand. People want to avoid negative outcomes. It meant more people, and particularly the managers, were more willing to prioritise implementing the changes than usual. Buy-in was more widespread.

Getting Ready to Implement

As all of the functions had taken part in the creation of the vision for change, we continued to involve them in the detailed planning of its implementation. What new behaviours would be needed to operate the company in the new model? What sort of leadership behaviours and types of managers were required? What kind of reward and recognition mechanisms would support the new model? And so on.

As part of Kotters' step 5, empowering action, each function began to analyse what was needed. The Operations team looked into the production process, raw materials and how materials could potentially be substituted. The Marketing team looked at the volumes and redesigned the look and feel of the product after raw materials were substituted. HR analysed what incentive structures should be put in place and how leadership development, coaching and promotions could be tailored to support the new behaviours. Many other teams were also busy at work.

In different forums, teams aligned their approaches. When there were major disagreements, issues were escalated to the executive team, who would recommend, approve and, at times, override. It was amazing how the company changed through this process. To see their full commitment combined with their usual positive can-do attitude. To observe their willingness to sacrifice what had, up until recently, been considered sacred cows for decades.

We shared the new business model with management in the London HQ. We received their full support and began implementation. We built a communications plans (step 4) to bring awareness to every part of the organisation. It involved a combination of top-down messaging, followed by more direct engagement in town-hall meetings and focus groups where people could ask questions and bring ideas.

Gradually, the new vision was implemented across the 1,500-person organisation, across all of the functions and site locations across Venezuela. We also engaged with our external stakeholders (e.g. the tax authorities, unions, and major clients) to ensure they understood the new strategy and how it would affect them. The last steps in the model, step 6-8, around creating quick wins, building on the change and making it stick were part of the implementation plan over the next year.

I had never seen a transformation of such a large and complex organisation implemented so quickly and with such commitment in my life. I believe it was as a result of the incredibly skilled and adaptable team. They were all used to adapting to unforeseen changes, both at a personal and professional level. Furthermore, the tough external environment seemed to dampen the ego issues typically activated by change. Finally, everyone could see that something had to change. Changes were therefore not seen as a barrier but a must do.

As the process involved so many in the organisation, it created a strong commitment and alignment across all the functions and their leaders. In parallel, it also addressed the need for changes in mindset, behaviour and culture – vital elements in leading transformational change.

Food for Thought

☞ Do you co-create in your life by involving others in designing the solution?

☞ How is your interest in a project affected by being a part of its creation rather than having it presented to you in its final form?

☞ Do you seek to meet people where they are and communicate in a way that motivates and includes them?

☞ What is your approach to risk and uncertainty?

☞ Are you typically proactive or reactive, risk averse or risk loving?

Chapter 25: Petronas Towers versus Count Dracula

After another Christmas break in Copenhagen, I was back in Caracas. The new strategy was in full implementation mode across the organisation. The usual year end reporting and annual appraisal processes had also been finalised.

By this point, we were running three full budgeting processes a year because of the hyperinflation (now at an annual rate of more than 700%). This meant we had to constantly revise the assumptions that went into the management reporting models. In addition, the new strategy, with its extreme measures also led to frequent updates to the budget as the market's reactions to our price and product changes were hard to predict. It meant several course corrections and having to stay agile. As the direction was clear, the course corrections did not derail the transformation process, but the end game was a moving target as the organisation constantly had to adapt to the unpredictable political decisions and reactions from consumers.

My assignment in Caracas was coming to an end. The company had a policy where assignments in tough environments like Venezuela were set for only two years compared to three or four years in most other assignments. I had already reached two years and was already discussing my next position within the company.

Having lived far and isolated from my family and closest friends, I expressed wanting to return to Europe. Perhaps an FD role in Europe would be good. The company did not agree. They thought I would be under-stimulated. By this point, most of Europe was operating with an above-market structure, i.e. many strategic activities were being carried out centrally at the regional level or HQ. Most production was centralised into a few factories across the region that supplied most countries within the EU. Transactional tasks were mostly executed in shared services.

The Group wanted me to go to Asia. After some reflection, I started to get excited about the possibility. A new continent and an important region for the company as Asia was where most of the growth was happening. An FD role in Asia could definitely be interesting. But again, the Group had other plans.

They suggested a role as GM of the regional shared services centre located in Malaysia. The shared services centre was in charge of executing transactional and operational tasks predominantly within the finance area. Activities that followed step-by-step manuals and not a lot of high-level thinking involved. It wasn't a large operation, albeit more activities were planned to be added in the coming years. This was not what I had in mind for my next career move or overall direction.

I couldn't see any excitement in that area, especially not after my thrilling FD experience in Venezuela where I had thrived after getting out of my finance box and seeing my role in a much broader context.

After long conversations with HQ in London, I agreed to go on a 'look and see', where the company sends you to the country on a visit to get a feel for it before you decide whether to take up the role or not. By this point, you would normally be pretty much accepting the role and the visit would just be to confirm the last bits of doubt. I wasn't quite there yet but I was definitely opening up to the idea. I researched the country to better understand where I would potentially be living. I was already in contact with the HR director who was planning the specifics of my visit. Gradually, my brain was tuning into the adventure of living there - the opportunity to explore the Asia region.

Two weeks before my trip, the Group came back with a new offer - a larger role as GM of the shared services centre in Romania. This was the Group's largest services centre and serviced more than half of the company's operating markets. It also hosted several global functions, with plans for further rapid expansion.

It had more than 700 employees and was growing. The centre in Asia only had around 200 employees. I could see the juicier challenges from a people perspective, but Romania?

I felt the Group was testing my ability to manage change at a personal level. I had spent weeks mentally preparing for a move to Asia. For joining the shared services centre there. Now, they suggested a totally different part of the world, in the region I originally asked for and they had said no to!

Having been raised in Western Europe at a time when Romania was part of the Soviet Union, my strongest memory of the country was of the horrific footage of the execution of its dictator, Nicolae Ceauşescu, and his wife, like dogs, in a backyard in 1989.

It was a poor country with many areas in need of substantial investment. I had visited the capital city, Bucharest, back in 2010 when I was the Treasury Transformation Change Manager. At the time, we already had some treasury employees in the centre who were great. A colourful crowd even back then. I had visited the during the bitterly cold and grey months of January and February. It had felt like being in a black and white movie as most buildings were grey concrete and any other colours were covered in snow. My recollection of the country was not of a picture-perfect dream, especially since I had now lived in Caracas for more than two years, with no winter and colours everywhere all year long. Kuala Lumpur would be fairly similar, so swapping that for black and white Romania did not sound appealing.

Growing in Leadership

What I have always loved the most about being in leadership is the people element. Working with people, managing, and empowering people, and developing people. It is amazing what you can achieve when you bring a group of talented individuals together and draw the best out of each of them.

What I liked about the Romania role was the challenge of leading the largest group of people I had ever had responsibility over and of turning around some of the problems the centre was facing. Given the rapid expansion of the centre in recent years, there were many day-to-day issues to be sorted, but I also relished the challenge of tackling them with a long-term strategic lens rather than just fire-fighting.

The role in Venezuela had given me the opportunity to lead around 80 people. The finance top team and I had worked very well together. We had really shifted the agenda and the department forward. But also, as I began to see my role in the wider context beyond finance, I had begun to enjoy the influence I had. It had been a great experience and I had gradually begun to understand how I could lead people I didn't directly oversee. The possibility of having more than 700 employees to try this out on really excited me.

On the negative side, my perception of shared services centres was extremely poor. During my time in Venezuela, we had our own shared services centre to begin with, but its reporting line was eventually moved under the regional centre in Costa Rica. Employees were still sitting in my building with a dotted reporting line to me, but was under the direct management of the regional centre. With all of Venezuela's complex legal and banking requirements, we had to keep certain jobs in the country and it didn't make sense to lay off people who were paid cheaper local salaries. Plus, we wouldn't have been able to buy US dollars to pay any employees offshore in any case.

Unfortunately, there were many incidences over the years following the reporting line change to Costa Rica. We had to align to the Group's standardised ways of working but that didn't work in an extreme environment like Venezuela's with its hyperinflation and scarcity problems. Task and process-oriented people in the regional centre blocked the execution of payments because the Group had standardised terms (e.g. paying on certain days of the month). Immediate payments were exceptions that had to be approved through multiple hoops. But if you can't pay immediately in an extreme scarcity environment, suppliers will just sell their goods to someone who can.

On a practical level, you could end up with no toilet paper in the building for the next month. An outcome that would not be well received. On a business level, you would rapidly run out of raw or packing materials. Flexibility is what is required when you operate in a country like Venezuela, but working with the shared services centres across the Group had taught me that they were everything *but* flexible. We'd had many fights and escalations over the years and my initial appetite to join this part of the organisation was not high.

Still, my UK manager wanted me to take up the position and asked me to go on a 'look and see' before deciding. He promised me that I would be impressed as it had changed a lot since 2010. With reluctance, I changed my ticket from Malaysia to Romania and, a week later, flew to Bucharest.

It was late May and summer was already in full swing. What met me as I entered the city was many new modern buildings and green trees everywhere. It felt like one of those film sequences where a black and white movie gradually turns into colour - the image gets clearer, the volume increases and my brain rapidly paints over its old memory.

The office was in a tall, modern building. It was the same one I had visited back in 2010, but vastly different. At the time, around 100 people occupied a single floor. Now, there were more than 700 people across four floors. It had grown a lot and I felt a great energy when I walked in.

As I hadn't accepted the role yet, I was officially visiting for some other reason. I didn't get much of an introduction to the people in the office apart from the HR Director, Alex, and her trusted sidekick. Alex was a well-dressed woman in her early forties. Like me, she had worked in many other countries, so was aware of the challenges of starting life again in a new place. We immediately hit it off. I sensed she was a woman of action and, if she committed herself to something, she would success.

In the evening, they invited me out for dinner. They had chosen a restaurant right on the River Herastrau, the river passing through Bucharest. The evening was nothing less than beautiful.

The weather was warm, the food and wine were exquisite, and the location was brilliant. We sat outside and a DJ played music whilst we watched people walking around the lake. It was far from the shortages and sense of danger I had gotten used to in Caracas. Alex and her sidekick both had dry and refined humours and they made me laugh a lot that night. By the time I got back to the hotel, I felt energised and started to think I could live there, especially after Caracas.

The best part was that there was a direct two and a half hour flight to and from Copenhagen on most days. I could see family and friends on the weekends and as and when I wanted to. I would not be able to do that if I was based in Asia.

New Home, New Adventure, New Memories

The company had already arranged for me to look at a flat during my short visit in case I liked it there. I dreaded it – the fourth relocation agent I'd had in seven years. Just the thought of another round of flat viewings exhausted me.

I had sent my specifications a few days earlier and was picked up by a young, energetic Romanian lady about 30 years old. Compared to my previous relocation agents, she had actually read what I had sent through. She reassured me that she had found several good options and on top of this, shared a lot of insight into how it was to live in Romania as a foreigner.

The first flat we saw was amazing. It was in a brand-new building on a quiet street in a lovely area of Bucharest, surrounded by big parks and boulevards. I immediately saw me living there. The commute to work and the airport was easy. I saw a few more just to be sure but the next day, before leaving the country, I asked to see the first flat again and it just felt right – my extensive experience with flat-searching had sped up my decision-making process!

My destiny was now sealed. My next home would be in the land of Count Dracula and not the Petronas Towers in Kuala Lumpur.

There was one other major consideration – what about Fran? We both took our relationship very seriously, but to ask Fran to move with me to another continent was another level of commitment. It was a big decision for both of us.

I had left my family and friends many years back in Denmark, but at least I was moving with a job and good prospects, knowing I could always return. Fran had never really considered leaving Venezuela and didn't speak English well. I knew my new job would not be a 9-5 role. Having to come home to someone under-stimulated and alone was not what I wished for, but I wasn't quite ready to give up on the relationship yet. In any case, getting a visa would take months, so for now, we decided to continue under the assumption that we would be moving together to Romania, but would make the final decision when the visa came through.

The following day, I returned to Caracas. This time, I was more relaxed. This would be the last time I would be entering the country and, the next time I'd be at the airport, I would be leaving for good. It felt like my sight had changed overnight. Now that I knew it was only for another month, I was not so emotionally impacted by the darkness and desperation around me. Even the annoying customs staff were less annoying. I could start to look at my surroundings with a curious mind, knowing that this would be my last opportunity to drink it up. Even *if* I were to visit again, which seemed highly unlikely, it would be as a tourist and that is never the same.

The Venezuelan company eventually announced that I would be moving on. People expected it. They knew the two-year policy and I was nearly at two and a half years. Many were sad to see me leave and I was incredibly sad to leave them. When I had left other jobs, I knew I would be back for a visit. I had returned to Buenos Aires numerous times and London frequently for work, but also to visit dear friends and colleagues. I knew that the likelihood that I would return to Caracas one day was close to zero, as least as long as the current regime was in power.

This meant that the goodbyes felt very different. It wasn't a 'goodbye till we meet again' but a 'goodbye, I wish you all the best for your life'. It was much harder than I thought it would be. I had lived with these people for several years under the toughest conditions I had experienced in my life. Each of them had meant something to me. Some had been life savers. Some had become dear friends and others were great people I had really enjoyed working with. Without each of them, I knew that I would not have managed this major challenge. In the western world, we seem to pride ourselves on our own independence, but in Latin American, that is not celebrated or desired. Moreover, in Venezuela, you just wouldn't survive.

I knew they would have to continue to live in this hostile environment which would get worse every day. They would continue with their warm smiles, greeting each other with a 'welcome to another day in paradise' in the morning.

The company arranged a farewell party for me – dinner and drinks. It went on late into the night. In usual Venezuelan style, there were lots of hugs, laughter and selfies. When it was time to go home, there were many emotional conversations and warm words from colleagues. I still cherish the heartwarming memories from that day.

The next morning, I went to the office to hand in my phone, computer, and keys. After a final lunch with my direct reports, I said goodbye and left straight for the airport. Fran came to wave me off. After checking in my bags, we had to say farewell. It was hard and emotional, but luckily we could look forward to meeting again in Bucharest, hopefully in a few months. I also gave a big hug to the three security guys who had taken such good care of me over the two and a half years. They had followed me all the way to the airport security control area.

Going through the usual hassle in the airport didn't bother me so much that day. Despite the offensive military who basically tried to daylight rob you every time you passed them, it was also a symptom of a society in total disarray. A society where every little helps and where most individuals are forced to think about themselves – an eat or be eaten world. So, it was not that I didn't understand where they came from or see the poverty they lived in, it just felt wrong to witness, having been brought up in a society so different and privileged, where corruption and threats are almost non-existent. Having experienced what I did in Venezuela, I would never see my own country of Denmark in the same way again.

As I reflected, it was a very different Kim who left Venezuela that afternoon. I could see the personal growth I had experienced from how I was as a person, how I led people, what unconscious biases I carried, and how I dealt with extreme challenges. In other words, I had undergone a personal transformation.

From a professional perspective, I would soon realise that some of the successes I had at work were not due to my skills in particular, but the result of the extreme circumstances in which the business transformational change had taken place. But for now, I left feeling proud of my results. As they say: You don't know what you don't know.

As I boarded the plane and the cabin door closed, a peace and quietness came over me. As I looked down on the slum areas along the coastal line from the sky, I felt a combination of sorrow, sadness, and happiness. Sorrow for a country that was once thriving and had so much to offer, but was now decaying. Sadness after having said goodbye to Fran. But also warm happiness for the beautiful people I had met during my time there.

I will always feel a certain belonging to Caracas, but as of today, writing this book in 2021, I have not returned to Venezuela.

Food for Thought

☞ How agile are you at making decisions in your own life?

☞ When under pressure, do you focus on the negatives or the positives?

☞ Does that help you?

Part 4

Leadership

Bucharest, Romania

Chapter 26: How Not to Make a First Impression

After a few days' rest in Copenhagen, it was time to head to Bucharest to set-up my new life there.

I knew the drill by now, but there were added complications. Over the first weeks, I would stay in a hotel while the company tried to get my furniture out of Venezuela. Corruption had made it very difficult to get goods through the ports. There were plenty of stories of belongings being vandalised or stolen while waiting to be shipped. Therefore, the Group had tried to airfreight my boxes out. This meant they would only be in customs at the airport for a few hours rather than weeks or months in a port. Venezuela was increasingly isolated. Only two international airlines still flew between Venezuela and Europe. Getting a ticket for a seat on the plane was difficult enough, let alone accessing the limited airfreight capacity.

I was staying in the Marriott Bucharest Grand Hotel. A massive concrete building that formed part of the former Ceausescu's urban building project in central Bucharest in the '70s and '80s. The hotel was close by the Palace of the Parliament – another imposing monster of concrete that holds the title for being the heaviest building in the world, as well as the second largest building after the Pentagon. The Marriott converted one of the nearby buildings in 2009 into the luxury five-star hotel that was now my temporary home, but you could still feel the history and legacy of the building. Luckily for me, everything worked well in the hotel, which I appreciated after Caracas.

After a good night's sleep, I was picked-up and driven to the office. It was my first official day. I felt a combination of nervousness and excitement. Alex and her team welcomed me. They took me on a tour around the building and I met my direct reports. It was overwhelming – my first role as a GM. A role that, in theory, has no direct portfolio other than to manage the entire organisation and ensure that effort and focus is channelled to the right areas.

Being a GM of a shared services centre differs from leading an operating company. You're not producing or selling a physical product, rather you're supplying a service to a customer and that customer is internal, i.e. other subsidiaries and teams within the Group. Even though the customers are internal, service level agreements are still in place to ensure quality and turnaround times match what is promised and agreed for the price charged. To a large degree, the set-up resembles that of call centres and service companies.

The centre operated with different service arms, providing many types of services to more than half of the Group's 200-plus operating markets. Services included paying bills and invoices, collecting and accounting for receipts, other financial reporting, compliance, HR administration and some recruitment activities. These areas ran as independent service lines but, due to the nature of finance, many were interlinked. On top of this, there was also a large function supporting the centre itself. The HR department was responsible for ensuring the best conditions for its employees, training, remuneration, etc. IT was responsible for the company's entire digital infrastructure and security. It had to be robust enough. Finance managed the budget and costs for the centre. And lastly, there were smaller functions such as legal, facility management, and procurement.

Like in any company, it won't work well if any of the functions is weak. Before I left Venezuela, Gabriel had given me some advice. I had also met with the GM of the Romanian operating company. Both had shared invaluable advice as to where I should focus first as a new GM.

In many aspects, Romanian culture resembles the Venezuelan more than the Danish. For instance, Romanians are high context in communication, hierarchical in leadership, and top-down in their decision-making style. It is also a relationships-based culture and flexible-time driven when it comes to scheduling. However, in areas like evaluating and disagreeing, Romanians are closer to the Danish culture. They give direct feedback and can be confrontational. However, it would likely be felt differently by me as their hierarchical and top-down driven culture would prevent many from giving direct feedback or confronting their manager. It would be interesting to experience this mix in an unfamiliar culture and pan out in reality.

My new line manager, who was based in London, had flown in to spend a few days in the Bucharest office. We had dinner that evening and spoke about the priorities of the role, as well as the future challenges we saw. My first day had been great but long; I was overstimulated with a brain full of impressions. I fell asleep like a baby that night.

The following day would be my big day. The company was holding a quarterly briefing meeting. It would be held in my hotel - the only venue in Bucharest that could host over 500 people in one big ballroom.

The idea behind the meeting was to have a short briefing from each of the functions, some discussion and socialising over drinks. I had never spoken in front of 500-plus people before. The largest group had been around 200 in Venezuela. I had managed it but never really liked it or felt relaxed. Now, on my second day on the job, I was to stand in front of a ballroom full of people and I only knew a few of them.

The session started with my manager giving a short pep talk and a warm introduction to me. People applauded as I stepped onto the stage. Despite being incredibly nervous, I managed to convince myself that they wouldn't notice. I had to nail it. The first impression always lasts the longest!

As I began my speech, I started with how much I had been looking forward to arriving and how much I was looking forward to meeting everyone. I went through a bit of my work background and what I'd done in the Group. I then shared a story about how, as FD in Venezuela, I had not been able to buy toilet paper for the office because of the overly process-oriented mindset of the shared services centre I was dealing with. I managed to get a few laughs. I carried on with how I saw many opportunities to address these challenges and how together, we would make shared services great. I ended my speech with saying how I really looked forward to working with them all.

As I left the stage, people applauded politely. I knew I had not nailed it. The complete opposite, in fact. The last few minutes on stage felt like a train crash in slow motion and I felt it in my stomach. In only 8 minutes, I had managed to generate bad will and a mixed impression of myself. Sitting there on the chair, my brain was in overdrive with the pressure. What should I do?

I listened to the next few presentations and learned new things about the centre. I realised just how many different internal areas they were focusing on and how much each function had actually improved over the past year. I felt increasingly bad. I had started my new role by criticising 700 people and I realised I had done so based on such little knowledge about what was actually happening. My experience had primarily been with a completely different shared services centre - an office in the Americas nearly 7,000 miles away. This one was five times bigger and far more complex. It had undergone a massive transformation over the last few years.

The presentations came to an end and Alex was about to close the session. I stopped her. I asked her to let me do the closing instead. I needed to correct my mistake and I needed to correct it whilst I had the opportunity.

She passed the microphone to me. I walked up, humbled and reflective. I started by saying, 'My first speech was bad. Really bad'.

As I paused, a few laughed quietly but otherwise there was total silence in the ballroom. I had everyone's full attention. I continued, 'I have come to a new organisation with my heavily biased views based on a reality that is not true. I built up a perception over the last few years. A perception that, for me, was reality, but now I see was naïve and only as an outsider.'

After a pause, I continued, 'Having heard how much you have achieved over the last few years, I feel terrible about my speech. I am sorry. Still, I know that my perception is widely shared across other parts of the Group. But perception is not necessarily reality, and I see that now. This shall be our focus - to change people's perception. To ensure that the rest of Group understands how much you have done and how much we will do together in the future.'

I emphasised, 'We will make sure to share all your fantastic achievements with the rest of the Group. And we will need to identify the behaviours that lead to the negative perception of us. This will be a journey for me to lead, but I hope each and every one of you will join with me.'

I ended by saying that over the next few months, I would use my time to thoroughly get to know the organisation and I hoped that everyone, irrespective of position, would be honest with me in providing insights. I explained that when I said my office door was open, that it truly was. Unless I was in a meeting, anyone could enter if they had a topic, concern or idea they wanted to discuss. As I left the stage, the applause was louder and the smiles wider. I had managed to partially repair my poor introduction.

I left the stage with a personal learning about, once again, reflecting on my biases and being clear what I know and what I do not know. I also realised that starting on a negative tone (i.e. 'we have so much to fix') is never going to bring people with you. That's the stick approach, and they'd had enough of that from the rest of the organisation. Language around 'we' and not 'you' and 'I' is also very important.

I hadn't understood my audience at all. I had basically made the same type of disastrous speech that the guys from HQ had made when they visited the Danish company back in 2008. They had talked about international careers because that was important to them. I spoke about my poor experiences because that was important to me. I didn't want to lead an organisation with such a bad reputation. But nether speech was made for the audience.

And I had not thought enough about what it was I wanted to achieve through my speech. I had saved it a little at the end but I still felt miserable that afternoon. At least, I learnt something, I guess.

Despite the terrible delivery, I believe I managed to lay a foundation for a 'burning platform' in change management terms – or rather a 'burning desire' which is much more impactful. A reason and desire for change for the individuals in the organisation to build towards what you want to achieve.

Over the rest of the afternoon, I met a lot of the employees. The average age of the 700-plus employees was around 27 years old. They each spoke at least two languages fluently – many spoke three. Everyone had a university degree of some form. How very different to my initial perception.

They would have grown up in the aftermath of the communism era in Romania - a very difficult period for many. The driven can-do attitude and desire to build a better life than their parents had is what I will remember most from that day. I felt the energy. I felt like I was going to enjoy being here.

Food for Thought

☞ We all screw up at times. When did you last time screw up a situation?

☞ When did you realise and how did you seek to rectify it?

☞ How did you deal with it personally and how did you deal with it professionally?

☞ What did you learn?

Chapter 27: Putting the Pieces of the Puzzle Together

Over the following weeks, I found out that it would take at least three months for my furniture to arrive. When I heard this, I panicked. Should I stay in the hotel for three months? I had tried this in Venezuela and I'd felt like a lion in a cage. I already had this beautiful flat that I just wanted to settle into. Luckily, the Group understood and they helped me furnish the flat with some basic IKEA furniture and I moved in. I missed my partner a lot and there was no progress on the visa front. That would also take at least another three months to sort.

I threw myself into the new role instead. I got to know the centre in Romania, but also visited centres of other corporates in nearby countries. I took note of things I wanted to bring back and things I knew needed to change.

The centre had originally been built as a finance shared services centre. As it matured, it began to expand its coverage to more geographic locations and functional areas like HR and recruitment, procurement and IT. On a global level, the Group had begun to consolidate the handful of regional centres and build a 'hub and spoke model'. In such a model, one of the centres becomes the main centre (i.e. the hub) and supports the other smaller centres (i.e. the spokes) that are still located in different regions due to time zone coverage or other country-specific legal requirements. The main centre becomes the centre with most of the specialist knowledge.

The Bucharest centre would now be the main centre, with most of the global functions concentrated there and supporting the other centres in the Americas and Asia Pacific. Lastly, it hosted several functions where the ownership and direction of the service was outside the centre, but many of the tasks were executed in Romania. The ultimate vision was to build the shared services centres into a Global Business Services (GBS) centre. This is an even more advanced set-up, where more and more tasks are onboarded from operating markets and HQ into the centres, leveraging economies of scale. It would involve a change in the leadership structure and entire power dynamic of the Group.

In an ideal set-up, the GBS centre would manage most of the daily tasks for operating markets. The stripped down local markets are then freed up to focus on winning in that market without the distraction of operational activities related to managing the 'engine' of the company. It also frees up HQ to focus on setting the vision. The operating markets execute the vision in the markets and GBS runs the backroom engine.

It was definitely an exciting time, but GBS would not be launched until a few years later. There was still a lot noise around shared services, both with regards to the services they took over and whether there were genuine cost savings and value added. For now, the priority was therefore on improving the existing services, with a focus on efficiency and utilising new technological solutions.

In my role, it was imperative to travel out and meet my customers to understand where they saw challenges and areas of improvement. My first visit was to the centre in Kuala Lumpur, Malaysia. It was located on the outskirts of the city in a tired-looking industrial complex. The people were very warm and I enjoyed the visit. Still, I couldn't help thinking how it would have been had I ended up there and concluded that it was good that I had chosen to lead the Bucharest centre. The challenges were much bigger and, well, much more challenging!

I also visited HQ in London, where I had many senior stakeholders. Some already had parts of their teams located in my centre. Others would potentially be moving parts of their teams there in the future. Having now thoroughly learned the importance of wider stakeholder management, I wanted to ensure that I got as much and as diverse input as possible.

Back in the office, I was getting to know my team well and getting a much better idea of the challenges the organisation was facing. I also sought their views around what they believed could and should be changed. The pieces of the bigger puzzle were slowly coming together.

Before my arrival, the centre had embarked on a journey to becoming 'world class'. Many consultants had been hired, especially by HQ, to drive a lot of these initiatives. As I've shared before, I have a pet hate of the term world class – do we need to be the best in the world or do we just need to be excellent? Many people think they are world class anyway, so who is arbiter of this nonsensical title?

Without a GM at the helm for many months, the consultants had come to play a major role in the direction and prioritisation of these improvement projects. This was not always for the better. Consultants, appointed by HQ, need to demonstrate successes to HQ. The success of local teams is often in delivering their day job. This mismatch often results in tension and resistance between the parties. Often changes are laid on top of an already stretched team. With little or no additional capacity to implement changes, this will lead to traffic jams across the organisation where changes are stuck with a particular person or team. This slows down the whole change process, resulting in loss of momentum and often frustration between teams. On top of this, a consultant from London costs materially more than a local employee in Romania. It became evident that the set-up needed to change.

My manager in London wanted me to take on the project lead role. I disagreed. I didn't have time to run a process improving project. It was an important one but it would be at the expense of my broad and strategic role as GM. Either I would become the bottle neck and slowdown the project or I would struggle to do my day job – that of leading the entire organisation and, importantly, to deliver on the key objective of making it more customer-oriented and changing the perception of the services centre amongst the rest of the Group.

The root of the problem was that this centre had grown from zero to over 700 employees in only seven years. There had been no thorough evaluation of the right set-up. It had grown in width (size) and depth (complexity). Gradually, more and more teams and managerial positions had been added but with no fresh look at the overall set-up. It had grown so quickly that it wasn't fully understood by senior managers outside the centre.

I sensed that there were other much more fundamental issues that needed to be addressed, even though I hadn't yet identified exactly what these were. But this is where I wanted to and needed to spend my time and energy. However, I also sensed that I would gain little by pushing back on my manager's request at such an early stage in my role. I took the lead as asked but decided I would lead by delegation and empowering of my direct reports. It would be in their respective functions that the improvements would be implemented, so it was natural that the responsibility was anchored there. This would also facilitate us getting to know each other as a top team.

Naturally, I joined all of the steering committees and monthly meetings. I let my direct reports know that I was available if they needed help but that they were in charge of their respective areas. I helped in the decision-making and ultimately demonstrated my sponsorship and backing of their initiatives.

Gradually, the use of expensive consultants was largely eliminated. The local team felt more empowered and it also reduced some of the tensions across the organisation.

Food for Thought

☞ Do you know who your key stakeholders are?

☞ Do you know what is important to them?

☞ Have you ever been given a task or project that you felt was not right for you or the organisation?

☞ How did it make you feel?

☞ What did you do about it?

Chapter 28: Leadership Agility

Over the following months, I gained more insights from our internal customers (senior managers across the organisation). It became clearer what worked well for them and what did not. Many shared how they thought the user experience could be improved and often it related to human behaviour rather than processes.

I shared the feedback with my top team. The response was mixed – some agreed and some didn't. Those who didn't felt that the initiatives that were in place would eventually start paying off and lead to improvements in customer satisfaction. They completely missed the point. It became clear that the dynamic in my new top team was different to any I'd experienced before. Perhaps it was because this was my first GM role. Or perhaps it was because I was new. There were days when I felt utterly frustrated. Why did people not buy into what was so clear to me – that something had to change?

Building a strong coalition of senior managers had definitely been easier in Venezuela. There were several possible reasons. Firstly, when I kicked off the strategy process there, I had already been in the company for more than a year and had built solid relationships with the various functions. I had already demonstrated my worth and value. Secondly, and I think more importantly, the composition of the top team members here was very different.

I'd inherited a top team in Bucharest that was a mixture of direct reports, indirect reports and some people not having any reporting line to me at all. Over the first couple of meetings, I remained quieter than normal and observed the group to understand the group dynamics and individuals' personalities. Only a few were seasoned senior managers. Most were relatively junior (both in age and grade) or only recently promoted. I had tried a number of different approaches in leadership previously. Some were more successful than others. I found the approach that gave me the best results was to coach and engage people, regardless of reporting line.

In Venezuela, Gabriel had taught me that when you are in a senior role, you will always be a role-model in the organisation. The first few times I had taken someone not in my direct team aside and given some feedback had felt unnatural, but gradually I realised that most people appreciate it. Helping more junior employees reframe situations and try new approaches had become one of the things I liked the most about my job. I felt I made a difference to that person's growth and hadn't cost me a lot to do it. What felt very different here was the feedback culture (or lack of) amongst most of the top team members and the lack of urgency for change. It made it difficult to even get to vision-building stage.

In their excellent *Leadership Agility* book, Joiner and Josephs mention five levels of leadership agility, from Expert to Synergist. According to their research, roughly 45% of managers operate at the first level (Expert), 35% at the second level (Achiever), and only 10% of managers operate at the higher Catalyst, Co-creator and Synergist levels. The remaining 10% of managers haven't even made it to the Expert level[10] (there are four pre-Expert levels - see Figure 3). [11]

If you expand the percentage distribution for the vertical development concept to the entire human population, you won't find such a high proportion at the Expert or Achiever level. Many will be found at the pre-Expert levels like Operator or Conformer.

It is worth noting that while in this context, vertical development refers to the defined five leadership agility levels, it can also be seen in its broader context, as every person develops 'vertically' from birth to adulthood.

It is also worth noting that whilst you may have reached a certain level (e.g. Achiever, the second leadership level), you may not always operate at that level on a day-to-day basis or in certain situations. It means you have the skillset associated with the level and the tools associated with the level are part of your toolkit. You will tend to operate at the highest level you have reached, but whether you do or not in a given situation depends on many things, including how your emotional, psychological and physical state at that time.

Figure 3. Joiner & Josephs's Developmental Stages

As mentioned earlier in the book the leadership levels are not reflecting intelligence, but the agility that a person has in leadership, e.g. in leading the self, leading teams, leading organisational change, managing pivotal conversations, conflicts, stakeholders etc. The leadership agility levels and the development through them are, to some extent, building on the thoughts and theory of Daniel Goleman in his book *Emotional Intelligence*[12].

Daniel Goleman has been a pioneer within the field of emotional intelligence. In his book, he talks about how developing emotional intelligence develops you as a person and improves your leadership capabilities across many of the areas covered above. What I like about Joiner and Josephs's approach is that it covers how these capabilities and typical behaviours are expressed in the different developmental stages. This provides a framework for comparing behaviours among leaders and understanding skills and limitations better.

Reaching the Expert level (the first management level) is most likely to happen only in adulthood as an individual develops stronger problem-solving abilities and a more analytical and independent mindset, often stimulated through higher education (e.g. learning about more complex issues) or work (e.g. learning from more experienced role models).

To reach even higher levels, people would typically have to learn through experience and have a desire to develop vertically.

Vertical development

You can develop vertically by actively working on it yourself, but it can also be helpful to be around a group of curious and open-minded people who both seek and give feedback, and who facilitate constructive debates.

According to Being First© institute, the first stage in vertical development is to become more **Self-aware**. To understand yourself and your beliefs better. In the Food for Thoughts that have ended most chapters, I have asked you to reflect on various situations, views on people and groups, but also about what feelings certain situations have triggered in you and what unconscious biases may influence you on a daily basis. The easier it has been for you to answer these questions and the more natural these questions have felt to you, the more self-aware you probably are as a person. If it didn't feel natural at all, spending time to think more deeply on such questions will help you to build self-awareness. Self-awareness is vital in vertical development.

The next stage of vertical development is **Self-management** or your ability to change how you see things in real time. It requires a profound self-awareness to be aware of your personal biases, emotional triggers and react upon them in the situation itself. If you are aware of your unconscious self, it is more likely that you will be able to stop being led by that part of yourself if it isn't helpful.

The third stage or capacity on the vertical leadership ladder is **Self-leadership**. To reach this level requires well-developed self-awareness and self-management skills and enables you to adjust your beliefs and ego issues in a more constructive way, that lead to new and better outcomes for you in given situations.

The final stage is **Self-mastery** - a stage only a few people reach. To reach this level requires strong performance in the first three stages. When performing at self-mastery stage, you often operate from your inner 'being'. You are consciously present in many different aspects of your life, which frees you from typical reactions from your ego, your personal beliefs system, etc. If you operate at this stage, you are most likely applying a certain form of meditation, spiritual belief, or other method to keep you centred in life. Even at self-leadership stage, many will have begun to explore or practice this in some form.

With a young average age of 27 in the Bucharest centre and with most managers in their late twenties or early thirties, it was natural that many operated at Expert level. I also did in my late twenties back in my first professional job in Denmark. It isn't that those in their twenties and thirties cannot in theory operate at a higher (or lower) level, but vertical development happens over time so even if you are focused on it, it would take many more years to reach the higher levels. This was visible from their behaviour. Only a few were operating at what distinguish the Achiever level or above.

Experts
Experts are excellent supervisors. They are task-oriented and have a methodical approach to problem solving. Improving processes and procedures are their core areas of strength and when they are on the job, they are often so focused on delivering that they do not pay much attention

to their surroundings or the broader picture of what is happening in other functions. Therefore, they tend to operate in silos. They lack strategic purpose in their initiatives. This applies both to their current role but also more generally to how they approach their career. Thinking more than one or two years ahead is not usual at the Expert level.

Some of the more senior leaders in the top team operated at the Achiever level.

Achievers
Achievers can zoom in and out of a given task or challenge to see the bigger picture. This helps them become more strategic and less task-oriented. Achievers can see the past and future more clearly, and have the capacity to imagine different possibilities. They understand the need to manage stakeholders and how vital it is to deliver over the medium as well as short term. They are typically more advanced leaders, with the ability to orchestrate and motivate people by challenging and developing them rather than just giving them tasks.

In my new top team, there were more Experts than Achievers. I needed people who would think more strategically, i.e. Achievers or higher. The Experts only engaged in areas of their own concern and responsibility. On other matters, they would be silent. How could I get the Experts to think broadly, to engage and pull together as a united team? There was work to be done.

I am a true believer that some of the best results are achieved when a team consists of a diverse group of people. Surveys also reveal that companies with diverse leadership teams financially outperform companies with limited diversity[13]. Besides earnings, it also has a positive impact on innovation, attracting and retaining talent, etc.

I had seen this working in a global organisation. I had experienced how a combination of different genders, age and functional expertise and backgrounds can deliver outstanding results. Most will say this is obvious. Yet so many corporates continue to operate with homogeneous leadership teams. The gender agenda pops up frequently across many different countries and work environments.

Besides benefiting from how men and women lead, there are many other diversity factors. Older people see opportunities through the eyes of experience and knowledge. Younger people are not as limited by history and previous failures. People with different functional expertise can challenge each other and bring different perspectives that those working within the same profession cannot due to tunnel blindness. Different cultures approach problems in different ways. Even diversity in sexuality, gender identity, political conviction, and religion can influence the belief system and thereby the group dynamics.

In my top team, I had many of the right ingredients, but still, most would stay silent during our meetings when we talked about topics outside their own area.

I could have chosen to change or streamline my top team, but I sensed that it would have resulted in even less cohesion around the new strategy. It would likely trigger negative emotions and justice issues amongst those who had been part of the top team but suddenly found themselves outside. Just putting myself in their shoes and thinking back to my twenties, I knew that wasn't the right move. Plus, how could I coach them if they were distant to me? I needed to create a safe forum in the top team where each member would feel able to actively input with whatever thoughts they had and could grow vertically over time. But also, I had to ensure that they took an active and leading part in the change journey within their respective areas - that we were a committed and aligned leadership team.

In Venezuela, I had seen what impact building a shared vision had on commitment and engagement across the organisation. Now, I had to differentiate between team members if I wanted to progress with the strategy and put it into motion. I had identified a few Achievers with the right capabilities who would play a larger role in the change project. It was not ideal to differentiate between team members, but it was the best approach for now.

Food for Thought

☞ What type of people do you surround yourself with in and outside work?

☞ Are they open-minded and curious to other people's views and ideas?

☞ Do they often provide and seek feedback?

☞ Do you know many who operate at the Expert level?

☞ How about the Achiever or higher levels?

☞ Do you belong to either category?

Chapter 29: The lost Train Wagons

It was September and I had now been in Bucharest for three months. There was still no news with regards to Fran's visa and whilst it frustrated me, I was so busy at work that it was probably better that I was alone for now. Most nights were busy either working late in the office or hosting dinners with various internal customers or stakeholders visiting the centre.

Over the following months, many of my friends and family would be visiting me. I had carefully built up a pipeline of fun visits where I wouldn't be alone for long. Just the anticipation alone filled me with joy. My parents would be the first to exploit the short flight for a long weekend visit. A week later, a close friend from London would be visiting, followed by another good friend from Copenhagen in October. It was so great being back in Europe and being able to do this – I had missed it. I put the visa application delays out of my mind.

In the office, we kicked off an extensive company-wide internal survey. Based on this, we began to identify what were the causes behind the poor performance and what led to frequent escalations that were not resolved once and for all. Gradually, some patterns became visible. They all related to softer areas such as the mindset of employees, the behaviours they exhibited, the culture of the centre (the sum of the individual's behaviour) and, not least, how the supporting system kept it all tied together.

There was a general feeling amongst employees that they were regarded as less valuable than their counterparts in the operating markets. Many believed that their role was limited to executing the tasks they'd been assigned and nothing more. They believed that to think more broadly would not be appreciated by others. Many employees' desire to innovate or take risks was limited. This makes sense if you hold a transactional position (you don't necessarily want your transactional employees to take risks), but it makes for a boring job and limited development prospects.

This mindset led to certain behaviours. Mistakes were not tolerated. The stick approach. Mistakes weren't used as learning opportunities, so the same ones kept being repeated. Unfortunately, in some cases, this led to the covering up of mistakes (thankfully not financial ones) or delays in owning up to errors, which lost precious time. Decision-making was often top-down. In some lucky cases, people were informed about the decision but not the reasoning behind the decision. Few people moved between functions. Moreover, some people would be prevented from moving because they held all the expertise and the manager couldn't live without them.

This fed into the culture. The organisation operated in strong silos. People were seldom aware of the challenges other teams or functions faced, despite sitting next to each other for years. How their tasks were interrelated was often only visible to more senior managers, so cross-functional problem-solving was rarely employed. Mostly people who were technically strong and didn't make mistakes were those who got promoted, but they didn't necessarily have broader leadership skills. At times, it would be the favourites (and friends) of the team manager.

The supporting systems around promotions and rewards reflected this too. Many promotions were made within a function by the functional management team. They were not challenged by other functions. The same applied to the identification of star performers. Few senior managers knew the talent in other functional silos, which meant that each silo ran almost independently. Suggestions by the HR leadership team to think more broadly were often ignored or considered a good suggestion but nothing to take too seriously.

However, we also discovered many positive elements of the mindset, behaviour, culture and supporting systems. Things that had led to great achievements so far. Still, they were sadly overridden by the negatives and it was the poor perception by the customers that we wanted to tackle.

The findings were certainly disappointing. They contradicted what the Group fostered - a winning organisation with a strong focus on learning, development, empowerment, consensus decision-making, and so on. This culture clash between two parts of the same global organisation was a major cause of the frustration and, now I realised, lack of understanding between the shared services centre and their customers.

As I reflected, it occurred to me that one of the major factors leading to this clash was found in how the shared services centre had grown over time. Its original purpose was to manage low-value transactional tasks. It is managed like a factory – you have X people to pay Y bills. You hire graduates because you don't need people with experience and you want it done cheaply. Success year-on-year is having fewer than X people paying the same Y bills. You gradually take on more tasks, e.g. collecting cash. As this task is also largely transactional, you hire more of the same kind of people.

Then you need managers to manage the growing number of people paying the bills and collecting the money. You promote one who is good at carrying out tasks and not making mistakes, expecting them now to be a good supervisors. But you don't invest much in their development as a manager.

You now have critical mass to onboard more tasks. You may service 50 markets and already have a few hundred people doing transactional tasks. The operating markets have equally reduced their headcount as you have onboarded their operational tasks. The operating markets are also in cost-cutting mode but for a while, they will keep a few relatively junior staff to manage the transition to the shared services centre. As many are operating at Expert level, the difference isn't noticeable. He or she can still relate to the Expert-level performers in the shared services. Everyone thinks everything is working well.

Then you bring more value-added tasks into the centre. This could be financial and management reporting, cost calculations, hiring people for the operating markets and so forth. These tasks require a different skillset to a purely transactional or technical one. This is where the Romanian centre was at now. More sophisticated leadership skills were now required and this is precisely where there had been little professional development in the centre. So, senior manager positions were largely populated by people operating at the Expert level.

It made absolute sense. Vertical development was needed. As I shared earlier, some will naturally develop vertically over time, especially if they are self-aware, curious and reflexive by nature. Whilst the organisation held some leadership training courses, the challenge was that there were only be a few people in the organisation operating at the higher leadership levels in order to act as role models. It is then difficult to lift the managerial population by role-modelling and coaching. Furthermore, if there isn't a strong feedback culture that encourages people to become more self-aware (the first and probably most important stage of vertical development), vertical development will be slow or not happen at all.

At this point, the operating markets had the opposite composition. They were largely composed of more senior managers, most of which were operating at the Achiever or higher levels. Some directors such as GMs and FDs operated at Catalyst or higher levels, although simply having reached such senior positions was not a guarantee of this. Growth in leadership agility does not come with your position but your personal development. Most junior managers in operating markets would have benefited from this role-modelling by managers mostly operating at predominantly higher levels.

Suddenly, senior managers or executives must communicate directly with employees in the shared services operating with a very different leadership mindset and capabilities. The gap in agility becomes evident to all. To make a simple comparison. Observe a child who has grown up with parents in their forties and another child who has been raised by parents in their early twenties. In most cases, there will be a visible difference in how the children operate when they are ten years old. How self-aware they are and how they react to situations and challenges will likely be different. This demonstrates the huge impact that role-modelling has on the growth of humans. We mirror and learn from our surroundings.

We had now understood why and how the frustration had developed. A transformation train had departed the station seven years ago and embarked on an exciting journey, adding more and more tasks. But the last wagons of the train – mindset, behaviour, culture and supporting systems – had been left on the platform. How were we going to address this on a large scale?

The leadership team put their heads together. We had to first tackle the mindset and behaviour. The culture would flow from this. We would need to do this with our own employees, but also with the Group. We also had to adapt the systems that reinforced the old ways into ones that supported the new mindset, behaviour and culture. We had to vertically develop an entire organisation!

It was more than just setting objectives for the year. It was an entirely different vision. And it wasn't developing a vision in the usual way where you mostly focus on business imperatives. I was aware from all of my previous work that a vision is, firstly, usually long term - something to be achieved over five to ten years. And secondly, a good vision focuses on where the company wants to be in the future. Here, it was more about creating a short term vision that could unite and motivate people to rapidly adjust their mindset and behaviour to catch-up with the overall vision and mission of the Group.

To get the organisation onboard, we would need a vision that spoke to people. One that would create a desire for change. A vision that could be easily visualised but also address many of the negative feelings people had expressed. We would eventually come to encapsulate the vision in the phrase: *Business Partners to the Group.*

It was a strong but simple vision. It would strengthen the internal feeling of belonging to the Group. It would underpin that shared services are equal partners to the business. It would facilitate the establishment of an equal and respectful relationship between employees in operating markets and shared services. In addition, it would promote shared services as value creating partners. This was in stark contrast to how it had been seen up until that point - a cost efficiency project.

We could have chosen to use a corporate power phrase like 'World Class Shared Services' or something similar referring to our deliverables, but by articulating the vision focused on *people* and how they would act, be seen and treated, it appealed to both the heart and the mind.

Most of the change would have to come from the shared services centre in terms of mindset and behavior at many levels. But equally, change was required from the operating markets in terms of their views and attitudes.

Food for Thought

☞ What processes are in place to gather feedback from your employees?

☞ How would you describe the mindset, behaviour and culture of your organisation?

☞ Can you think of organisations with a different culture?

☞ What mindset do you think lies behind the different corporate cultures?

☞ Who typically gets promoted and rewarded in what cultures?

Chapter 30: All Coming Together...

It was November and the first steps of the high-level design work on the vision had been completed. It had resulted in us defining a new set of capabilities and behaviours. More work on each of these was being carried out by various groups. The plan was to launch and implement it early the following year. We were making good progress and we rode on the momentum.

I was on my way to Costa Rica to visit the shared services centre there. I looked forward to getting back to the Americas region. I knew several people in the centre already – some were former Venezuelan employees who the Group had managed to relocate there.

The Costa Rica office was the smaller of the two 'spoke' centres and my centre provided a lot of secondary services to them. The purpose of the trip was to cover two main topics - the new vision and improving the relationship between our centres. As the ultimate goal from the new vision was to deliver a better service to operating markets, it wouldn't be possible unless the three centres worked well together. The response to it was positive. The team provided some valuable feedback on the new capabilities and behaviours and insight into how their centre matched up on each of them.

Interestingly, they felt that the mindset of the employees in the Costa Rican centre was different from the Romanian centre. In many ways, they were more solutions-oriented and holistic in their thinking. I could see how this could be. Their centre was much smaller and the average employee age was also higher. A high proportion of their employees originally came from operating markets across the region. The Central American cluster of countries was managed out of the same office and employees were actively encouraged to move between the operating business and the shared services centre for career development. I also sensed that they had a higher proportion of Achievers versus Experts than we did. And Achievers operate more naturally in the field of cross-functional solutioning and wider stakeholder management.

As I reflected later, I also believe national cultures played a major part. Romanians tend to give negative feedback more directly and are more confrontational than Latin Americans. Romanians are also hierarchical and employ top-down decision-making. Given this dynamic amongst a large group of Experts who don't reflect deeply or have a good understanding their own biases, you will not tend to find an empathetic and sensitive group of people.

At that time, I also visited some operating markets (e.g. Spain and Nigeria) and attended the regional finance leadership meetings of Europe, Africa, the Middle East and Russia. The support for the new vision was strong. It resonated with people and useful inputs were provided, especially around the quality of the centres stakeholder engagement.

It had been an intense first five months in Romania in the new role, with lots of exciting but also exhausting business travel. Finally, good news on the personal front. The visa had been approved. It had been difficult to attain but one of the HR business partners had worked intensely with the authorities.

Fran would arrive in mid-December. I felt a warm happiness spread inside. I had landed well in the organisation, there were lots of exciting projects, the bigger picture was getting clearer and soon I would also be able to welcome my partner and we could enjoy the city together – basically living a normal life!

The Group had been helpful in providing Fran with English lessons. Still, it was not at a good level – about sufficient to survive going into shops and restaurants. I had another concern though. Fran wouldn't be able to work and I had never been in the situation where I would be living with a partner who would likely feel under-stimulated during the day. How dependent would Fran be on me? How would I balance my work and private life in regards to time and energy?

Arrival day came soon enough. After spending Christmas together in Copenhagen, we returned to a freezing cold Bucharest. I knew I would be very busy at work and hoped it would not result in any challenges on the relationship front. My partner (well, really both of us) would need to find a daily rhythm in the new city after the 'honeymoon' break in Copenhagen. How would Fran take it being alone most of the time?

I didn't have time to think too much about it. Back in the office, it was full speed as soon as I arrived. It was accounting year end, time for the annual performance review process and the setting of new targets for the year. In addition, there were multiple deadlines for the various efficiency and performance projects we were running.

On the transformation project we were now looking at the detailed design. Fleshing out exactly what culture, behaviours and mindset would be required. But also how the centre's systems could support it all and whether any changes in organisational design were needed.

Firstly, if we wanted to become business partners to the Group, we needed to act like the rest of the Group. This meant a number of changes, but primarily building a culture of engagement, consensus-building, learning and development, feedback and coaching, and a high-performance culture constantly seeking solutions and focused on delivering results.

This culture would translate into behaviour at the individual level such that people would ask others for input but also give input to others, with the intention of helping each other grow and improve. Learning would be prioritised by managers and everyone would receive frequent feedback and be encouraged to reflect upon their behaviours – not just at the annual performance review. Inappropriate behaviours, failures and poor performance would be addressed promptly and in a positive way, with a way forward and clear timelines and expectations.

The mindset required to support such behaviours would include: 'I am equal to everyone else in this Group', 'I can do it.

If I cannot right now, I will learn', 'I will engage with my colleagues and other functions to deliver results', 'I will actively listen and learn from the input I receive', 'when I fail and I inevitably will, rather than beating myself up, I will take it as a learning', 'I will treat other people with the same kindness when they experience failures', and 'I will drive for excellence and expect others to do the same'.

As much as possible, the structures would support this culture and mindset. For example, HR would ensure that relevant learning and development options were available for all to access. They would set-up a coaching and mentoring programme, both inside the centre but also with colleagues working in the operating markets. Promotions and remuneration would be awarded based on alignment with the desired behaviours and culture. The top team would have oversight over performance reviews and talent development to ensure there was a fair calibration across functions. To mention just a few.

The organisational design also required some changes. Many role descriptions had to be updated especially where they involved direct engagement with customers. Where it made sense, certain tasks were moved to new sub-functions. It was a revamp that was much needed.

Approach to Change

Whilst Part 4 of the book largely focuses on vertical development and leadership, it would be difficult not to briefly touch upon change management and transformation as well, since a large driver behind the need for vertical development was the need for transforming the organisation and its employees.

Change models are not an exact science. One is not more correct or rigorous than another, but different models have different approaches and emphases to managing change. Some focus on the whole transformation process and are very broad in their coverage, whereas others only cover certain parts of the change journey.

In Venezuela, I used Kotter's 8-step model, which captures many of the vital parts of leading change. There are many other models that can be used. There is no one *simple* model fits all - it just depends on your specific change requirement and what works for you. But also, how mindful you are around other steps typically needed.

For the transformation project in Romania, I would like to bring in the ADKAR model designed by Jeffrey Hiatt. This model is very powerful for implementing change in individual's behaviour, which was one of the main objectives of the project. It's not a perfect model. It has some obvious shortfalls compared to other models. In particular, it is light on the preparatory steps required to ensure a successful outcome. Many of these steps have been mentioned already in previous chapters, but it would be pertinent to remind ourselves of them now before introducing the ADKAR model.

Firstly, it is imperative to understand the high level vision. To understand what the organisation or your sponsors and stakeholders wish to achieve. What is causing the obstacles the organisation is facing now? What would a successful change result in and what behaviours are needed to support this? Most of this exercise was carried out in my first few months in Romania, as I touched upon in Chapters 27 and 28.

The next important step is to obtain internal alignment and identify key players. This needs to happen early on in the process, both internally among the leadership team and the teams who'll be carrying out the change, but equally with external executives, stakeholders and sponsors. It needs to be clear what challenges you are trying to address and how they should be addressed. In other words, what are we trying to accomplish and who will do what? There needs to be alignment across the board on this. Chapter 28 touched on parts of this.

The next step is to carry out an organisational assessment to understand where you are now, before you can assess the change required to reach the endgame. Such an assessment captures 'hard' and 'soft' elements such as systems, culture, behaviour, mindset, challenges, pitfalls, and, importantly, what type of resistance can be expected and from where. Much of this was captured in Chapter 29 (and more will be covered in later chapters).

This leads you to the organisational design phase. What is the endgame. This includes analysing roles and responsibilities, reviewing role descriptions (what skills and behaviour is needed), and organisational structure. I covered this earlier in this chapter. You can now identify the gap between the current state (as is) and the endgame (to be).

It is worth noting that many of these steps are executed in parallel, so timing is less of an issue. What is important for a successful transformation is that these pre-steps are carried out or planned for early on in the process.

Then comes the question: what change is actually required to bridge the gap between the 'as is' and the 'to be'? During this phase, it is helpful to try to anticipate what resistance may arise and have a plan as to how to transition people. This is where the ADKAR model becomes very powerful with its focus on the process around changing people's behaviour (see Figure 4).[14]

In our case, the foundation for the first two steps (awareness ('A') and desire ('D')), had been established during my first speech at the hotel, but much more of the same was needed. We decided the vision would be officially launched at the next quarterly engagement session. A few weeks later, around 600 people joined in Bucharest and similar events were held in Costa Rica and Malaysia.

I used a few simple slides to illustrate the story I was telling. I wanted to tell a compelling story that would convince people that change was needed, but also to motivate people to join in the transformation – create a desire and interest. I highlighted the potential for our organisation and how an investment from each employee would benefit themselves as well as the centre and the Group.

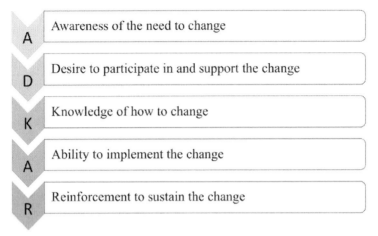

A — Awareness of the need to change

D — Desire to participate in and support the change

K — Knowledge of how to change

A — Ability to implement the change

R — Reinforcement to sustain the change

Figure 4. Jeffrey Hiatt's ADKAR Model

In short, the centre had been on a transformation journey since it was founded. This latest transformation was just the piece that had been missing in the journey - the culture piece. It helped tremendously that I had sown the first seed six months prior (at my foot-in-mouth speech) around building a shared services centre that was not perceived inferior to the rest of the Group. Since then, the desire for change amongst the people had only grown.

We were now at 'K' – increasing knowledge across the shared services organisation of how we were going to change. I ran through the focus areas we had defined but also stressed that we would work together to make the change more tangible and relatable to their everyday work.

After my presentation, we held breakout sessions where each function met with their functional leads (my top team members) to discuss exactly what this would mean and to ask questions in a more intimate setting. This exercise revealed that what it would mean for the individual was unclear for many. We were expecting this. We had worked on this for many months. To expect that others, after a presentation and some small group discussions, would be completely onboard would be unrealistic.

We had therefore planned that over the next year, there would be focus groups and more sessions, top-down and bottom-up, on the various behaviours and capabilities. We would make use of lots of different communication modes to gain broad support across the organisation. Working on behaviours is a time-consuming task.

The release of the vision and the inclusive nature of the project gave the organisation a new lease of life. Many were positive about the direction and outlook for their job, even though they knew it meant more work in the short term.

As part of the implementation plan, each employee was to identify the two capabilities they considered most relevant to them in their development. For some, it may be strengthening their leadership capabilities. For others, it could be effectively implementing changes. For others still, how to communicate and interact effectively with customers. People would agree these with their manager.

The reason for limiting it to two areas is that if you focus on too many things, nothing will change. If I were to ask you to change the following when making a presentation: speak louder, stop touching your leg with you left hand, gesture more with your hands to underpin your points, speak more slowly, don't say 'hmmm' when you are pausing, and please try to smile once in a while during your speech as you appear tense when you look so serious all the time! How much of this list do you think you would manage to do? Most likely none of it!

If instead, I asked you to speak more slowly and use your hands more, you have a chance of accomplishing them. When those two are achieved, you can start working two new ones. Human behaviours take time to change and only with dedicated focus can you make long-lasting change.

Food for Thought

☞ When you want to change something (e.g. mindset, behaviour, etc), how do you approach it?

☞ Do you tend to be too ambitious or not ambitious at all?

☞ What are your personal developmental areas right now?

☞ Have they been highlighted by someone else or have you identified them yourself by reflecting?

☞ What two areas would you focus on first?

Chapter 31: The Elephant in the Room

I had just received a report on my desk that made for uncomfortable reading. It had been produced by some external consultants the Group had hired to evaluate some of the initiatives we had implemented. Apparently, on one of the key initiatives - the daily whiteboard – the Romanian centre was showing the lowest scores on commitment and engagement out of the three centres. It had been fully implemented across most functions by the time I landed in Romania and I thought it had been running successfully.

The concept was simple. At the start of the day, each team would meet for 15 minutes in a huddle in front of a whiteboard that captured a broad range of points and data. The team leaders would run through everything that needed to be done that day - tasks, challenges, escalations, successes, and anything else that was relevant and the team needed to know about. It had already delivered synergies in the form of a substantial headcount reduction. It was an idea brought by the external consultants and it had worked wonders in other large service companies.

Several managers, including senior managers, disapproved of it. It had been a high profile project so most would not have aired their views publicly. When they heard critique and complaints from the employees, they would often just park it with a 'it's early days – let's see how it develops'. Whilst this may sound harmless, a statement like this leaves space in people's minds for discontent to grow, i.e. I don't expect it to get better either but we'll have to live with it.

Given how busy I had been getting up to speed, building relationships, working on the new vision, visiting customers, etc, I had not spent much time following up on the initiative. And without knowing it, I had inadvertently joined the group of dissenters. Some managers continued to persist with the initiative but many didn't. Given I didn't show much interest in it, even the supporters started to doubt whether it was worth the effort of carrying on. The lack of explicit commitment from my side had been interpreted as a lack of support for the initiative. Honestly, I had failed in this area as GM. In my defence, I thought I had bigger fish to fry, but I couldn't think like this. I was GM. Everything fell ultimately under my purview.

It was one of the important change initiatives in that it impacted around 70% of employees. Implementation had started before my arrival and we had already banked the headcount reduction gains. The growing resistance had dragged down the benefits but perhaps we'd also been too quick to call it a success. What frustrated me was that I had not noticed there was a problem until it was raised in black and white in the report. And an external consultant's report – a double blow! The performance of the initiative should have been discussed in the top team, but it was never brought up. I think it became the elephant in the room that I didn't know was there, and now there it stood – impossible to miss.

I was not happy with myself. What I needed to do now was to address it head on and see what learnings I could derive from it. I asked for a longer session with the coaches who had implemented the initiative in the first place. They explained the concept to me again. They spoke a lot about synergies and efficiencies. For several hours. I was impressed with how they could turn such a simple concept into such a complex one, with flowery consultancy language and graphs. But it didn't motivate me. What they said made sense. It would have been perfect for selling a project to an executive team. But did it resonate with a 25 year old newly promoted manager?

Repetition Blindness

When I was 18 years old, I had a summer job in a sugar factory in Copenhagen. I was in charge of operating a machine that packed 150 bags of sugar per minute. We operated in 30-minute shifts, as repetitive tasks make you 'blind'. We had to rest our eyes and brain regularly. In the longer term, your brain gets tired of non-stimulating work and easily oversees errors after a while. It's human nature and as factories know this, they rotate people around different tasks to create variety. It was not a hard job but it was interesting to try and it paid well.

Today, I am thankful I got to try so many different jobs when I was younger. It broadened my understanding of the world and has helped me to see different situations through different lenses. I think this has helped me as my career has progressed. When else do you get the chance to try such a variety of different roles? When you are more senior, you don't get to just try things out and you can also easily lose touch with the daily working lives of the 'average worker' in your company.

My sugar factory work experience helped me in Venezuela when I spoke with factory workers and knew the right questions to ask. I shared with them that I had operated a similar machine in my youth. My work experience helped me more readily understand why errors sometimes happen in service centres. Many researchers confirm that when people are asked to do or check the same thing all day every day, like in a factory, you gradually become blind.

It also helped me understand how productivity is hugely dependent on work processes, measurement and rotation in tasks. So when I was listening to them talk about synergies and efficiencies, my brain and ears blocked it out. The concepts were too familiar to me. It was corporate speech that bored me.

In many ways, as I shared earlier, a shared services organisation operates like a factory. It is all about scale, efficiency and control. However, now we were asking employees to think more strategically and not like a factory worker. What the coaches did not consider was the leadership capabilities that were now required and which were indirectly embedded into the whiteboard process. They weren't mentioned at all.

Sharing this with them, they agreed. One problem with management consultants is they've all gone to the same business schools. They develop knowledge about the same areas of management but in most cases, 80-90% of what they are taught relates to managing tasks and processes - not people. They build skills in areas like project management, creating key performance indicators and how to measure them smartly. Much less effort is placed on softer management skills like self-awareness and empathy. Some consultants have never managed a larger team themselves, despite teaching others to do so. The softer skills (read empathy) are more and more important as you grow as a leader. Most people can be taught to manage by spreadsheets and schedules, but fewer can lead with emotional intelligence, motivation and reflection. These require an entirely different skillset.

Whilst some may have a natural talent in these softer skills, anyone can grow in them as they go through life. Typically, those who mature into great leaders are those who master self-awareness and self-leadership. They stay curious all of their lives, whether that is in work or in their personal lives. They often reflect on themselves, situations, their own behaviour and seek feedback from others.

Think about it - if you try to marginally improve yourself every day and learn something new, after ten or twenty years, you will likely be materially smarter and more rounded as a person than the ones who are not curious. Some people call this having a growth mindset rather than a fixed mindset[15]. It doesn't even necessarily matter what you learn. It could be something about nature, history, science or psychology. You name it. If you aim to grow each day and learn something new, you will benefit from the compound interest (interest-on-interest) over time. As your brain works like a muscle, the more you flex that muscle, the stronger it becomes.

Of course there are the managers who don't need to reflect. They have a long track record of experience that enables them to do the right thing at the right time. Because they have done it all before, they know exactly how to cope with the situation in front of them. Or at least, that is what they think. These people will typically be operating at an Expert leadership level or even lower levels. We always need to grow. The learnings are never done.

Managers who think they have it all sussed are often amongst the worst managers. They manage on autopilot and haven't developed what I consider to be one of the most important skills of management - the ability to empathise, reflect, and self-correct. Because they believe they know how to lead and that their way is the only way, they are not open to input from others. They may insist they are listening, but in fact they are not.

They surround themselves with people who think the same way as they do. They promote junior managers who are 'mini-mes' and thereby confirm to themselves that they are great at leading. This type of manager was more usual in the past. Today, they fit poorly into most organisations, although some still exist. Maduro was such a manager.

Although it's not necessarily age specific, younger people tend to seek out learnings more actively and are more open to guidance, so the whiteboard initiative was a perfect opportunity to accelerate the vertical development of the young team leaders. In short, the whiteboard contained 10-15 parameters that were important to the team.

The parameters differed according to the tasks carried out by the team. They related to measurable areas like performance, error rate, issues to be escalated, skills capabilities, a mood tracker, coaching, etc.

At its basic, it was helpful data, but combining several data points (e.g. employee performance, error rate, mood and competencies), one could paint an interesting holistic picture of the function, and strengthen a young manager's holistic understanding of what was going on and where they should focus. Links to other teams were also explicitly highlighted on the board, so the team would remember to look outside their silo.

However, like most things, the benefits of the initiative depended on the team lead – how engaged they were, whether they were using it effectively, and so on. That included me on a centre-wide level. I was the team lead of the whole thing. I had to correct my own behaviour. Some of my senior managers also had to adjust their behaviour. And so did the coaches training the team leads. We ran a half-day workshop where we only focused on the whiteboard initiative and how it could be used to drive results and vertically develop leaders across the organisation. As a top team, we agreed to regularly go out onto the floor and join different teams for their 15-minute huddles. We would openly coach the team and team leads, thus leading by example. Soon, energy returned to the daily huddles and efficiency sky-rocketed. The entire building began to embed this way of working into their daily routines. It was very satisfying to see.

So, what did I learn from this experience? Leading by example is powerful. You cannot say one thing and do something else. Even remaining quiet about something can show passive agreement. People notice what you do, not what you say. And also, sometimes you need to get hands on, even in a task you deem small fish.

Food for Thought

☞ Have you always worked in the same profession or did you have other jobs when you were younger?

☞ What have those other roles taught you that you can benefit from today?

☞ Do you try to keep challenging yourself and keeping your brain stimulated with new things?

☞ Can you identify managers with a fixed and a growth mindset?

☞ What are the benefits of one versus the other?

Chapter 32: The Tricky Thing with Travelling Cattle-class

There were several criticisms that our services centre repeatedly received from operating markets. One was that they were too process-oriented and not flexible enough (i.e. not service-oriented). Having been on the other side, I could agree. I had announced the same in my foot-in-mouth opening speech on my second day! Many of our stakeholders also shared that they didn't get the same level of service or expertise from a service centre employee as they would from a local employee.

Now, seeing the lay of the land from the inside, I understood what tight cost measures such centres operated under and the continual pressures for further cost efficiencies compared to operating markets. That was the whole point of its set-up. However, we had to shift this thinking because we were trying to evolve up the value curve with more sophisticated tasks and more high-value services. That was the vision of the new shared services organisation.

I have always known the power of story-telling. It takes a skilled story-teller to present a problem without implicating the parties in the story. This 'other-ing' of the problem enables the audience to listen to the message from a more neutral position and thus be more receptive to its message.

Had I reverted to our stakeholders with all the good things we were doing and complained about HQ cutting our budget each year, they would have immediately said that they experienced the same pressures and we should get over it and do better, as they were. Instead, I told the following story: Assume you have always travelled on business class for work. Now, due to cost cutting measures across the company, you are only allowed to fly on coach (economy) class unless it is a long-haul flight.

You arrive at Heathrow Airport. You head to the check-in queue as usual. You join the longer queue for coach class, even though the business class queue is empty. You're now in front of security and you realise you've lost your fast-track access badge. At the gate, you're the last group to be called to board the plane because, not only does your ticket not allow for priority boarding, your seat is three rows from the toilet in the back. When you finally get into the cabin, you first pass the business class passengers. There is plenty of leg space and you remember when you used to be smug too. When you get to your seat, you struggle to find space in the overhead locker for your cabin bag. Soon after you take off, the curtain is closed separating the business customers from the cattle-class, where you are now seated.

Behind the curtain, you hear the clink of glasses as champagne is poured. You suspect warm towels are being passed around (face pat optional, armpit pat definitely optional), another pre-dinner drink, dinner with wine, coffee and after-dinner drinks follow. The only difference is you are not part of it. Eventually, the smiling air hostess reaches your seat with the drinks trolley. She apologises for taking so long. And asks if you want to buy something. You are annoyed. It was much better in the old days.

The question now is: Should you be angry with the airline and its employees? They have given you exactly what you paid for. Or should you be angry with the management in your company who changed the policy on air travel and reduced the budget?

The point is that often, people complain that the service levels of their service centres are not up to scratch and definitely lower than they were used to with their local employees. However, it isn't the centres or the employees who decide the service levels in large organisations. It is senior management in HQ. They made the decision to cut costs and to move the activity away. Should you expect the same level of service? At least in the short and medium term, there is likely to be a dip.

Likewise, would I, now sat in cattle-class, complain to the airline for the lack of free beverages and longer wait? Would I think the airline had dropped its service levels? No. I would understand that I'm now sat in economy. Now, over time, I would hope that the service provided would improve, but my base expectations are adjusted. Whether this is right or wrong, whether I'm happy with this or not, the senior management team at HQ have decided this is the Group's new strategy. The way to change this would be to communicate to senior managers in HQ. They are the ones who hold the purse strings.

Again, this is not to say that the airline should not seek to improve the service in economy class, but without recognising that there has been a fundamental shift that was decided by neither of the parties most affected, the discussion leads nowhere. The GMs and FDs in the operating markets hear one thing – that things have worsened. Senior management in HQ only hear some of this because the message is somewhat managed – it has to be a success, doesn't it? Shared services are in the middle – managing the different expectations. When I spoke to other corporates with large service centres, I repeatedly heard this pattern.

I used different versions of the business/cattle class analogy when I met with operating markets. Often, they said it helped them readjust their expectations and that they now perceived the service more positively. During the meetings, we would run through various key performance indicators. With expectations now more realistic, they could see more clearly that the service provided was mostly within the limits agreed in the service level agreements. Managers in the operating markets began to actively support us. When their employees expressed frustrations, they were able to explain and shift views within their teams.

On top of this, a lot of the initiatives we had launched earlier that year began to yield returns. The combination of addressing the mismatch in expectations whilst promising to improve service levels via the new business partnering vision worked well together. Both were necessary.

Change your Environment, Change your Mindset

The implementation of the new vision was progressing. There was little I could do to accelerate the process as most of the initiatives were being carried out by employees. However, one area I tackled that spring was the physical working environment, with the aim of adjusting the employees' perception of themselves.

As I said earlier, I believe one's environment and immediate surroundings hugely impacts one's energy, creativity and motivation. Studies on office ambience (e.g. on noise, lighting, temperature, the presence of windows, etc) suggest that such elements influence employees' attitudes, mindset, behaviour, levels of satisfaction and ultimately performance.

During my time in Venezuela, I initiated a minor refurbishment of the Finance and HR floor – the basement floor. Even though it was mostly decorative changes (e.g. new carpets, paint, softer lighting and some new office equipment), it hugely boosted employees' energy and readiness for change. I felt it almost worked like a visual reset of the status quo and matched the general environment of change that was around. It suggested a new beginning.

In the same way, a new logo and rebranding can have some of the same impacts for companies. An investment in the working environment gives off positive signals, e.g. the Group is investing in your wellbeing and job satisfaction, we are a winning organisation and we are going places.

The current office in Romania looked and felt different to the offices I had known in the operating markets. Given the mass of global activity that had been concentrated there, employees were now engaging with senior managers in the operating markets on a daily basis. We needed offices that looked and felt like they were part of the same Group.

Over the next year, we revamped all of the (now) five floors. We hired an interior design company with expertise in creating energetic and dynamic office environments. We shared with them the culture we wanted to build. Everything was changed, from the reception area to the rest rooms, the canteen, the open offices, and the managers' offices. Fewer people would sit in closed offices and more pods were established to cater for private meetings. The branding, the look and the feel of the offices matched those of the Group and the visual cultural gap was closed.

As the physical transformation began to take shape, it began to energise the people in it. People started to see themselves as valuable employees working in a dynamic hub part of a successful, multinational Group. It also helped erase some of the old visual cues that kept mindsets and behaviours locked in the old ways of doing things by their brains' System 1s. Many senior managers across the Group visited the centre and they were blown away by the set-up. They expected to see transactional people sitting in a boring dusty office endlessly inputting data. Instead, what they saw was a vibrant, young organisation with a can-do attitude in a physical environment just like their own. They started to view the employees as colleagues and as business partners in the Group.

Food for Thought

☞ Do you think your expectations of others (e.g. colleagues, business partners, stakeholders, bosses) is reasonable?

☞ What emotions are triggered when working with them?

☞ Why do you think this is the case?

☞ How important is your physical environment to you?

☞ Do you notice a difference in your mindset and behaviour in different environments?

☞ Is the way you act and feel different when entering a discount shop versus an exclusive high-end one?

Chapter 33: The Power of Role-Modelling

It was beautiful weather in Bucharest. The temperature was around 30°C. Summer was basically upon us. I was looking forward to it after the cold winter, especially having gotten used to the temperate weather of Latin America. Different groups of friends from London and Copenhagen had visited in the last few months and they had all loved it.

Soon, my parents would visit again, followed by my cousin, then my brother and his family. Despite having survived the isolation of Venezuela, I knew that the frequent physical presence of dear friends and family was vital for my wellbeing. It had only fully dawned on me once I had gotten some of it back in Europe.

It would have been even harder in Venezuela had I not met Fran. Unfortunately, no one from Venezuela would be visiting. It was difficult. It was the first time my partner had lived outside the country. I could empathise with the loneliness. Despite living in relative freedom compared to Caracas, there were many negatives. I worked long hours and travelled frequently, meaning we didn't spend much time together. The language was still a problem and it had been difficult to connect with new people.

I had suggested Fran take up some hobbies or enrol in a course but for now, the only hobby was going to the gym, taking some English classes, and looking after our home. This seeming passivity triggered some strong negative emotions in me that I didn't expect and didn't like. I'd need to reflect on where those emotions had come from. For now, the many visits from friends helped us both and, in a few months' time, we would be taking a three-week holiday to drive through Europe to Denmark. I hoped it would lift the mood and dynamic between us.

Before that though, there were many things to attend to at work. Besides an extensive survey that Alex had conducted and was thoroughly analysing, we had agreed that all managers would be going through a 360-degree feedback process. Leadership behaviour had been identified as one of the key areas that needed to be strengthened. It is fundamental to changing organisational culture and behaviour, especially if you want to vertically develop your organisation. You need strong role models to demonstrate certain behaviours. This supported the knowledge and ability elements (steps 'K' and 'A') of the ADKAR model around addressing skills, monitoring performance and providing constructive feedback.

I mentioned the 360-degrees evaluation earlier in the book. For those not that familiar, it is a process through which feedback is sought from an employee's manager, peers and subordinates, as well as from the employee themselves. Feedback may also be sought from external customers or stakeholders (in this case, from the operating markets). Information is typically collected through surveys and focuses on the employee's behaviour in different situations and with people. Hence, its aim is not to collect information on professional or technical knowledge, but look solely at behavioural aspects. Organisations commonly use such reviews to develop their staff.

It is worth noting that what you get is a snapshot of how you are perceived at that point of time. It may look different a year later. It is a powerful tool that helps you identify your strengths and weaknesses according to others who know you, but it also helps you calibrate your self-perception. As follows the quote earlier in the book, 'perception is reality', you may be good at something, but if those around you disagree, then something has gone wrong. In order to be an effective manager, you have to be good *and* perceived to be good.

It may be that only small adjustments are needed. Or it may spur more fundamental changes, e.g. around your general mood, the way you talk to people or your general professionalism, etc. You may totally disagree with the findings and not be interested in making any changes, but then you need to calibrate your self-perception to match with how people actually see you.

There will always be some subjectivity to such feedback. Some people have a tendency to pick out everything that is wrong and not focus on any of the positives. Others will not understand the full picture behind certain decisions you may have made. Yet others may have personal motives behind their feedback. This is why it is important to get multiple views from all sides (i.e. a 360-degree view). When many people evaluate a person in a certain way, you should probably pay attention. But even if only one person says something, it's still useful information to have.

More than 200 managers in the centre, including myself, took part in the survey, with many more giving feedback. The results were not overwhelmingly encouraging and confirmed the previous observation that many of the managers operated at Expert level, with only a few at Achiever or higher levels.

Expert level leaders are critical in a centre operating daily transactional tasks as they are often excellent at supervising people and problem-solving within their specific areas. The problem we found was that even the more senior leaders were operating at the Expert level. Such leaders have to deal with a lot of stakeholder engagement. It is a key part of their job. Yet many had not evolved in their leadership capabilities. I sensed that many were hungry to develop but because the centre had grown so quickly, many had been promoted too soon and it was all made more difficult by the fact that there weren't enough good senior role models in the organisation.

So, what distinguishes you as an Achiever rather than an Expert?

Achievers versus Experts
Achievers are characterised by having a better understanding of themselves and their surroundings – both within the organisation but also for the external environment, e.g. competitors, the industry, society at large, etc. This means they hold a much broader view than

Experts. They can zoom in and out of a given situation, which helps them to see things not only practically but also strategically.

Their self-awareness typically helps them to understand others better too. They are able to put themselves into other people's shoes, making them more empathetic leaders. They understand that you can lead in more ways than by direct authority, which also helps them to manage their stakeholders more effectively.

They have more tools available to them in their leadership toolbox, including coaching and building organisational motivation by creating a shared vision that employees buy-in to. Lastly, their superior understanding of the political dynamics that exist in all organisations means they are better equipped to solve problems across functions and locations.

With our centre operating directly with directors and other senior managers across operating markets, having more Achiever level managers would be the difference between success and failure. Having more Achievers in senior positions was not only imperative to deliver the new vision we had set, but also to ensure more junior managers had good role-models to look up to and emulate. In a healthy organisation, this should happen at all levels, with directors coaching senior managers, who are coaching more junior managers, who are coaching team members, and so on.

We implemented a raft of changes. Enhanced leadership training programmes were developed for all managers. Mentor and mentee programs were already in place for more experienced managers, but they were expanded to include junior managers. Newly promoted managers could access more senior managers. In these one-to-one relationships, mentees could raise issues, incidences, and challenges that they would like another more experienced perspective on. We also paired senior managers and other high potential talent with mentors outside the centre. Such employees would get an even broader view of the organisation. Finally, we encouraged informal mentoring across the organisation. After all, mentoring others is good for the mentor as well as the mentee (when the pairing is good).

To accelerate the role-modelling, some senior positions in the centre were filled by strong managers rotating in from operating markets. Besides coming in with strong Achiever behaviours, they also brought the cultural mindset of the Group, further accelerating the change in culture.

All of these initiatives and changes understandably triggered a lot of different emotions among employees. Core ego needs for security, inclusion, power, control, competence, and justice were triggered to varying degrees. That there was now a new set of capabilities and expectations that would be valued and ultimately feed into promotions and career progression challenged them. We had changed the goal posts. Imagine it's nearly your turn to be promoted. You have been working hard on your technical and supervisor capabilities, but now we've changed what is expected and we haven't equipped you well enough to build those other skills – leadership, empathy, etc. Your peers were recently promoted off the old set of capabilities. Now, how long will you have to wait?

It was difficult for many managers to manage these emotions in their teams. We sought to address it by the senior managers, myself included, explicitly talking about what the new focus capabilities would bring to the organisation and why this type of leadership was needed for us to succeed. We also highlighted how employees could take ownership of their own development and grow as leaders.

To help them, a lot of support initiatives to accelerate the vertical development that we were asking for were put in place. However, ultimately, it depended on the individual and their appetite for development. To vertically develop, you must have some self-awareness and reflexivity, and when you identify an area that requires works, you have to take action. You have to be good at managing yourself as well as others.

Let's take for example that you find it difficult providing feedback to others (observing). Your self-awareness will help you uncover the underlying behaviour and root of the behaviour. Perhaps it is a lack of confidence or a desire to please that causes you to feel uncomfortable (analysing). Once you've rooted this out, what will you do about it? Perhaps you could set a goal to give feedback to three colleagues over the next month. Perhaps you role play with a friend before approaching the first colleague (strategising). And eventually, you execute your strategy (taking actions). Finally, and importantly, the loop starts again. You observe and assess the outcome of your actions - what went well and what you should do differently next time. You set another goal that builds on your learnings and you make a new strategy. It is a cycle that will vertically develop you by repeatedly (see Figure 5);

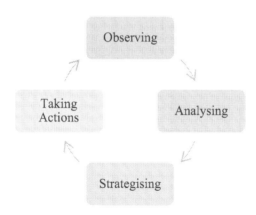

Figure 5. Behavioural Change Model

Mentors, colleagues, friends or family (especially if they operate at higher leadership levels themselves) can help you to identify the areas that are most vital for you to work first. As progress is made in these areas, new ones will appear. It's like an orange. You can peel it, but despite having removed the first obvious outer layer, you will continue to see areas where you can remove

white peal. By refining the peeling, it gradually becomes a
beautifully peeled orange.

Food for Thought

☞ Are you able to initiate a 360-degree process for yourself?

☞ If your organisation doesn't run them, can you ask for
feedback from your manager, peers, subordinates and
external stakeholders in other ways (hint: use of web tools)?

☞ What do you expect to find?

☞ Which areas are you working on right now?

☞ Are you using the four-step approach of observing,
analysing, strategising and taking actions?

Chapter 34: Communication - Content or Style?

With the focus on leadership behaviour came a related focus area: communication and engagement.

From my experience, there are two elements of an effective communication: content and delivery.

Expert level managers' beliefs on leadership are often based on being knowledgeable and knowing the details. Many will try to emulate other managers who come across as strong in their specific technical area. They themselves seek appreciation that comes from others admiring their knowledge.

It naturally leads, therefore, to presentations that are very detailed and heavy on data. The more you can show the audience you know a given topic, the better. All details are equally important and there's little that can be left out. This type of presentation is powerful when used for an audience of peers (e.g. other Experts). It can also be well received by those outside your area as you are seen as a technical expert.

However, often the message is lost. The audience is left with the feeling that a lot has been packed into the half hour, but they don't know what to take away with them. The presenter's inability to put themself in their audience's shoes means that they are probably not used to reflecting on the question: Will this be interesting or useful to this person?

When it come to delivery, the Expert has not yet appreciated the power of visioning and engaging others through story-telling. Thus, their delivery and language often lacks creativity or passion. At worst, it will be received by the audience as boring.

With a lot of the communication now being with senior managers from the operating markets (most of whom would be operating solidly as Achievers or Catalysts), the repeated feedback we received was that employees' communications were far too wordy, lacking focus, and didn't captivate those receiving the messages in the markets. At times, the audience had not understood what our employees were trying to say as the main messages were drowned out by all the details that came with them.

I could completely empathise. Having worked in HQs or operating markets for most of my career, it was a wake-up call to land in a shared services centre. In operating markets, presentations to senior managers are targeted, carefully scripted and, irrespective of the topic, always had a marketing spin. The messages would be direct and punchy, with sparing use of detail.

In the shared services centre, most slides included long tables with performance metrics in red, amber and green (traffic lights). In order to fit the long tables in, the font would be size 8 or smaller. Other slides would be lengthy and almost totally filled with text – often in full sentences and paragraphs. Again, in some small font size that required squinting or a magnifying glass.

Where the presenter in the operating market would stand up confidently next to the screen and present their carefully worded presentation, the preferred approach in the service centre was to run through the presentation slides whilst remaining sat in their chair. Sometimes you didn't need the presenter at all as the entire script was basically written on the slides. Perhaps that is harsh, but this was my experience.

I used to be terrible at presentations. In my 20s, I could barely speak in front of a group of four at a team meeting. I was nervous and worried that if I opened my mouth and shared my view, I would be trapped by a question that I didn't know the answer to or detail that I hadn't remembered. Opening my mouth was an opportunity to be caught out. My beliefs around being a good manager were linked entirely to my skills within my specialist field. It did not help that my manager at that time that operated solidly as an Expert and didn't appreciate the softer leadership skills. If I couldn't answer a question within my area of responsibility, he would write a little mental note in his black book. It meant I spent days preparing for each presentation, making sure I covered everything that could possibly be asked.

Somehow, he always managed to find a weak spot and I would get that little note in his mental black book.

Over the years, I learned to move on from that. Numerous courses in presentation skills by coaches helped. Being filmed and receiving critique from the other course participants helped my self-confidence and recalibrate my own understanding of what I could do in front of others. Still, I didn't have any good role models to look up to in terms of both content *and* delivery.

Over many years, I prepared many PowerPoint presentations for senior managers in my different roles. I thought that I was OK at it. That understanding came to an end when I worked in London. I had spent weeks putting together a pretty treasury transformation slide pack. In the end, it was 48 pages long. I showed it to Miles. He was not impressed. It was a read-it-yourself slide deck (or I-have-written-it-all-on-the-slides-so-I-am-sure-I-will-not-forget-any-important-messages slides). This was the first time I realised what actually makes for effective slides. None of my original slides made it into the final presentation in front of Miles' peers.

Up till then, I had mostly presented the treasury transformation project to other treasury specialists. My slides contained information they would care about but were sometimes highly technical. I applied no filter for relevance and didn't attempt to show the bigger picture.

In the end, Miles used six simple slides – slides that he put together himself. In them, he laid out a simple narrative of the main points and used his storytelling skills to build the rest of the story and captivate the audience. He used the slides to help his story, rather than the other way round. Now I paid attention.

His body language was calm and deliberate. There was some gesturing and moving around, but it was well placed. He leaned into the audience when he wanted their full attention and he moved back when their full attention was not required. At times, he made people laugh. At other times, he employed a soft tone and pauses to give the audience time to reflect.

I was deeply impressed. He basically took the audience, including myself, along with him from the start to end of his story. He drew our senses and emotions in. I had been looking for a role-model just like him and from that day on, I would pay attention each time he spoke in order to pick up more tips.

When I was in Venezuela and presented to 200 people, my largest audience at that time, I had butterflies in my stomach for hours before. I did my best and sought feedback from others. I gave more presentations. Some were recorded for wider broadcast, so I watched them and tried, as objectively as I could, to evaluate how I had done. I analysed my body language and considered what worked well and what didn't. At the next presentation, I would put into practice what I had learnt and try new things. This process helped me to strengthen my presenting skills and calibrate how I viewed myself.

One of the most challenging presentations I had to give at that time was one in Spanish to 80 people. Despite many hours of language lessons, I still didn't speak that well. Somehow, I still managed to make people laugh and get my messages across. I realised that I compensated a lot for my poor language skills with gestures and using my body language to emphasise what I was saying. It seemed to work and I would make use of both these things more in my future speeches, even in English.

Of course, when I came to Romania, I screwed up big time. It the first of many presentations to audiences of 500 or more people and I was underprepared, not thinking through the story or being clear what messages I wanted the audience to take away with them. I had thought about the style (e.g. remember to smile and engage the audience with open body language), but I had not thought through the content enough. I learned a tough lesson that day. Both style and content are needed. It doesn't have to take hours to prepare for a presentation, especially when you're giving so many, but you do need to think through your content (e.g. story, tone, emphasis, slides, etc) and match it with your style.

Thankfully, most of the presentations I subsequently gave in Romania were recorded so that all the employees in the centre could catch up on it if they missed it live. I always chose to see each of them afterwards. It was incredibly uncomfortable to watch them and hear myself speak (who likes to do this?) but it was necessary. Over the years, I reminded myself that what I saw on the video was what everyone else had already seen, and what they saw and heard every day. I just wasn't used to being on the receiving end of myself! I began to evaluate myself with more self-compassion. I could now note my intonation, body language and whether it was captivating the audience or losing them. I always found points where I could do better next time, but I could also see that I was improving with practice.

Now, in Romania, we needed to create an environment where role-modelling was the norm, especially among those managers who, in many ways, operated at Achiever level but when it came to communication and engagement, were more Experts. By raising their skills in the area, they would become aspirational leaders for their younger peers.

Know Your Audience

How do you know what content is relevant to your audience? It is a common challenge for people who work in specialist or technical roles to judge this. Such people tend to overcommunicate just in case something is important, but in doing so, lose their audience early on in the presentation. The content may be absolutely correct and the work behind it brilliant, but too many details will drown out the main points. There is only so much someone can take in, especially in a one-way interaction. An article published by TIME magazine in 2015[16] quoted research from Microsoft suggesting that humans now have an attention span of just eight seconds –allegedly less than a goldfish.

I have attended many formal dinners that go like this - your main course has just been served, someone announces they want to make a speech, you put your knife and fork down, you sit and listen to them talk about nothing and everything. You wonder how it is relevant to you. And more importantly, you think about how your dinner is getting cold. Will they ever finish what they're saying? As soon as the presenter is done, everyone applauds – because we are polite human beings. Unfortunately, we will recall none of the speech and tell our partner later that evening that we had to eat our steak cold.

Taking all that the top team and I had learned, we decided to coach people to make better presentations. For example, presentations to end customers should be more marketing or sales-oriented and less technical. If you were in their shoes, what would you want to know? If you or they were short on time, what would you absolutely need to convey? What would their main concerns be? What would reassure them that you are competent and will get things sorted? Often this meant not sharing every little detail about what happened in the 'engine room' (e.g. processes, steps, every communication or timing).

When we failed or made mistakes, the speech would not be so much about why we failed (e.g. finding excuses) but we would instead focus on what we had learned and what we would do to avoid making the same mistake again. This reshaping of communication helped many employees, especially the younger employees, to communicate more effectively with their customers in the operating markets. But it also laid a foundation for a new culture around how failures should be treated by people – as learning opportunities.

When it came to delivery, we spoke about body language and intonation. We encouraged our high potential employees to present at top team or extended leadership team (100-plus people) meetings for training purpose after receiving coaching from their managers. We, the top team, would also provide feedback to the presenters.

At the start, some found it very difficult to receive the feedback. Many of those operating at Expert level are not good at hearing feedback and few will actively seek it. There was also a cultural element to it in that feedback, regardless of whether it was constructive or not, was generally perceived as something negative to Romanians. Even to those in senior positions. Some explained that the school system and their parents' generations were not trained in providing constructive feedback, so it often came across as harsh. It reminded me that, even though there are vertical development stages, there are also other dimensions that add complexity such as culture, personality traits and past experience.

Food for Thought

☞ How would you rate your ability to present?

☞ What do you do to prepare for a presentation or a speech?

☞ Do you consider both the content and style?

☞ What body language and intonation do you make use of?

☞ Do you actively seek feedback from others and how receptive are you to feedback?

Chapter 35: The Problem with a Revolving Door

During that autumn, a topic that was consistently raised by our customers was the problem of attrition and the resulting loss of knowledge - the last leadership challenge I will dive into.

Attrition refers to people who leave the company for reasons other than being fired (or retiring). They may move to other companies, seek a change of career. Perhaps they have secured a more senior or better paid position elsewhere, moved to a different city or didn't like their manager or felt there was a lack of appreciation. There are many reasons for attrition.

Not all leavers are a loss for the company. Some flow is always healthy for a company as it opens the opportunity for new blood and fresh energy to come in. If you think about it, the opposite (i.e. a stagnant team) is not good. We benefited from natural attrition, either bringing onboard fresh graduates who were sponges ready and eager to absorb the teaching, or hiring experienced mid-career professionals who shook up the leadership composition in a good way.

The challenges come when attrition rates are too high. So high that the knowledge base is eroded, the team dynamic is constantly changing and the remaining employees start to wonder why they haven't left too. When attrition is too high, employees who aren't ready to be promoted or moved to new positions are moved prematurely to fill gaps. It also makes it harder to maintain a strong corporate culture.

Another challenge with high attrition is that it weakens networks that have been built. Employees at the centre had worked hard at building relationships with the key people in the operating markets. Not only does this make for better business partnering, it also improves productivity as tacit understanding is built up over time. It takes time to build strong and valuable networks. There is a large amount of literature on this topic that I won't go through in this book, but the importance of networking for building an effective team and coherent culture is clear.

There is a common misconception that people who are often at the coffee machine chatting to people are the lazy ones in the company. That that is all they do. But some of the most efficient people I have worked with spend a lot of time building informal networks. The short conversation with the marketing manager probably has little payback now, but you have made a connection with someone in the marketing department and it is easier to reach out in the future when you need some data at short notice.

Some of my managers have been incredibly strong networkers and I have managed people who have been better than me at it, by far. I learnt by seeing them do it well. In my earlier years, I was terrible at networking. I knew I had to do it but I would only do it within the barriers of my functional silo. This is very common among managers at the Expert level, where the understanding of networking is not well developed. With time and experience, I have seen the importance of networking and now more actively do it. My approach was shallow and short-termist in the past. I mostly considered it a waste of time as I couldn't see the benefit of it so clearly. Today, I can.

An attrition rate of 5-10% is healthy for most organisations. In the shared services centre in Bucharest, it was 20%. This is within the typical range of service centres (20-35% range) but I wasn't comfortable with the rate and I felt it shouldn't be a foregone conclusion. A rate of 35% broadly means one in every three employees will resign each year. Our one in five was manageable but in addition, we were growing by almost 100 new employees each year. With both factors at play, this meant we had around 250 new hires a year, out of a base of 800-900. Attrition became one of the largest threats to the successful implementation of our new vision.

I would love to say we identified a silver bullet that solved it. In reality, it was many different things that helped, but often it felt like a sticky plaster.

To deal with the loss of knowledge, we started to build a structured knowledge management system where key information was stored, updated and made accessible to all employees in the team and, if needed, across different teams. Gradually, it began to help raise the basic level of knowledge of our markets.

However, the frequent turnover meant, that most employees had limited networks and wouldn't know who to go to in the operating markets. Eager to solve a given issue or find certain information combined with their can-do attitude, they would often send emails to whoever they could locate in the operating market. Often that person would be helpful, but after three emails from three different new hires in three months on the same topic, patience understandably wore thin.

Email ping pong

Different types of communication serve different purposes. Effective communication is vital, especially when time is short and relationships have not yet been built. One of the issues that came up during our review of behaviours was how employees tended to send emails rather than pick up the phone or walk over to the person's desk (if in the same office). It really provoked and annoyed many receivers in terms of the high number of emails (hence the term 'email ping pong') and the tone of the emails.

There are many challenges with written communication. Much is lost in translation. We read messages through our own cultural lens and, because we're not picking up on visual cues or tone as you would in person, you are often left to figure these out yourself. I only had to recall my experience with the global roll-out during my time in London, where I realised that one size fits no-one. Or, from the same time, how much I initially misinterpreted some of the written messages I received from my British colleagues. On top of this, you add context and differences in seniority, leadership level and communication ability, and it's a minefield!

As we communicated with markets across the globe, it was certainly a minefield for us. We asked employees to work through a *communication thought process*. Their first option should be to do a video call. This was the best substitute for in-person communication, as you get facial expression, body language, tone, and message. When you communicate with cultures very different to your own, you need all the cues you can get. If video calls weren't appropriate or possible, they should make a phone call. That way, you would still get tone and message. Only if both were not possible, should they send an email. With email, you only really get the message and the field for misinterpretations is wide open. This didn't apply to every communication but it should be their thought process.

We invested in several new video meeting rooms over the five floors for larger meetings, while smaller meetings were managed with Zoom.

Immediately, the video calls made a huge difference to how we were perceived by the operating markets and accelerated the build-up of networks outside of the centre. It is inevitably easier to build a relationship with someone once you have 'seen' them and 'felt' their personality.

Almost one year had passed since we launched the business partnering vision with its pairing mindset, behaviours, culture and systems. Progress had been made in all areas, especially in communications, stakeholder engagement, and leadership style and capabilities. The whole organisation was developing vertically. This, combined with the technical improvement on the systems side that ran as part of the efficiency improvement project, meant a noticeable uplift in satisfaction ratings from our end market and HQ customers.

As a part of the reinforcement of the change (ADKAR step 'R'), senior stakeholders in the markets were invited to Bucharest to share their views on our progress and what impact it had had on their business.

Several referred to our former out-of-sync communication style and how much the video and phone calls had reduced misunderstandings, altered the perception of our centre and our capabilities among them and their teams. When communicating with up to 100 different cultures daily, choosing the relevant content and most effective communication style is key. The positive feedback and signals from the customers really fuelled the energy in the centre.

Food for Thought

☞ For what reasons have you left a company or organisation before?

☞ Do you tend to stay for many years in one place or do you like frequent change?

☞ Why is that so?

☞ How do you feel about networking?

☞ Do you have formal and informal networks?

☞ What type of communication and engagement do you prefer? Why is that?

Part 5

Purpose in Life

Chapter 36: What is 30 Centimetres?

Christmas was fast approaching. On the organisational front, the Group had identified the external candidate who would take up the role of building the GBS organisation. It meant that in time, we would onboard more functional areas beyond Finance, HR, and IT into our centres. The candidate had already visited my centre during the autumn but hadn't relocated to London yet. Equally, I had visited her in Asia to get to know her better, build our working relationship, and understand her ideas and plans for the GBS organisation. The journey sounded exciting and the following year looked prosperous.

In early December, I was able to combine a business trip to London with a long weekend with my parents. I had tried to get a visa for Fran to visit as well but for unknown reasons it had been rejected by the UK immigration office. I went alone and resolved that we would instead have to enjoy Christmas shopping together in Copenhagen in a few weeks' time. As always, I had a great time with my parents in London despite missing my partner.

One evening, Mum shared that she was having some problems with her digestive system and would be getting it tested upon her return to Denmark the following week. She never complained about her health and she didn't want any of the London trip to be affected by it. We enjoyed the rest of our days there, after which I returned to Romania and they to Denmark. A week later, Mum rang me. She had received the results from her tests – colon cancer.

I was in shock. I know survival rates have greatly improved over the years, but nothing prepares you for the shock when cancer hits someone close to you. This wasn't happening.

In Denmark, everyone is looked after by the public healthcare system. Like most other similar systems, there are waiting lists but for cancer treatments, there was a guarantee that you would be treated immediately. It was mid-December and Mum had already received some dates for the operation. She chose the date in early January. She wanted a fun and joyful Christmas and New Year's Eve with the family.

Fran and I were supposed to travel to Copenhagen in a week's time. There was a family wedding and we would be joining. I was exhausted. My work days were long. On many of my evenings, I hosted work dinners. On the weekends, I often had to answer emails and take work calls. On top of this, I was travelling frequently. There was no let up and it barely gave me time to rest or spend time with Fran.

Fran's feelings of loneliness and frustration had grown and it impacted both of us. Whilst my job in Venezuela also involved long working hours, Fran had had an independent life. And in Venezuela, I rarely travelled abroad and there weren't many evening obligations – there was little you could do! We struggled to find a new rhythm that worked for both of us in Romania.

I felt torn between prioritising my work and my partner. It wasn't as straightforward as choosing love. I was leading a major organisation and many depended on me. The reason we were there together at all was due to the company – they had helped make it happen. It led to a constant feeling of guilt as I loved both. After many long discussions and lots of tears, we made the difficult decision to end the relationship.

Fran wouldn't travel to Copenhagen but would head back to Venezuela before Christmas. Early on Saturday morning, we drove to the airport. A three-year relationship had come to an end. I returned home, packed, and left for the airport in the early afternoon. On the plane, I was filled with profound sadness. How could something that worked so well in Venezuela not work at all in Romania? It was the right decision but one thing is logic and another is emotions. The last thing I was in the mood for was attending a wedding.

I arrived in Copenhagen and managed to speak to my parents before heading to the wedding party together. Their comfort and love really helped. I somehow made it through the wedding celebration.

Over Christmas, we had more time to speak. I talked about the sadness I felt at the loss of my partner and the challenges of choosing an international career and trying to have a relationship. Was it an either-or choice? This Christmas was not really what I had hoped for and I felt Fran's absence profoundly. My parents listened to me and gave me space without making me feel bad for not being on top form.

I also tried to ask Mum about her upcoming operation, but soon sensed that she didn't want to be reminded too often of it. She said she thought about it here and there, but it wouldn't change anything to worry and she didn't want it to affect her mood.

She has always been stoic. The cancer was outside her circle of influence, so she placed her hope in a highly skilled doctor who would do her or his job as well as they could. As she said, 'Thinking and worrying about the outlook will not change the outcome, but it will impact my life up to then, so that's what I can control'.

We celebrated Christmas in the evening on 24th December, as is usual in Denmark. Dad made the traditional and utterly deliciously Danish Christmas dinner, which is normally either pork roast or duck served with caramelized potatoes and gravy. We had both. And a Danish version of a rice pudding for dessert. Mum had tastefully decorated the house and set the scene perfectly for a lovely *hygge* Christmas with me, my brother and his family.

In many ways, it felt like all the other Christmases we'd had, apart from the loneliness I felt. Over the days in between Christmas and New Year, we saw the extended family and I caught up with precious friends too, which distracted me sufficiently. I spent as much time with my parents as possible. I felt I needed to get as much out of my time in Copenhagen before returning to Bucharest a few days later.

On 3 January, Dad drove Mum to the hospital. I think we were all nervous although, having googled colon cancer and seen the likelihood of success, I was reasonably calm. My dad would call me when the operation was over. He hadn't yet. Why hadn't he?

Less than an hour later, he rang me. The operation had taken longer than expected. They had removed 30 centimetres of her colon, nearly double what they had planned. Mum was now waking up after the anaesthesia and was feeling OK. She would stay for a few days for monitoring. I was so relieved.

In the evening, I drove to the hospital and found her room. She was in a lot of pain but overall, was well. I didn't stay long as she was tired, but I came back the following day with my dad and brother and she was feeling much better. She was pleased that the operation had not resulted in a colostomy bag. We laughed a little. Now, I knew how terrified she must have been.

After my brother left, I stayed with my dad for another hour. We spoke about all of the things they would do when she was fully recovered, including a trip to New York, which was Dad's 70-year-old birthday present to himself! They wanted me to join and we spoke about going there in the late summer as it would not be possible for me to take a vacation beforehand. It was good to have something fun to look forward to and I think my mum needed that too.

A few days later, Mum rang me. Her voice was cheerful and warm. She was sitting in her living room. In an armchair, but delighted to have been discharged, mending well and finally home. It was good to hear her sound more herself and I could sense her joy through the telephone. I would come for dinner the next night – my last in Copenhagen. I was leaving for Romania on Monday morning.

It had been a tough few weeks – breaking up with my partner, Mum being diagnosed with cancer and undergoing surgery. With Mum doing better, it felt like a weight had been lifted off. I was glad and could allow myself to relax a little that afternoon.

I began looking forward to getting back to my flat in Romania and the work at hand. I missed my colleagues, all the challenges that awaited and not least the enormous energy there was in the vibrant office. Yes, I also feared getting back to my flat, which was now emptier. I'd have to redecorate and rearrange the empty spots. For now, it was time to stockpile the usual Danish products that I could not get in the supermarkets in Bucharest. It was already dark outside and it felt colder due to the light rain but I didn't mind – it made me feel alive.

Chapter 37: Make the Bad Dream Go Away

'*Kim, Kim, I think Mum is dying.*'

'What do you mean? What's happening?'

'I'm not sure. When I got back to the living room, I found her paralysed in her armchair.'

I knew it was true.

'Which hospital are you going to?'

'Glostrup... No – I mean Bispebjerg. We're going to Bispebjerg Hospital', my dad stumbled out. I had never heard him talk this way before.

'I'll drive straight to the hospital and meet you there'.

I arrived at the hospital 30 minutes later. I asked the receptionist where my mum was but they couldn't find her in the system. When I explained that she just come in by ambulance, I was directed to the thrombolysis department.

Arriving there moments later, I found it empty apart from my dad. He was pacing up and down the hallway, visibly shocked. I went to him and gave him a long tight hug. He explained that he was preparing dinner and Mum was fine in the living room. When he returned 15 minutes later, he found her lying in her armchair paralysed. Her eyes were wide open and he could see that she was trying to communicate something, but she couldn't move or speak.

My dad instantly rang the emergency services. They arrived within 15 minutes. In the ambulance, the paramedics immediately began preparing her for thrombolysis therapy. She had had a stroke in her brain. She would need urgent treatment to thin her blood and dissolve the dangerous clots in her blood vessels. This would prevent further damage to her brain.

Now my brother arrived. He looked just as scared as we did. We all hugged. Soon after, more family arrived. My dad had called the closest family when he was in the ambulance. So, there we all sat, in disbelief and feeling helpless. We could only hope for the best.

Eventually, the doctor came in and explained that the initial MRI scan did not indicate a major stroke. But the bad news was there wasn't much else they could do at this point. Mum had undergone serious surgery only three days before, so they wouldn't give her the thrombolysis treatment. According to the doctor, the risk of her dying from internal bleeding was greater than the benefits of the therapy.

Over the next few days, we would know how severe the damage was. I was devastated.

Mum was transferred to an intensive care unit, which is where I first saw her. She was awake now. I could see in her eyes a fear and a pain that I have never seen before. It was unbearable. Just standing there and not being able to do anything.

We tried to speak to her. But she couldn't move her lips. We asked her to try to move her body. She could move her left side a little, but the right side was completely paralysed. From her face to her right arm and leg, she couldn't feel or move a thing. Eventually, she fell asleep.

It was past midnight now. We could do no more and she was sleeping. We left the ward together and hugged before saying goodbye to each other. Sitting in the cold car and driving back home through empty streets in the middle of the night, I began to cry. The emotions were overwhelming. And yet I felt empty as well. A feeling of profound loneliness. A feeling of mourning and expectation of more mourning to come. How can life change so drastically in the split of a second?

When I got home, I poured myself a large stiff drink. I needed something to calm my nerves. It didn't help so I poured myself another one. I walked around and around the house. I couldn't find peace. I played loud music, cried more, made more drinks and around 3 or 4 a.m., the alcohol or something else finally worked and I crashed into bed.

The following morning, I woke up with a horrible headache. I hoped it had just been a bad dream. But no such luck. I rang my dad. He had hardly slept as well. The sadness in his voice chilled me. We agreed to meet at the hospital.

Again, at the hospital, we tried to speak to Mum and hoped for a little reaction or movement. But there wasn't any. She just looked at us. She was transferred to another ward – one where she would stay for the next weeks and where she would receive neurological treatment. Everyone else in the ward had had a similar story. I had never thought about how many families each day are devastated by news of a stroke.

The doctors explained that she would sleep a lot during the first few days as the brain seeks to recover from the damage and, in its own way, try to gain back control of the body. That Mum could not move her right side or speak indicated the damage was most likely severe.

When I got home later that evening, I rang my office. I spoke to Alex and explained the situation. I wouldn't be able to return to Romania yet and I didn't know when I'd be able to. She offered only support and compassion. Later that evening, I rang the new head of GBS. She also offered her support. She said I should take time as needed and get back to her in a few weeks.

I was grateful that I worked in a company where there were such care and understanding. I didn't know where my mind was but I knew where I had to be and that was with my family. Being able to put work aside gave me breathing space to do that.

A Joint Action Plan

The next few days, I went back to the hospital daily. As did my dad and brother. Mum mostly slept but still, it helped us just to be there and every time she opened her eyes, someone loving was sitting next to her and holding her hand.

This pattern continued the following week. It was the hardest few weeks of my entire life. Most nights when driving home, I would only cry. If I could just speak with her for another hour. Why had I hung up so quickly that Saturday when she rang? I could surely have spoken for a bit longer. If I could just get her advice about how to handle this situation… If I could only get her support and a big hug. The line of 'ifs' felt infinite. It was too much to take in and I had not foreseen this at all.

Over the coming weeks, Mum received physiotherapy and speech therapy in the hospital. The staff in the hospital were well-coordinated on her training. Once a week, there was an all-party meeting which they named 'The Involving Rounds Conversation' (literal translation from Danish) where the doctors, nurses, physiotherapist, speech therapist, social and health assistants, relatives, and patient (i.e. Mum) were present. This is where the different partners would share their observations and agree an action plan. The plan was then written on a big whiteboard in her room. Everyone who looked after her could see what they should focus on.

It made me think of the whiteboard initiative we had in Romania. It was a strong coalition involving all the right people. It impressed me to see such an approach at a public hospital. It reminded me of leading change and transformation over my work career. Of the importance of getting the right stakeholders aligned and committed to a joint action plan. It gave me comfort knowing that they all took it so seriously.

Over the following weeks, it became evident that the stroke was worse than they initially thought. The part of the brain that plans all of your actions - movements, facial expressions, talking, eating, coordination, etc - was damaged.

We had to lower our expectations for recovery. We agreed as a team to focus first on a few tiny improvements. At this point, just to get her to nod or shake her head was a struggle. Everyone in the team, including the relatives, were focused on helping her regain control over saying 'yes' or 'no', whether verbally or by nodding or shaking. We were not to focus on too many things at the same time. It reminded me of the work we'd done with employees in Romania in getting them to identify two areas of improvement first. That I could draw parallels to experiences from my own life helped me a lot in a situation where everything seemed unfamiliar and hopeless.

Some nights, when I was alone there, I pushed her wheelchair to a part of the ward that was empty. We sat there – just her and I. I tried to help her make sounds. I was desperate. I so wanted to help, but I had no idea how to. Gradually, I realised that it would take a long time before I would have a normal conversation with her again. Being there alone with her in the silence was particularly hard. At the start, I talked like a waterfall. I think I was trying to compensate for her lack of speech. I would bring *all* the conversation, I felt. I would be all the entertainment. But I couldn't be myself, so I gradually chilled out.

The impact of the stroke on my mum was devastating, but my dad's life was also turned upside down overnight. My brother and I tried to support him as much as possible but he often preferred to go home himself. I believe this was his way of coping.

In Chapter 4, I introduced the Kübler-Ross change curve model. If you remember, the five stages are: denial, anger, bargaining, depression, and acceptance. However, this was built on the original model, which contains the same five stages but refers to grief from losing a loved one. Knowing what I knew from my experience of the change curve, I knew that each stage could last for many months and be very messy. Just when you think you're past one stage, you circle back to an earlier one again. I knew the next year or few years would be extremely difficult for my family, not least for my mum.

For now, I could see that we were all still largely in the 'denial' stage. None of us could believe what had happened and accept that we had lost Mum (or the Mum we had known for our whole lives). I reflected a lot on the experiences and history my Mum and I had shared. Big moments and the little day-to-day things. I wondered how I was going to move forward in life without her. Or again, the 'her' I knew. It was difficult to know what were the right words to use. The thoughts were unbearable. I can cope with a lot of stress but I need to be on top of the problem and know what I can and can't do, what to expect, what is normal and what isn't.

Soon, I began to apply the techniques I had learned from my professional life around managing tough and uncertain situations. One thing I had learned in Argentina and Venezuela was that I cannot escape bad emotions irrespective of how much I wanted to. So, it was best for me to accept them. To occasionally feel them in my body and let them rush through without resisting them. Even allowing myself to cry in the car was part of this process of acceptance. I never normally cried.

To address the 'what' and 'how', I began to research strokes and recovery from strokes. I googled and read dozens and dozens of articles. I watched many YouTube videos of people explaining how they had recovered and what the process was like. I asked the doctors and nurses questions that I couldn't find answers to. What I found out gave me some hope, as I could see it was not a death sentence. And it helped me to do something productive rather than just sit and stew in my own thoughts.

After a few weeks, I had to go back to Romania. I had taken a few weeks of compassionate leave and my colleagues had kept things going in my absence. Time and space I will always be grateful for. But I had to head back. I could not stay in Denmark forever.

When I told my dad that I would need to return to Bucharest, I saw the sadness all over his face. He was still in denial and feeling helpless. His life partner of 49 years was just lying in a hospital bed, occasionally getting up for some training or tests. He only lived to go to the hospital every day. My brother would still be around and do as much as he could, but he had his own family to take care of. I felt so bad about leaving them.

I spoke with the company and we made an agreement. I would be in Romania during the week but fly to Copenhagen every weekend. There were only a few direct flights each week though, so I would be in the Bucharest office on Tuesdays, Wednesdays, and Thursdays, and either work from home or the Copenhagen office on Mondays and Fridays. This way, I would be able to support my family from Friday to Monday, and focus 100% on my job from Tuesday to Thursday.

It was tough going back. My flat in Bucharest was still decorated from pre-Christmas and many things reminded me of my now ex-partner. The first weeks of the new schedule, flying back and forth between Copenhagen and Bucharest, continued to be tough - I was always tired wherever I was. The emotional impact of the break-up and Mum's stroke drained me. Adding the ten hours of additional commute each week and intensive, long days at work nearly tipped me over, but I knew that this was just how it had to be right now.

Food for Thought

☞ What mechanisms or support do you turn to in a crisis?

☞ What have you learned from previous crises that can help you prepare for future ones?

☞ How prepared are you for the unknown?

Chapter 38: The Power of Visioning

The positive thing with me being in Copenhagen so much was that I could attend the weekly 'involving rounds conversations' in the hospital.

I continued to read more about recovery from strokes to better understand what we were up against. On a daily basis, there is a lot we don't think about. We just do them - walking, eating, drinking, brushing our teeth. We've stored it all away somewhere in our brains. After a severe stroke, neurological connections linking different parts of the brain may be broken and new pathways need to be established as you learn to do even the most basic things again. It is like starting all over.

To do even the basic tasks takes a lot of effort and you have to do most things consciously. Think of a child tying their shoelaces or speaking a full sentence. To get an idea, try to do everything with the opposite hand for a few hours and you'll notice how it drains your brain. Gradually, through repetition, it gets easier and you need to think less and less about it. This reminded me of the brain's two systems - the unconscious System 1 and the conscious System 2.

I also read that the recovery and learning curves after a stroke are steepest in the first six months and thereafter progress is slower and more difficult. One Friday morning, I returned to Copenhagen on my usual morning flight from Bucharest to join the 'involving rounds conversation'. My dad had mentioned to me that most of Mum's training sessions had been cancelled that week. Overall, the care and support from the hospital was great, but resources were limited in the state system.

At first, I was angry. I had managed to contain a lot of the anger (stage 2 in grief process) I felt during the first few weeks. Although even small situations could trigger very strong emotions in me, I usually managed to contain them well. I wanted to express my frustration at the meeting about the cancelled trainings, but knew that it would likely not be the right approach. Everyone did their best. But for me, it wasn't good enough. They needed to do better – this was important. The first six months were vital.

On the plane, I thought about how to express my frustrations without pissing off the staff team. I tried to put myself in their shoes. I knew there were budget restraints. That it was a stressful environment. But I also felt that several doctors did not exhibit much empathy or understand how we, the relatives, felt. Or maybe they did, but blocked it out as a way of maintaining healthy boundaries. Most of the doctors used language that other doctors and medical professionals would understand. I only understood most of what they were saying because of my extensive research, but other patients and family members may not have.

I also, frustratingly, felt that several of the staff team were exhibiting more Expert level mentalities than Achiever or higher levels of leadership capabilities. I already knew that most Expert level leaders are not good at receiving critique and even worse at receiving it in front of other people. After thinking it through, I decided to be as empathetic as possible, but also to openly share my thoughts. Honesty and authenticity was required here.

We started the meeting in the usual way, with the different teams sharing their observations and recommendations. Then it was my turn to speak. I praised and thanked them for their care and support of my mum. I said that as a senior manager, I was used to being in control and taking action when something was not how I liked it. I knew that they were working under tight budget constraints and were doing what they could within those limits.

I shared that I had read that Mum's potential to improve was greatest right now, straight after the stroke, and that as the months passed, her progress would inevitably slow down. I mentioned that most of her scheduled trainings had been cancelled that past week, so she had barely received any training. I then asked, 'Would you be satisfied with this if it were your mum sitting in the wheelchair at the end of this table?' I paused and continued, 'I know you can only do so much with the external restrictions put on you. I have some funds and I would like to bring in external professionals who could provide additional training and support to my mum. Why? Because I have a wish or dream that she will get back to where she was prior to the stroke.' That was my vision for Mum.

Everyone was quiet and several members of the staff team looked around to see who would speak first. Eventually, the senior doctor responded, 'We don't support having other people come into the hospital to train *our* patients'. He didn't comment on the cancelled training, but said that the physiotherapists, occupational therapists, and speech therapists would review her training programme. I sensed he was offended.

Thankfully, the other team members were not. After the meeting ended, several came up to me and said that they understood where I was coming from. One nurse even admitted that, at times, things fall into routines and they forget that behind each patient lies a full and rich life. A life that has been altered in a split second.

After that meeting, Mum received more training. The conversation had achieved its purpose and I was relieved. We didn't end up bringing in additional professional help, but I kept a close eye on it.

When coping with loss, it isn't unusual to feel desperate and like you would do things you wouldn't normally have considered. 'Bargaining' for a better outcome is stage 3 in the grief process. Some will pray to God and ask for support, or promise to change their ways of living if their loved one gets better. My way of bargaining became influencing the support from the hospital - to make sure Mum's health was kept as a top priority by the staff. I also continued to research and ask questions, even if it resulted in only tiny gains. Many times, I had to accept my limitations. In reality, I couldn't do much, but to painfully accept this was also out of my hands. I had to work through the grief process.

After a month in hospital, Mum's condition stabilised to a point where she could be moved to the rehabilitation centre. At the centre, she would receive daily training by different therapists. Slowly, over the next few months, I saw some of her personality coming back. It was nice to see but there was still a long way to go.

Gradually, I also began to find a new rhythm to my life. Mixing my professional life in Bucharest with my family life in Copenhagen helped me cope. In a way, the change of scenery and focus on work mid-week gave me a break from the emotionally heavy burden of looking after family and space to see it from a distance. I felt some joy in the little things, but I also felt little joy in most things. It was a bit of a rollercoaster and very usual to feel these symptoms in stage 4 of the grief process – 'depression'.

At work, the Group had just embarked on the GBS journey. In late February 2018, the global top team for shared services gathered in Bucharest for three days to work on the overall GBS vision and mission. This is the part of management I have always loved and where I feel I make a substantial contribution.

We brought in an external coach to help facilitate the workshop. The crowd was now more senior. Over the last year, more senior people (with higher grades) had been added to the GBS structure globally. We were now a crowd of a few Experts, a larger group of Achievers, and a couple of Catalysts. It elevated the strategy work to a different level that I had only experienced a few times before.

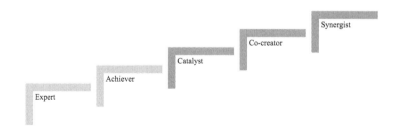

Figure 6. Joiner & Josephs's Stages of Leadership

Individuals operating at the top three management levels - Catalysts, Co-creators, and Synergists - are better placed to lead complex changes and transformations in organisations. This is largely down to the greater understanding they have of themselves and others, which means they are not as coloured by prejudices and worldviews. They also have a broader understanding of the time dimension and are able to spot the many interdependencies that exist in complex projects. This, combined with their ability to hold several perspectives at the same time, means they are well placed to take the lead on more complex leadership tasks. Some of the characteristics that distinguish this group from Achievers are:

Catalysts (and higher) versus Achievers

Catalysts (and higher) take change and uncertainty in their stride. They have developed a far more holistic approach to problems, time, and the environment. Their self-awareness and understanding of their own biases and beliefs is more advanced, enabling them to be more open to new thoughts, feelings, and behaviours. Even those that conflict with their own.

They naturally seek feedback and input from others, and make active use of this to develop themselves and deal with new and uncertain situations. This also enables them to try on frames that differ from their own and understand that even well-thought through actions, with the best of intentions, can have unintended consequences. This makes them more affirming towards themselves and others.

They also excel in creating positive environments and inviting others in to participate and bring their own initiatives to those environments. They typically seek greater meaning in the things they do and this becomes their motivating factor. They are visionaries who see the future in creative and imaginative ways. In many ways, this motivates and captivates others. They are those who see things ahead of time and catalyse others to come alongside them to implement that future vision.

At the end of the three days, we had a strong vision that we articulated in a clear statement. We wanted to unite the various business lines within GBS into one organisation. Even less working in silos or geographic boundaries, hence the 'Global' in Global Business Services. There were many steps before we could get it off the ground, though there were an eagerness amongst some to launch it straight away.

I would normally have found this all very exciting, and it was, but it was the first time I sensed something had changed in me. I wasn't 100% there. I was torn between my work and family. I had always been self-motivated but now, even projects that would have energised me previously didn't have the same effect now. Yes, I was exhausted. That was only to be expected given the last few devastating months. But was it more than that?

I decided to park it for now and carry on as best I could. I don't think anyone at work noticed, so I would ride it out for now. Over the following months, Mum also found a good rhythm. The training in the rehabilitation centre was intense and followed a strict framework, but she was making progress. This meant that on some weekends, I could stay in Bucharest, knowing that she was in good hands.

Spring was approaching and things began to look better everywhere. I have always loved the season of spring - the feeling of the days getting longer, the sun on my face, and slowly seeing the parks turn green again. It's the feeling of new beginnings, a new season, and for me, this year more than ever. That feeling wasn't to last long.

One Friday in April, I returned to Copenhagen to find that my mum had once again been hospitalised. This time, with very low blood volume. I began to fear for her life again. My research had told me that statistically, there is a 20-30% risk that people who have a stroke in their brain die within the first year. The doctors feared that she had some inner bleeding somewhere in her body, but couldn't find any sign of this in the scans. Thankfully, the medication they gave her brought her blood volumes back up and after a few stable days, she was discharged back to the rehabilitation centre.

It was hard to leave the family again the following week to go to a work conference in Berlin. I sensed my rightful place was to be near them and not on a business trip. It just didn't seem to matter so much anymore. The company had shown so much support and understanding that I also had to consider what I could continue to ask for.

After Berlin, I flew to Bucharest to host another global top team meeting for GBS. We would soon launch the new GBS vision and structure. Things had moved quickly. It had largely been driven by the global head of GBS. I had supported the best I could from Romania, but ultimately ownership was with the head of GBS.

This suited me well. I would normally have wanted to be in the driving seat but with everything else going on, it released me to attend to those other things. In parallel, I began to reflect on my true values. What was most important to me in life? What really mattered? What life did I see myself living in the future? I felt torn between two worlds and I couldn't ignore it much longer.

Food for Thought

☞ How do you approach difficult conversations?

☞ How do you prepare for them?

☞ Identify someone you think operates at the Catalyst level or higher (if any). What traits and behaviours do they have that you would like to develop too?

☞ Does their behaviour and approach stimulate or trigger a different behaviour and thought process in yourself?

Chapter 39: Paving the Way

It was nearly summer in Denmark and the progress Mum had made was impressive. The physiotherapists had been amazing. From not being able to move to now being able to walk short distances, wash her hands, go to the bathroom herself, and feed herself.

The speech therapist trained her to make sounds and express whole words. They helped her recall what things are called (basic things like a chair, table and house) through a range of creative exercises. By repeating the same words over and over, her brain slowly began to learn grammar again. Gradually, Mum started communicating in simple sentences. It brought me such joy to see how excited she got about her own progress.

She had now been living in the rehabilitation centre for more than five months. The intense training had paved the way for her to finally be discharged. It was mid-June. She would head home but still receive training as an out-patient. My dad was overjoyed. For almost six months, he had gotten up early every morning, driven to the rehabilitation centre and visited Mum at least twice a day, all whilst trying to keep his own one person company running.

They had now been married for 49 years. The marriage vow 'for better or worse' had been thoroughly tested and held a new meaning for both of them.

I was incredibly proud of Dad. He had managed to keep his spirit up and was forever supportive of Mum. He had gone home alone every night for six months. The next morning, he'd be up again and repeat his routine. He had done so well, but it had visibly worn him out.

It was late June and I had just returned to Copenhagen. Dad rang on Sunday morning. His speech was slow and his voice weak. I asked, 'What's happening?' He responded that he was lying on the floor and couldn't get up. He didn't feel well at all. I heard Mum in the background trying to communicate but I couldn't pick it up. I rushed over to their home immediately.

In the car, I rang the emergency services, sharing his symptoms and explaining that I was about 20 minutes away. When I got to the house, I found Dad still lying on the floor. Thankfully, he was conscious. His speech was still disturbed and I helped him into a chair. Mum was visibly distressed. Trapped in her body without the ability to communicate clearly, there was nothing she could do but watch her husband struggling.

The ambulance came and the medics helped him into the ambulance. They said they thought he had had a stroke. The ambulance left with him. I couldn't leave Mum alone – she had only been home a week. She was devastated.

Later that afternoon, I drove to the hospital on my own. As I drove, I thought how I wouldn't be able to take it if he would now go through the same as Mum had the last six months. I wouldn't be able to cope.

At the hospital, Dad looked fresher. It had been a minor stroke and the doctors didn't think he would suffer any severe side effects. He would be able to return home within the next 24 hours.

Relief flooded through me. I can't even express how I felt at that time. It felt like I had stopped breathing all the way to the hospital and I had to remind myself again that it was OK. I spent the rest of that week in Copenhagen and checked in on my parents frequently.

I had to return to Bucharest though. I began to realise that although I had hoped I could re-establish a normal routine with working abroad and travelling to Denmark, it was looking increasingly difficult to continue like this. Working abroad had become too great an obstacle and I started the conversation with the Group about finding a longer term solution for me in Denmark.

I also knew that I had lacked a sense of purpose in my work and that I had felt that for months now. Circumstances had forced me to consider my true values.

True Values

True values are the values that trump all others. It means more to you that these are satisfied over and above many others that you may also feel are important. There are different ways to identify your true or core values, but reflecting on turning points and highlights in your life is one approach, amongst many.

First of all, identify key turning points in your life – events and situations that led to pivotal personal and professional change and growth. Analyse how these points led to change and what core values they therefore point to. One example is my moving from Denmark to Argentina when I was 36. The change in job situation that was forced on me triggered a strong reaction. Gaining back control meant more to me than, for instance, feeling 'safe' in Denmark, even though I value safety too. Thus, control is a core value of mine. The opposite, not having control, triggered clear ego issues for me. Whilst many may argue that control is one of their values, if losing control does not typically lead to much of a reaction besides discomfort, perhaps it isn't a *core* value. Other values may be more dominant.

Reflect on your life's highlights. When did you experience being in a flow state? When you felt you were in harmony, where you didn't notice time passing? When you were totally absorbed in a situation and experienced true joy, satisfaction, and happiness? When I thought back, many of these situations related to being with family and dear friends – for instance like my parents visit to Venezuela. But also in working with and developing people, etc. It revealed to me that values around relationships and connections are vital for my well-being and therefore among my core values. Again, I could see that not having strong connections (e.g. feelings of exclusion in Argentina with the senior management team) triggered strong core ego issues in me.

For more on identifying your true values, I would highly recommend a book by Fredens og Prehn[17].

It was great living in other countries when my friends and family were all well. They could come and visit me, and vice versa. And I knew we could always see more of each other in the future. But suddenly that future was now.

I needed to be back in Denmark. What I valued most in life was to be together with my dear family and friends. Not the career, the money, the travelling around the world. But all the personal relationships that cannot be bought at any money or easily replaced. Being newly single meant that all the dearest people I held in my heart were in Denmark.

Once again, I had to bargain for a better outcome for my future. Like I had done all those years ago when the Danish company had been acquired and I found myself suddenly in a new reality. Like I had done when the position in Venezuela was delayed and I bargained for a move to Buenos Aires in the interim. I was now in the same situation, but the need was triggered by a change in personal rather than professional circumstances.

Clearly, the ideal solution would be to get a senior position within the Group in Copenhagen. If that wasn't possible, I would have to explore other possibilities. Over the following months, I had many discussions with the Group. It became clearer that there wouldn't be a suitable senior job in Denmark for me, at least in the short term. Over the last few years, the Group had aggressively driven efficiencies across all of the operating markets, ironically, into the GBS organisation I was now part of. There weren't sufficient senior roles in the operating markets. Eventually, we agreed that the only option was for me to leave the Group. It wasn't an easy decision, but it was a clear one.

I would move back to Denmark at the end of September 2018, nine months after that devastating Saturday afternoon when Mum had her stroke. Having made the decision and began to prepare for the move back, I realised with relief that the 'depression' stage of grief that I had been in for many months now was passing to 'acceptance' (stage 5). I still felt pain, but I began to come to terms with the new reality and I believed that, with time, it would all be good again.

My last couple of months in Romania were still exciting but, in many ways, also frustrating. We were on a major change journey. So much progress had been made over the last two years and I felt I had so much more buy-in from the organisation than at the start. Things were moving and it finally felt easier. But I'd have to leave it mid-project – to let someone else take it over and bring it to completion.

'The graveyards are full of indispensable men'
Charles De Gaulle

And, I would be just another one. Life goes on. When you're working in an organisation and you're completely invested, it can feel like everything. You can't imagine not being there, turning up each day to the same office and seeing the same people day in day out. There is an adrenaline to working that I enjoy, even though it would tip into stress frequently.

I was leaving on a high. My strong team and I had achieved great results in a short period of time. The progress had been noticed across the Group. The last day in the company coincidently fell on a quarterly engagement meeting, like the one I had presented at on my second day in Romania. I had come full circle. This time, I would not be playing a major role. I was leaving the organisation.

Still, I got to say a proper goodbye. In my farewell speech, I started by thanking all the amazing people I had worked with. I reflected on my poor speech when I arrived and once again acknowledged how wrong I had been in my perception of the capabilities of the crowd. How I had loved every day in the office. How I had felt and appreciated the energy from the 1,000-

plus employees who came in to work with a desire and will to make a difference. They had become like a big family to me and I would miss them. However, my family in Denmark needed me more right now and they could not be replaced. The rest of that afternoon, I got to catch up with many employees and say a proper farewell before leaving the next morning.

Food for Thought

☞ When have you had to make a difficult decision between work and personal life?

☞ What factors drove your decision?

☞ What values are most important to you?

☞ How are you living those out right now in your life?

Chapter 40: Choose Your Life

As I landed in Copenhagen airport, I realised a major chapter of my life had ended. It had been a ten-year international career adventure. It had granted me the opportunity to live in four different countries across two continents. In total, I had visited more than thirty countries across all of the continents apart from Antarctica. Most importantly, I had gotten to know such interesting people from so many different cultures. Today, I can truly appreciate how different but also similar we are across the world. How our fundamental desires, feelings, emotions, and dreams are alike – but often are expressed in different ways. I could see that I had grown a lot as a person and developed vertically in ways I didn't know that I would when I left Denmark ten years prior.

So, what would I do now?

Firstly, I would give a period of my life to supporting my parents. They had given so much support to me in my life. Not only in love but also patience, role-modelling, coaching and unconditionally supporting me through my life, all of which had set me up for success. I wanted to give back to them while I could, and what better thing to give than time.

Over the first few weeks that I was back in Copenhagen, I began to see how I could best help my mum and dad. A lot of great results had been achieved in the short-term with the therapy and training. Consistent baby steps (e.g. wiggling her right foot or saying A, B, C) had accumulated over time and now she could move around the house by herself and express her needs with words. She could even manage a short simple phrase. Still, there was much she could not yet express. For a person who had had a 40-year career as a healthcare worker within psychiatry and helped people her entire life by talking to them and listening to them, this had to be the biggest loss for her. I decided that I would use my time and energy helping her improve her speech and communication.

I asked her if she would like this and she accepted with gratitude. My dad is dyslexic so he had struggled with this part of her therapy. He did so many other things anyway that it only felt right that this would be the part I would focus on.

I decided I wouldn't work during my first year back home. I would support my parents, settle back into Copenhagen life, visit friends abroad, and give myself time to decompress from the last ten hectic years and reflect on what I wanted to do going forward.

I began to attend the speech therapy sessions with Mum. I asked the therapist how I could help and she suggested multiple exercises we could do in-between lessons. Slowly, Mum began to say smaller sentences – still very basic, but progress. When the official training from the speech therapist came to an end, I took over the training.

Seeing Mum on such a regular basis meant I could observe from a close distance how she was coping. For a long period, she was stuck in denial. She didn't acknowledge how severe the damage had been. She had unrealistically high expectations of how fast she would return to normal life. She got angry or sad with herself and others easily. And as the severity of her state gradually dawned on her, a period of depression came. On some days, her mood and energy were so low that it all felt impossible.

Many people rush to offer solutions to other people's problems. The only problem with this is they are rarely welcomed and rarely work. Solutions in your universe rarely work in mine. And solutions that work in mine may well not work in yours. What is more effective is to work together to uncover appropriate solutions. This is what good coaches do. They often don't tell you what you should do but ask you questions that help you find good solutions yourself. They can also help you refocus or reframe a situation. This is what Mum had done with me my whole life. If you wish to learn this for yourself, I would again recommend the book by Fredens og Prehn.

With Mum, what helped was not to focus on all the things she couldn't do or how long it would take before she could them again, but to focus on all the things she was now able to do and what things she'd soon be able to do. This seemingly small reframing exercise often helped to bring her back into a positive space, where she usually was.

We also needed to celebrate her successes. From leading change in my professional life, I knew how important it was to set clear targets and celebrate them when achieved. Doing so helps with building motivation, reinforces positive messages, and allows for a well-deserved break on the long journey. When leading change, there can be a risk that celebration has the opposite effect as it can give the impression that the change journey is over and people can take their foot off the pedal. That risk didn't exist here. Mum knew that *much* more would be required on an ongoing basis before she reached a stage where she would be satisfied.

In September that year, I told my parents I would be taking them to London in December to celebrate their 49th wedding anniversary. I wanted them to have something to look forward too. A 'well done' for both of their hard work over the past year and a 'we got through it' celebration. I also wanted them to know that life, as they used to know it, was not dead. It would come back gradually. It helped to boost our energy as a whole team. Half the fun is in the anticipation!

As Mum's condition noticeably improved over the next year and she was needing my help less and less, I began to think about my future. We only have one life, so I guess we'd better make the most of it. Up till the stroke, I loved my working life, even with its high demands. You can't work for 60-plus hours a week for too long if you don't enjoy it.

My move to Argentina 11 years earlier helped me to learn more about myself than if I had stayed in Denmark moving from company to company. I knew I could do it – to set-up life elsewhere and start afresh with no friends, home, or even language skills.

My years in London taught me how to navigate a large multinational organisation as just another big fish in an even bigger pond. With work, I got to travel to so many new countries and work with so many people of different cultures.

My time in Venezuela was about living in uncertainty and insecurity, and managing change in an ever-changing environment – both personally and professionally. It was about building resilience without the support systems I relied on back in Denmark. It was about growing out of the functional silo and into a general leader. I confronted my conscious and unconscious biases about people and groups that had built up from my youth.

Romania was about leading a massive organisation with its unique challenges. It was about motivating and leading transformation through focusing on the vertical development of people. It also helped elevate my understanding of how all the different dimensions interact - dimensions like culture (organisational and national), mindset, behaviour, leadership agility and so on. Through all of these experiences, I also experienced a lot of vertical development myself.

I really loved the professional life. When I was in it.

Now, I see life slightly differently. The last few years made me realise that there are some things I cannot compromise on. I need to ensure a better balance between work and personal life. That doesn't mean I cannot work 60 hours a week – just not all year round and not at the expense of existing and new relationships.

I still miss the international lifestyle. I miss working in a professional environment, the challenges and the different cultures. But right now, I need to find the right balance that includes all the different aspects of life that I appreciate. A balance that fuels a deeper happiness inside of me. Life is fragile and we do not know how many years we have. I don't want to waste any of it. I want to try to live every day to its fullest.

I made the decision to put my career on hold. To move back to Denmark. To focus on helping my parents through the toughest period of their lives, and mine. I am aware that this is a privilege not everyone has available to them. I also know that had it not been for the adventure I'd been on over the ten years I'd worked abroad, I would not have been in such a position - financially or emotionally.

The learnings I'd gained as I moved countries and jobs over the last decade became invaluable to me as I sought to manage the huge change that was to come. The change that came from taking a pause from it all and supporting my parents through the pause that life had forced on them. Wherever I was now or wherever I would go in the future, I know it was the right decision to say 'yes' to moving to Argentina back in 2008. Through the ups and downs, the experiences I gained made it all worth it. It's a big world out there. If you don't go and experience it, you'll never know!

Food for Thought

☞ Is there a bold decision you need to make soon?

☞ Have you stopped and reflected while reading this book?

☞ What have you learned about yourself or others that you want to take away with you?

☞ Will you continue to ask yourself questions that help you grow?

☞ Will you seek to grow vertically, both professionally and personally?

Afterword

Eighteen months later…

Having had more time to reflect on what I love and what drives me, I realise that I have a passion for transformation, for vertically developing leaders, for understanding how culture and human psychology leads to successful results for an organisation, team or individual.

I began reading and researching these areas to deepen and supplement the practical knowledge I had gained over my career. I have included a Recommended Book List at the end of the book for those who want to read up more about these areas. I also started to write this book which, in many ways, has been a therapeutical process. How the book looks now is not how it started. I'd like to thank many dear friends in Denmark and abroad who agreed to be test readers for their honest and bold feedback (see Acknowledgements).

I also completed a three month training course at the Being First © institute. We focused on catalysing transformations and learnt key strategies that have, for Being First©, delivered breakthrough results. It would have been great to have gotten this teaching years earlier as I would have managed the transformations much better, but I realised also that the course had such an impact on me because I could relate the teachings to my personal experiences. The course only helped me put into perspective what I had learned and witnessed over many years. Some lessons can only be truly learnt by going through them yourself.

I have written this book through the lens of how I saw things at a given time in the past. When I was younger, my thinking wasn't so developed. As I have grown older, I have become more reflective and I think more rounded in my thinking and approach to different situations. I hope you sensed that development in me through the book too. The questions I have continually asked myself over that time have been key for my development. If you already reflect a lot, most of the questions in the Food for Thought sections may be obvious, but if you do not generally reflect, I hope it has inspired you to do more of it. You often need to pause to get to know yourself better!

When I reflect on the last ten years, I see a clear pattern of how I have managed situations in spite of a lack of deep understanding of myself and the factors around me. At times, I reacted as I would have done at the start of my career – irrationally, emotionally and not at all how I wanted to. But I also realised that I was often able to save a situation before it was too late. Like when I realised that my bad mood in Venezuela was impacting others or when I gave the terrible first presentation in front of the whole company in Romania. Vertical development only enhances the palette of tools and capabilities we have as human beings, but it does not mean we always use them.

I have been blessed with great role-models throughout my life. I was born to a mum who taught me to be reflective and empathetic since childhood. To put myself in other people's shoes even when they weren't nice to me. Both my mum and dad motivated and inspired me to take chances, but given me the reassurance that they would be there to catch me should I fall. Managers have taught me new ways of leading and managing myself and others. Colleagues have inspired me and kept me humble. Both dear friends and colleagues have helped me through life by providing honest feedback – at times when I didn't want it and when I did. It has all helped me to grow!

Many have pointed out this blessing to me and, as I know many who sadly lack good role-models, I wrote my lessons, mistakes and learnings in this book in the hopes that it can inspire or motivate you to carry on growing. Perhaps some of the questions have helped you to understand yourself better. To become more aware of your worldviews, hidden biases, and emotions. To identify areas and behaviours that block your progression forward. Or perhaps they have inspired you to take chances in life and go even without knowing the future.

To help you understand how much my vertical development has really helped me both professionally and personally, I have chosen to share many private parts of my life. Both positive and negative ones. I have, of course, reflected a lot on whether this was right or not. Most people will happily share their successes but behind every success lies many failures. If at the least all you realise from reading this book is that no one is perfect or infallible, but you can keep going and you can keep growing, then that's a job well done in my opinion.

My final pieces of advice for you are:

✓ Stay curious

✓ Take calculated risks

✓ Ask questions

✓ Accept your mistakes and learn from them

✓ Seek feedback from others

✓ Acknowledge your emotions and learn to accept them – even the difficult ones

✓ Clarify your values and live them out

✓ Stay present in life, and

✓ Enjoy every moment!

Acknowledgements

This book was around two years in the making. It is the combined result of many people who have supported me through the process and, each in their own way, brought value to the book.

The idea to write a book first came up when a dear friend, Marinela Tanase, suggested that I should share my learnings over the many hard fought years. She believed that it would benefit other managers, especially more junior ones. She mentioned it many times (she's wonderfully persistent!) and said I should write it in the story-telling Kim-way that she knew from my presentations and general communication style.

That seed grew over the following years and, as I left the corporate world in late 2018 and moved back to Denmark, I kept it in mind as a project for 'sometime in the future'. After setting aside the first year back in Copenhagen to help Mum improve her communication skills, both of my parents (especially Dad) pushed me to once again do something meaningful. Having reflected on my life and all the adventures I still wanted to embark on, I did, at times, doubt whether my story would be interesting to others. Each time, Dad affirmed that it surely would be – not many people get to lead and drive transformational change all over the world and with people from so many different cultures.

Soon enough, I knew it was time to get going. I researched and read a lot of books about writing books. *On Writing* by Stephen King was particularly helpful. A writer friend, Kaare Thomsen, shared helpful insight into the process, but also challenged me to be clear as to why anybody should read my book in the first instance. A fair challenge! It helped me strengthen my own belief that I had valuable things to share.

And so, I began.

I brainstormed the content and structure, and then put pen to paper. Page after page, I poured out my learnings from different periods of my life, rich descriptions of the places I'd lived in and, not least, the emotional impact that Mum's stroke had on me. In the middle of this, the COVID crisis hit and Denmark, along with the rest of the world, was shut down for several months. My newly found hunger for writing and the ink on the pages dried up. The isolation didn't inspire me at all. Luckily, in the late summer, as restrictions began to lift, I found my energy and inspiration again. During late autumn 2020, the first draft was finished.

I connected with an editor, Ameesha Green, who provided me with an editorial assessment of the book. Her feedback was clear – she had never read a book like this before, she found it interesting (in a positive way!), but didn't know which category to place it in or what sort of audience it would appeal to. It was somewhere in between a professional business memoir, travel novel and self-development book. Not being that clear myself, I asked nine dear friends dotted around the world to test read it. Each had different professional and cultural backgrounds, and I wanted a good mix to get the most useful feedback.

It was a big ask to get these nine people to dedicate so much time to help me realise my personal project. High-level feedback was provided by Jesper Møller and Henrik Valdi Rindom Nielsen on key sections of the book, and by Sunil Panray and Thomas B. Andersen on the full draft. They liked it. Enough to move onto the next stage, but it definitely needed more work.

More detailed chapter-by-chapter feedback was given by Marinela Tanase, Henry Faughnan, Carolina Vilchis, Thomas Hadrup, and Karen Pluess. The feedback was: there are some great stories and valuable learnings in the book, but it lacked focus. Overall, it was what I expected for a first time author. I followed up with each of the reviewers to understand their views in more depth, and this sparked fresh ideas. The process was lengthy but also helped me get some distance from my book 'baby' and see it more objectively.

Through the four-month-long feedback process, Thomas Hadrup and Jesper Møller were especially helpful in being a sounding board for me talking through the reflections I had and giving me further thoughts to factor in. Gradually, it became clearer what I wanted to achieve through the book. I also had to make some bold decisions around sharing more about myself to connect (hopefully) with the reader. Story-telling only really works if you, the audience, feel a connection with me, and you feel that I am someone you can learn something off. As you can imagine, this is quite exposing and not what is typically found in the corporate world.

The second write-through took about six weeks. At least a third of the original content was entirely rewritten. The structure was changed too. I couldn't bother all my friends once more, but Marinela offered to test read some of it and her insights were invaluable. Yet, it was too wordy and despite my many years working abroad, my English was not at the level that was required to publish a book in English.

Then, Karen Pluess offered to become my developmental editor. Luckily for me, she was in an exciting transition phase of her own, and had time to help me. Having worked with her for almost four years during my treasury career, I knew her high standards and brilliant humour (often resembling mine). I was pleased to accept her offer and over the following months, she thoroughly uplifted the book. She made it much more focused, challenged me and suggested deletions of many irrelevant parts. Most importantly, she brought the language to life. After several iterations and versions back and forth, plus a copy edit, the final book came together.

In parallel, Linda Balle began to work on the book cover based on some initial thoughts I had. Her design skills are amazing and she took my own ideas to a new level. In addition, her experience in publishing meant that I got solid advice on what was needed to ensure the book was at a suitable standard for publishing.

Lastly, had it not been for my parents, who have supported me through my life and career, I would not be here. Their hard work and wonderful upbringing gave me the best start in life. And even as an adult, they have always let me be myself, believed in me, and pushed me when I needed it. I thank them for their support, love, and eternal trust in my skills and abilities. To Mor and Far, I love you so much and I dedicate this book to you.

Recommended Book List

Andersson, D & Ackerman Andersson, L. 2010. The Change Leaders Roadmap – how to navigate your organizations' transformation. Pfeiffer.

Andersson, D & Ackerman Andersson, L. 2010. Beyond change management – how to achieve breakthrough results through conscious change leadership (2. Edition). John Wiley & Sons, Inc.

Andersson, D & Ackerman Andersson, L. 2018. Nøglen til ledelse af forandring – Strategier for bevidst forandringslederskab (Dall, H. & Fischer, T.) (2. edition). Gyldendahl Business.

Fredens, K & Prehn, A. 2009. Coach dig selv – og få hjernen med til en forandring. Gyldendal Business.

Fredens, K & Prehn, A. 2012. Play your brain – Adopt a musician's mindset and create the change you want in your life and career. Marshall Cavendish Corp/Ccb,

Furr, N., Nel, K., & Ramsøy, T. Z. 2018. Leading Transformation – how to take change of your company's future. Harvard Business Review Press.

Goleman, D. 1995. Emotional Intelligence – Why it can matter more than IQ. Bantam Books

HBR's 10 Must reads. 2011. On Change Management. Harvard Business Review Press.

HBR's 10 Must reads. 2011. On Leadership. Harvard Business Review Press.

HBR's 10 Must reads. 2011. On Managing People. Harvard Business Review Press.

Hiatt, Jeffrey M. 2006. ADKAR, How to Implement Successful Change in Our Personal Lives and Professional Careers. Prosci Research.

Joiner, B & Josephs, S. 2007. Leadership Agility – Five Levels of Mastery for Anticipating and Initiating Change. John Wiley & Sons, Inc.

Kahneman, D., 2011. Thinking, fast and slow. Macmillan.

Kotter, John P. 1997. Leading Change. Howard Business School Press

Kübler-Ross, E. & Kessler, D. 2014. Life Lessons - Two Experts on Death & Dying Teach Us about the Mysteries of Life & Living. Scribner

MacDonald, M. G. 2015. Start Writing Your Book Today – A Step-By-Step Plan to Write Your Nonfiction Book, From First Draft to Finished Manuscript. Amazon.

Meyer, E. 2014. The Culture Map – Breaking through the invisible boundaries of global business. PublicAffairs[tm].

Münster, M. 2017. Jytte fra marketing er desværre gået for I dag., Gyldendal Business.

Münster, M. 2019. I'm afraid that Debbie from marketing has left for the day. Gyldendal Business.

Münster, M. 2020. Jytte vender tilbage - Den umoderne guide til at skabe forandringer imod alle odds. Gyldendal Business.

Overgaard, N. 2020. Det hele handler ikke om dig – Antikke principper for et liv med sindsro, frihed og mening. PeoplesPress.

Penn, J. 2018. How to Write Non-Fiction – Turn Your Knowledge Into Words. CurlUpPress.

Svenstrup, J. 2012. Du bliver hvad du tænker. Gyldendahl Business.

Notes

1   How our personality develops depends on both our genes and our environment. In relation to working with change, Being First © institute, which specialises in conscious change leadership, has defined six core ego issues that changes can trigger in individuals.

2   *Life Lessons - Two Experts on Death & Dying Teach Us about the Mysteries of Life & Living*, by Elisabeth Kübler-Ross & David Kessler, 2014.

3   Developmental change is typically a change from A to B. Transitional change is slightly more complex and can be seen a little like a caterpillar transforming into a butterfly. Transformational change is the most complex and is recognised by the fact that only the direction, not the end game, is normally known from the outset. This sort of change typically takes years.

4   For more on the brain systems 1 and 2, see *Thinking Fast and Slow*, by Daniel Kahneman.

5   Data from numbeo.com: Cost of living/country price rankings

6   Data from 'Salary experts salary assessor platform', converted into GBP, August 2021.

7   *Leading Change*, by John P. Kotter in Howard Business School Press, 1997.

8   Francis J. Aguilar created the stepping stone back in 1967 with his critical novel: *Scanning the Business Environment*. It began as ETPS and encompassed four broad factors of the environment: Economic, Technical, Political and Social influences. Since then, it has been developed by other authors into the PEST that we know today.

    PEST and SWOT are closely related approaches to business analysis. PEST is an acronym that stands for political,
economic, social and technological influences on a business. SWOT is a situational analysis tool for company

leaders that involves assessing strengths, weaknesses, opportunities and threats. There is plenty of literature on both topics.

9 Vertical development is widely covered by different authors, including Bill Joiner & Stephen Josephs, Susanne Cook-Greuter & Benna Sharma, Being First © Institute and many others.

10 The survey was conducted by Joiner & Josephs among 604 managers over a four-year period, of which:
- 384 of the managers were from Torberts' study detailed in *The Power of Balance: Transforming Self, Society and Scientific Inquiry* (1993)
- 220 were from interviews with managers by Joiner and Josephs in 'Leadership Agility' (2007).

Another strong researcher in the field of ego and its developmental stages is Susanne Cook-Greuter. In *Ego Development Theory*, she talks of stages (instead of levels) but broadly found the same distribution among 4,510 individuals.

11 *Explorer* covers the earliest stage of life – think of a baby exploring everything around them. *Enthusiast* is the next level, covering the early childhood years (2-7 years). The *Operator* stage, typically experienced during the school years, is characterised by limited attention to one's own feelings, a black and white thinking, and short time horizons with a focus on immediate needs. Operators rarely take the blame for situations. The *Conformer* stage typically emerges in the teenage years. Conformers work hard to avoid disapproval from the groups they identify with and want to belong to. This stage is characterised by an 'us and them' mindset. They prefer stability and the familiar. They are typically pleasant to hang out with, as long as you come from the same group, etc.

You can also find adult Enthusiasts, most often in the form of people with narcissistic traits and a distinct 'everything is about me' view. If you dare disagree with an adult Enthusiast, you are the enemy. Adult Conformers are most often seen in professional groups where they thrive among like-minded people. They see a lot of the world from the point of view of the group they identify and interact with. Unfortunately, this means they receive limited input and stimuli from outside groups, which limits their own view and approaches to situations in life.

12 Goleman, D. 1995. Emotional Intelligence – Why it can matter more than IQ. Bantam Books.

13 Diversity Wins, How inclusion matters, by McKinsey & Company, May 2020.

14 *ADKAR, How to Implement Successful Change in Our Personal Lives and Professional Careers*, by Jeffrey M. Hiatt, 2006.

15 Mindset: The New Psychology of Success, by Carol S Dweck, 2006.

16 https://time.com/3858309/attention-spans-goldfish/

17 The book that has meant the most to me in learning to self-coach is *Coach dig selv – og få hjernen med til en forandring*, by Fredens og Prehn in Gyldendal Business, 2009. For the English version, see *Play your brain – Adopt a musician's mindset and create the change you want in your life and career*, by Annette Prehn in Marshall Cavendish Corp/Ccb, 2012.

Printed in Poland
by Amazon Fulfillment
Poland Sp. z o.o., Wrocław

83235790R00200